The Rise of the Woman Novelist

From Aphra Behn to Jane Austen

JANE SPENCER

The Rise of
the Woman Novelist

From Aphra Behn to Jane Austen

Basil Blackwell

First published 1986
Reprinted 1987, 1989

Basil Blackwell Ltd
108 Cowley Road, Oxford OX4 1JF, UK

Basil Blackwell Inc.
432 Park Avenue South, Suite 1503
New York, NY 10016, USA

British Library Cataloguing in Publication Data
Spencer, Jane
The rise of the woman novelist: from Aphra Behn to
Jane Austen.
1. English literature—Early modern, 1500–1700—
History and criticism 2. English literature—
18th century—History and criticism 3. English
literature—19th century—History and criticism
4. English literature—Women authors—History
and criticism
I. Title
823'.009'9287 PR438.W65
ISBN 0–631–13915–X
ISBN 0–631–13916–8 Pbk

Library of Congress Cataloging in Publication Data
Spencer, Jane.
The rise of the woman novelist.
Bibliography: p.
Includes index.
1. English fiction—Women authors—History and
criticism. 2. English fiction—18th century—History
and criticism. 3. Women in literature. 4. Feminism and
literature. I. Title.
PR113.S6 1986 823'.009'9287 86–4242
ISBN 0–631–13915–X
ISBN 0–631–13916–8 (pbk.)

Typeset by Photographics, Honiton, Devon
Printed in Great Britain by Page Bros (Norwich), Ltd

Contents

Acknowledgements

I am especially grateful to Marilyn Butler for the help she has given me both as supervisor of my D.Phil. thesis and as reader of my work since.

Much of the book was written while I held a Junior Research Fellowship at Trinity College, Oxford, and I am grateful for the opportunity this gave me for research and writing.

Some material in Chapter 2 is taken from my article 'Creating the Woman Writer: The Autobiographical Works of Jane Barker', which appeared in *Tulsa Studies in Women's Literature*, Vol. 2, no. 2 (Fall, 1983). I would like to thank the editor for permission to use it here. I am obliged to the Curators of the Bodleian Library for permission to quote from a manuscript letter by Charlotte Smith, and to the President and Fellows of Magdalen College, Oxford, for permission to quote from the manuscript book of Jane Barker's poetry in Magdalen College Library.

I should like to thank Dennis Burden, Ian Campbell, Sarah Carpenter, Margaret Doody, Terry Eagleton, Elaine Hobby, Sandra Kemp and Ruth Perry for the help they have given by reading and commenting on my drafts at various stages; I am very grateful to Sandy Maxwell for lending me her copy of *The Victim of Prejudice*; and many thanks go to Jacquie Rawes for checking references, to Jackie McRae for proof reading, and to Hugh Glover for all his help, especially his valiant work with scissors and paste despite a broken arm.

Jane Spencer
Edinburgh, 1986

Introduction

Eighteenth-century England witnessed two remarkable and inter-connected literary events: the emergence of the novel and the estab-lishment of the professional woman writer. The first of these has been extensively documented and debated, while the second has been largely ignored. Yet the rise of the novel cannot be understood fully without considering how its conventions were shaped by the contributions of a large number of women, their writing deeply marked by the 'femininity' insistently demanded of them by the culture to which they belonged. This book is, to some extent, an attempt to provide that consideration. In the first part, I try to describe and account for the (conditional) acceptance of the woman novelist by the eighteenth-century critical establishment. In the second part, I trace the development of certain themes in women's novels, themes which they treated in a way signi-ficantly different from their male counterparts and which entitle us to refer to 'women's traditions' in the novel. These traditions, however, far from being isolated from a main tradition, were important agents in its formation.

It is not only an attempt to understand the rise of the novel that lies behind this book. My primary concern arises from the fact that women's role in the novel's rise has been underestimated. Eighteenth-century periodical reviewers, who tended to have a low opinion of the novel, emphasized and even exaggerated its connection with women writers, but modern critics, whose respect for the form is so much greater, usually concentrate on the five male 'greats'—Defoe, Richardson, Fielding, Smollett, and Sterne. As the novel has gained critical prestige women's part in it has been as far as possible edited out of the historical account, in a familiar move to belittle and suppress women's achievements.[1] My intention is to recall some of these achievements, and thus contribute to the feminist project of uncovering women's history.

If women's writing is important to the history of the novel, the novel is no less important to the history of women's search for a public voice. In the eighteenth century it was an important medium for the articulation of women's concerns, and its rise was centrally bound up with the growth of a female literary voice acceptable within patriarchal society. For despite the continuing tendency to disparage or forget them, women writers do have a voice in our society, and have had, publicly, since the period under discussion. It is crucially important for feminists to look at the implications for women of the development of that voice.

Any study which treats of women writers as a separate group needs to explain the reasoning behind such a procedure. The writers considered in this study entered a realm of discourse that had long been dominated by men; their work imitated, or counteracted, or (a point often over-looked) influenced the work of their male contemporaries, and it might be argued that they would be better studied alongside those men, whose work is mentioned only briefly here. Feminist critics have countered such arguments by reference to the 'specificity' of women's writing, that is, the claim that women's writing is significantly different from men's because of the authors' gender. We need to be careful here. I do not claim that in any respect, thematic or stylistic, women's writing is *essentially* different from men's: indeed the most crucial insight afforded by feminism is in my opinion the deconstruction of the opposition masculine–feminine as essential categories. But if women writers exhibit no essential 'femininity', they are still working within a patriarchal society that defines and judges them according to its notions of what femininity is. They may internalize their society's standards of femininity and reflect this in their writing. Or they may write in opposition to those standards. In short, women writers are in a special *position* because of society's attitude to their sex; and their work is likely to be affected by their *response* to that position (even when the response is an attempt to ignore a situation which might be debilitating if acknowledged). Women having been oppressed *as* women, it is not only reasonable but necessary to consider women as forming a group with significant interests in common.

The first part of my study then, charts the establishment of a certain position for women writers in the eighteenth century, a 'respectable' position granted them in return for the display of a number of positively valued 'feminine' characteristics. The discussion, therefore, focuses on changes in the ideology of womanhood from the late seventeenth to the late eighteenth centuries; on the reactions of the male cultural establishment to women writers and their work; and on women's own conception of themselves as writers within this ideological climate. The second part (chapters 4–6) focuses on women's novels as responses to the position outlined in the first; each chapter considering one kind of possible response, and suggesting its effect on women's novels throughout the century. I have called the responses protest, conformity, and escape;

but I hope it will be clear that I do not consider these as mutually exclusive strategies informing three entirely separate traditions. Rather they indicate tendencies each of which influences a particular development within the novel, while remaining mingled in any one writer's work with the other responses.

By focusing on women's response to women's position I am obviously centrally concerned with the problem of whether, and to what extent, eighteenth-century women's writing is to be read as feminist writing. It is a complicated question. Of course no woman of the time thought of herself as 'feminist', as the word was not in use then; but woman's nature and proper role were subjects of serious debate, and many women took up positions which we might usefully describe as feminist. As Hilda L. Smith demonstrates in her excellent study *Reason's Disciples: Seventeenth-Century Feminists* (1982) some women writers of the seventeenth century identified women as an oppressed group (rather than a naturally inferior sex), and with that crucial argument laid the foundations for modern feminist theory. A feminist discourse, then, was possible, and was recognized (though not by that name) as part of the intellectual debate in the period under discussion. There was a problem, though, then as now, in defining the relation of the woman writer *as* a woman to this discourse. Because of the very low opinion of women's intellectual capacities generally held in the male cultural tradition, a woman writer seemed, by the very act of writing, to be challenging received notions of womanhood; and to this extent all early women writers, whatever their own opinions on women's position, were engaged willy-nilly in feminist discourse. As I shall show, however, the gradual acceptance of the woman writer which took place during the eighteenth century considerably weakened this early link between women's writing and feminism. Once writing was no longer considered necessarily unfeminine, the woman writer was no longer necessarily offering a challenge to male domination. I have, therefore, used both 'feminist' and 'anti-feminist' to describe tendencies in eighteenth-century women's writing, depending on whether their work seems to me to argue against or in favour of male control and domination over women. I do not by this mean to label certain writers as 'feminists' or 'anti-feminists' in simplistic fashion: many women, writing in conscious support of current doctrines of female inferiority, left by implication a feminist message, while others, genuinely concerned to improve women's position, made suggestions which we would now judge as anti-feminist in tendency.

The relationship between the rise of the woman writer and the progress of the women's movement is a problematic one. Feminist critics concerned about the dearth of women in the critical canon of great writers have been rightly concerned with remembering forgotten women writers and explaining why their achievement has not seemed 'great' to established criticism, as well as with re-evaluating the better-known women writers in the light of their position as women. They have shown how women writers have needed to overcome tremendous odds in order to write.[2] In a work like Gilbert and Gubar's *The Madwoman in the Attic*, women's writing appears as an immensely difficult achievement in patriarchal society, and must therefore be celebrated, when successful, as a feminist gain. Hence their concern to 'uncover' feminist intention in the most apparently conformist texts. They may well be right to do so in many instances; but the underlying assumption that women's writing *must* have a feminist meaning, must in all cases be a gain for feminism, needs to be questioned. If my analysis of the eighteenth-century acceptance of the woman writer is correct, the relation between women's writing and patriarchal society is not simply one of opposition. Women's writing has not been totally suppressed, but on the contrary has (in certain forms) been encouraged; and it is capable of being appropriated for male domination.

Nancy Armstrong has pointed out that feminist analyses of the obstacles to female creativity in patriarchal society may leave women's actual achievements unexplained.[3] To explain why women were sometimes successful and highly acclaimed writers not only in the nineteenth century but for over 100 years before that, we could postulate that the oppressive ideology excluding women from writing has been neither consistent nor entirely successful. In the eighteenth century we can detect the presence of a view of writing that links it to the feminine role rather than opposing the two. This, as I will show, encouraged the expansion of women's professional writing. But at the same time as encouraging women to write, this feminization of literature defined literature as a special category supposedly outside the political arena, with an influence on the world as indirect as women's was supposed to be. Women's new status as authors did not necessarily mean new powers for women in general. *The Rise of the Woman Novelist*, then, is centrally concerned with the paradox that women writers may well be rising at a time when women's condition in general is deteriorating. My view of women's novels in the eighteenth century is in one sense positive: I am claiming that they occupy a much more important place in the development of the novel than is usually believed, and that they contributed a great deal to women's entry into public discourse. But I am wary of viewing that success as a simple gain: the terms on which women writers were accepted worked in some ways to suppress feminist opposition. Women's writing is not the same thing as women's rights.

NOTES

1. There are exceptions to this, and I am greatly indebted to those critics who have considered the work of the early women novelists. R. A. Day, *Told in Letters: Epistolary Fiction Before Richardson* (Ann Arbor: University of Michigan Press, 1966) and John J. Richetti, *Popular Fiction Before Richardson: Narrative Patterns 1700–39* (Oxford: Clarendon Press, 1969) include discussions of some women novelists, though neither focuses on the importance of the author's gender. Margaret Doody in *A Natural Passion: A Study of the Novels of Samuel Richardson* (Oxford: Clarendon Press, 1974) offers a welcome consideration of the early women novelists. Two important works which, though not centrally concerned with women writers, illuminate the connection between the early novel and the eighteenth-century ideology of femininity are Ruth Perry, *Women, Letters and the Novel* (New York: AMS Press, 1980), which describes the early letter-novel as offering women readers romantic fantasy to compensate for women's narrowed sphere, and Nancy K. Miller, *The Heroine's Text: Readings in the French and English Novel 1722–1782* (New York: Columbia University Press, 1980), which concentrates on male writers who adopt a 'feminine' voice. Both works have influenced my own view of the position of the eighteenth-century woman writer.

2. Ellen Moers' *Literary Women: The Great Writers* (New York, 1976; rpt London: Women's Press, 1980), Elaine Showalter's *A Literature of Their Own: British Women Novelists from Brontë to Lessing* (Princeton: Princeton University Press, 1977; rpt London: Virago Press, 1978), and Sandra Gilbert and Susan Gubar's *The Madwoman in the Attic: The Woman Writer and the Nineteenth-Century Literary Imagination* (New Haven: Yale University Press, 1979) are important works of feminist re-appraisal of women writers. Showalter's work is especially noteworthy for its concentration on lesser-known figures.

3. See Nancy Armstrong, 'The Rise of Feminine Authority in the Novel', *Novel* **15**, no. 2 (Winter, 1982), pp. 127–45.

PART 1
The Woman Novelist as Heroine

I

Wit's Mild Empire: The Rise of Women's Writing

In the late eighteenth century, many English writers were fond of congratulating their time for being an Age of Progress. 'Never did so many valuable improvements take place, never were so many prejudices abolished, in so short a time', glowed one man as he reviewed a volume of poetry written by a woman. Mrs Savage's *Poems on various Subjects and Occasions* had made him ponder on one of the more remarkable changes for the better he had witnessed: the proliferation of women writers. 'Instead of the single Sappho of antiquity, we can muster many names of equal, and some of superior value, in our little island, who, far from confining their abilities to the narrow limits of lyric poetry, stand foremost in various species of writing, both in prose and verse'.[1] *The New Lady's Magazine* took a similar line in an article entitled 'Female Literature', which rejoiced in the impossibility of forgetting 'a Cockburn, a Rowe, a Montagu, a Carter, a Chapone, a More, and a Barbauld ... a Seward and a Williams ... a Burney'.[2] Its optimistic tone may ring ironically in our ears today, when our society's tendency to amnesia about women's achievements has all but obliterated many of these names. They were illustrious in their time, though. Catharine Trotter Cockburn was known as a playwright and later for her philosophical writings; Elizabeth Singer Rowe for religious verse and prose; Elizabeth Montagu as the central figure in the literary and intellectual group known as the bluestockings; Elizabeth Carter as an intellectual, the author of a translation of the Stoic Epictetus; Hester Mulso Chapone for her didactic prose; Hannah More for plays and poetry; Anna Laetitia Barbauld for essays; Anna Seward and Helen Maria Williams for poetry.

Only Fanny Burney, of all these, had risen to fame as a novelist.[3] This bias in the list suggests the relatively low status of the novel rather than any dearth of women novelists. In fact it was the novel which more than any other literary form attracted large numbers of women into the male-dominated world of publishing. The market for novels, like the market for newspapers, magazines, tracts and pamphlets, expanded enormously during the century. From reviewing perhaps three or four novels a month in its early years, the *Monthly Review* (begun in 1749) soon found itself inundated with ten or a dozen, and the reviewers foresaw that their early plan of describing every book published would not be feasible much longer. 'The most we can do,' explained one writer in 1759, 'with respect to those numerous novels, that issue continually from the press, is to give rather a character than an account of each. To do even this, however, we find no easy task; since we might say of them, as Pope, with less justice, says of the *ladies*, "Most novels have no character at all."'⁴ It is interesting to note that while gallantly repudiating Pope's low opinion of women, the reviewer implies that ladies and novels belong together. This was a common belief. Critics (mostly male) presented themselves as upholders of cultural standards, bewailing the popularity of such a low (and, they believed, female) amusement as fiction. 'So long as our British Ladies continue to encourage our hackney Scriblers, by reading every Romance that appears, we need not wonder that the Press should swarm with such poor insignificant productions', they sighed.⁵ The debasement of literature in the marketplace was made even worse when women were successful sellers, and 'this branch of the literary *trade*', sniffed one reviewer (meaning novel-writing), 'appears, now, to be almost entirely engrossed by the Ladies'.⁶

It is hard to tell how far he was right. We do not know how many of the anonymous novels were by women nor how many writers adopted a pseudonym, or the designation 'lady' or 'gentleman' from the opposite sex. Women novelists were there in increasing numbers, though, and if they wrote, as one literary historian has estimated, between two-thirds and three-quarters of epistolary novels between 1760 and 1790, that was more than enough to give a general impression that they were taking over, whether this was felt as a threat or a cause for celebration.⁷ It was also enough to give a basis for the growth of a strong women's tradition in the novel by the end of the century. Moreover, some of the women novelists did a good deal to raise the genre in critical esteem. By the time Sir Walter Scott wrote his appreciative memoir of the novelist Charlotte Smith, he could reflect on 'the number of highly-talented women, who have, within our time of novel-reading, distinguished them-selves advantageously in this department of literature'. Jane Austen, Fanny Burney, Maria Edgeworth, Ann Radcliffe and several more were on his list, and, he added 'it would be impossible to match against these names the same number of masculine competitors, arising within the same space of time.'⁸ From being a frivolous and disreputable genre the novel had gained a certain amount of prestige. Women writers had had a similar rise in status, beginning somewhat earlier. The woman novelist in the early years of the nineteenth century benefited from a rise in public esteem for both her gender and her genre.

The rise of the woman writer, like the rise of the novel, encountered plenty of opposition. We have seen how reviewers tended to scorn fiction: but this is nothing to the abuse men sometimes gave to women writers. The popular novelist Eliza Haywood figured in the *Dunciad* as a 'Juno of majestic size,/With cow-like udders, and with ox-like eyes', her sexual favours offered as a prize in a urinating contest held between the booksellers Edmund Curll and William Chetwood. She was depicted with 'Two babes of love close clinging to her waste', and she and the playwright Susanna Centlivre were described as 'slip-shod Muses' with unkempt hair.[9] In one version Haywood appeared with 'Pearls on her neck, and roses in her hair,/And her fore-buttocks on the navel bare'.[10] Pope, of course, made equally virulent attacks on many male writers, but for his attack on Haywood he could draw on an existing stereotype of the woman writer, according to which she was unclean, untidy, disgustingly sexual and a whore.

Haywood encountered this kind of attack because she was a full member of the public world of hacks and scribblers, writing many scandalous pieces herself. Women who could afford to write without entering that world were understandably nervous about publishing their work.

> Did I my lines intend for public view,
> How many censures would their faults pursue!

mused the poet Anne Finch, Countess of Winchilsea. Certain that the main censure would be that they were 'by a woman writ', she suggested an explanation for men's hostility to women's writing:

> Alas! a woman that attempts the pen,
> Such an intruder on the rights of men,
> Such a presumptuous creature is esteemed,
> The fault can by no virtue be redeemed.[11]

Another woman writer, Margaret Cavendish (the Marchioness, and later the Duchess, of Newcastle) had suggested the same thing in 1653. Men, she argued, opposed women's writing 'because they think thereby, *Women* incroach too much upon their *Prerogatives*; for they hold *Books* as their *Crowne*, and the *Sword* their *Scepter*, by which they rule, and governe'.[12] With male dominance supposedly justified by man's greater powers of reason, evidence of women's intellectual capacities was obviously going to inspire fears, or hopes (depending on point of view) of a female rebellion.

The most extreme male reaction, then as now, was to deny women's ability to write at all. Theories excluding women from writing could be erected in the face of evidence of a growing number of women writers. Here is Chagrin the Critick in 1702, claiming that a woman writer is a contradiction in terms: 'I hate these Petticoat-Authors; 'tis false Grammar, there's no Feminine for the *Latin* word, 'tis entirely of the Masculine Gender, and the Language won't bear such a thing as a She-Author.' Chagrin, however, an imaginary character in the anonymous *Comparison Between the Two Stages*, is exposed as a pedantic Latinist living in the past, and his imaginary companions correct him by citing examples of real women living and writing plays in eighteenth-century England— Delariviere Manley, Mary Pix, and Catharine Trotter.[13]

The spirit of Chagrin the Critick is not entirely dead in the twentieth century. It haunted Virginia Woolf, who embodied it in Charles Tansley with his refrain 'women can't paint, women can't write', and exorcized it by the very writing of *To The Lighthouse*. It still haunts some women today; but it has been permanently weakened, as Woolf herself gratefully acknowledged, by the events of the eighteenth century.[14] Eighteenth-century women belied Chagrin's words in huge numbers, and they rose so much in public esteem that as we have seen, to some commentators their existence seemed almost the occasion for national celebration. Why were there so many more women writers, why did attitudes towards them change, and how did women gain their prominent position among novelists? These are questions which, as Scott remarked in his study of Charlotte Smith, could lead us far.

WOMEN NOVELISTS AND THE LITERARY MARKET

The expansion of the reading public to include the urban middle classes—tradesmen, shopkeepers, clerks, and their families—and also, to some extent, servants, has long been seen as the underlying social condition of the novel's rise.[15] Upper- and middle-class women with time on their hands probably formed a significant proportion of novel readers. Some of them also became novelists. Some formal education for women, however inadequate, was beginning to spread, causing some fears that class hierarchy was being threatened. By 1759, 'every description of tradesmen sent their children to be instructed, not in the useful attainments necessary for humble life, but the arts of coquetry and self-consequence, in short, those of a *young lady*,' complained one writer.[16] From such a background, according to the critics, came the typical, frivolous novel-reader. Perhaps some of the novelists did too. As a new form, apparently easy to write and not guarded by classical tradition,

it must have appealed to women without classical education. The epistolary novel, especially, seemed open almost to anyone who could write
a letter. Some people were afraid that their 'very Cook-wenches' would
become writers.[17] This was unlikely. Susanna Harrison was a domestic
servant who taught herself to read and write, and had her poems
published; while another writer remarkable for her low class-status was
Ann Yearsley, poet, playwright and 'Bristol milkwoman'. One novel was
announced as being by 'a Farmer's Daughter in Gloucestershire', leading
the reviewers to scold its author for wasting time on fiction that could
have been spent working at home;[18] while another farmer's daughter,
Elizabeth Inchbald, became a highly respected playwright and novelist.
These writers, though, were exceptions.

The novel might appeal particularly to the self-taught (though they
wrote poems and plays too) but it was also written by many women like
Sarah Fielding and Sarah Scott, who had had the benefit of an unusually
good education. Women who could translate Xenophon's *Memoirs of
Socrates* (Fielding) or write three works of history that gained contemporary praise (Scott), did not turn to the lowly novel as the only
form of writing they could manage. They turned to it because they could
make money from it.

Most women novelists shared their motive. Some, like Fanny Burney
and Ann Radcliffe, began to write fiction for pleasure, not profit, but
even Burney later depended on her writing and built a home for herself
and her penniless husband on the proceeds of *Camilla*, while the £900
reputedly paid for *The Italian* must have been useful in the Radcliffe
household. Critics were happy enough about writing they could charac-
terize as a leisured lady's amusement, but some of them thought that
only the leisured lady should write. 'A few ladies of high rank, who have
distinguished themselves of late years by their writings, exhibit by that
means, to their country women, a very dangerous object of emulation',
explained one writer. 'Those of superior fortunes, who are in the capacity
of always living above the cares of a family, however numerous, may
be allowed the privilege of commanding their own amusements and
pursuits; but surely such as are not in the most easy and affluent
circumstances, can scarcely indulge any inclination, more palpably
erroneous, than a preference for literature.'[19] But if women's writing did
not confirm its critics' worst fears by spreading to every servant girl and
labouring woman in the land, it did not obey their behests to confine
itself to rich high-born ladies either. Well-born or not, most women
novelists needed the money.

At this time money could be made from writing in new ways. Aristocratic patronage of writers was declining. This system, involving as it
often did court or government posts for writers, was not very helpful to

the sex barred from public office.[20] The new ways and means included publication by subscription, a sort of diffused patronage, whereby a number of people sponsored a book and had their names listed in the front. This clearly appealed to those women who had some connections with wealthy and titled readers, and seems to have been used as a genteel alternative to the literary marketplace. Selling a work outright to a bookseller, though, was more common. Prices rose throughout the century, and there are some cases of very high prices being paid to established novelists—Henry Fielding had £1,000 for *Amelia* in 1753. In most cases rewards were much lower—Jane Austen, as an unknown, got 10 guineas for *Sense and Sensibility*. They were large enough, however, to make fiction an attractive proposition to women barred from most other means of employment.

The career of Eliza Haywood (1693?–1756) shows how a woman could support herself by writing in the early eighteenth century.[21] Born Eliza Fowler, the daughter of a small shopkeeper in London, she was at the lower end of the women writers' social spectrum, but she claimed to have been given a good education, and certainly her learning included enough French to publish some translations. She married a clergyman, Valentine Haywood, and they had at least one child, a son baptised in 1711. The marriage was very probably stormy: certainly Eliza Haywood's desire for an independent life soon emerged. She made her acting debut in Smock Alley, Dublin, in 1715, and published her first novel, the phenomenally successful *Love in Excess*, in 1719. This went through several editions and was one of the most widely read novels of the period before 1740.[22] Her *Ten Letters from a Young Lady of Quality*, translated from French, was published by subscription in 1720 and had 309 subscribers. Perhaps encouraged by this evidence of her ability to survive without her husband she left him soon afterwards, and he put an advert in the *Post Boy* for 7 January 1721 announcing her disappearance and disclaiming responsibility for her debts. Two months afterwards her tragedy *The Fair Captive* was being performed at Lincoln's Inn Fields. Thereafter Eliza Haywood supported herself by writing, and occasionally acting. She performed in her own comedy, *A Wife To Be Lett*, in 1723. She wrote another tragedy, *Frederick, Duke of Brunswick-Lunenburgh*, performed in 1729, and collaborated with the playwright William Hatchett on an adaptation of Fielding's *Tom Thumb* in 1733. Most of the 38 works she published between 1720 and 1730 were novels. The first part of *Love in Excess* was followed by two further parts, and by *The British Recluse* (1722), *Idalia* (1723), *The Fatal Secret* (1724), *Lasselia* (1724) and many more. We do not know how many copies were sold of these novels, whose prices ranged from one to three shillings, but clearly the booksellers were making enough money from her work to keep on buying it, and we can assume that they were not paying her much since she evidently needed to keep up a considerable output. She probably hoped to increase her income from the various dedications of her works, combining old-style patronage with the new literary market as many writers did. Her novels were very popular, and a collected edition in four volumes appeared in 1724 and again, with additions, in 1725 and 1732. In some of her works, like *Memoirs of a Certain Island* (1725), she used a popular but greatly-scorned form, scandal about public figures disguised as fiction. This is what Pope attacked her for—she libelled some of his friends. She did not publish much in the 1730s, and it has been suggested that this is because she was less popular after her appearance in the *Dunciad*, though changes in the novel-market may well be a contributory factor. She turned instead to acting, and the casting may have been influenced by her sexual reputation—she tended to play cast-off mistresses.[23] In the 1740s and 1750s she returned to fiction with a new tone, and wrote several of the long, didactic novels then in vogue. She also tried periodicals, like *The Female Spectator*, 1744–46, and works of moral advice like *The Wife* and *The Husband* in 1756. She was writing until shortly before her death.

Haywood's long career shows that provided she was prolific and versatile, a woman could make her living by writing in the first half of the century. Just how far her income stretched is not clear. We cannot tell whether she had any financial help from the lovers she was reputed to have, nor whether she supported anyone besides herself. We do not know if the illegitimate children Pope referred to really existed, or if they did, whether they survived, nor do we know what happened to the son of her marriage. We can tell much more about the income and family circumstances of Charlotte Smith (1749–1806), whose career it is interesting to compare with Haywood's, because it shows what a woman dependent on her writing could achieve by the end of the century.

Like Eliza Haywood, Charlotte Smith left her husband. In her case it was after over 20 years of marriage and 12 children, eight of them (the youngest aged two) dependent on her for support after the separation in 1787.[24] Smith had had literary ambitions from an early age, sending her poems to the *Lady's Magazine* at 14; and during her marriage had made a profit from *Elegiac Sonnets*, published at her own expense in 1784. These poems were evidently very popular, as successive editions, with additional sonnets, appeared throughout the eighties and nineties; a second volume came out in 1797 and a ninth edition of the first volume in 1800. Novels, though, brought in most of the money. The first, *Emmeline*, was so popular when it appeared in 1788 that the publisher, Cadell, increased his original payment to her. *Ethelinde* (1789), *Celestina* (1791), *Desmond* (1792), *The Old Manor House* (1793), *The Banished Man* (1794), *The Wanderings of Warwick* (1794), *Montalbert* (1795),

Marchmont (1796) and *The Young Philosopher* (1798) followed. All are long works in three, four or even (*Ethelinde*) five volumes. They sold at three or four shillings a volume, and Smith was usually paid about £50 a volume. This was nowhere near the sums Ann Radcliffe was getting but well above the amount paid to most novelists at this time, and this indicates Smith's popularity and high reputation. Later in the nineties and in the 1800s she diversified her output with children's stories, works of history and natural history for children, and a five-volume collection of narratives (*Letters of a Solitary Wanderer*, 1799–1802).

It was only with a struggle that Charlotte Smith made enough money for her family. She was of a much higher social position than Eliza Haywood—her parents were landowning gentry, her husband the son of a rich man with a West Indian estate—and she wanted to educate her children to professions. Her husband had control of the fortune she had brought him, and was continually fleeing his creditors or being imprisoned for debt. After they parted she occasionally sent him money, and as her children grew up their financial burden on her was not always lightened. At one time she was supporting one of her daughters, her son-in-law (who had given up his college fellowship to marry and was studying) and her grandchild. Charlotte Smith was very bitter about her life because she considered that a woman of her class ought not to be reduced to writing novels for a living; and it was all made worse by a struggle with the lawyers about the terms of her rich father-in-law's will. (It was eventually settled, as she had hoped, in favour of her children, but not until after her death.) Her feelings were often vividly expressed in her letters.

> My situation is extremely terrible [she wrote in 1791]—for I have no means whatever of supporting my Children during the Holidays, nor of paying their Bills when they return to School: & I am so harassed with Duns, that I cannot write with any hope of getting any thing done by that time—I know not where I find resolution to go on from day to day—Especially under the idea of Mr. Smith's being in London, liable every hour to imprisonment [presumably for debt].[25]

She did go on, though, obtaining advances, writing in haste, and making enough to support her family; and unlike Haywood, was treated to public esteem instead of abuse. Deserting Mr Smith, and writing for money, did no harm to her reputation: people in general seem to have agreed with Elizabeth Carter's sympathetic report that she had been 'obliged to purchase her freedom from a vile husband'.[26] Her higher social status, and unblemished reputation, had a great deal to do with this difference of reception; but general changes in the literary world also helped. In Haywood's time it would have been much more difficult for a woman of Smith's background to write novels for a living and remain high in public esteem.

Haywood's and Smith's experiences show how important a source of money the novel could be, but they were exceptionally successful writers, and a more common pattern was for writing novels to provide a smaller proportion of the writer's income. Mary Davys tried, after her husband's death, to make money from plays and fiction, and made five guineas from her first novel in 1705; but the coffee-shop she set up in Cambridge seems to have provided a more regular support, and she was still in enough financial distress to send begging letters to Swift, an old friend of her husband's. Later in the century Sarah Scott, of very good family and with enough to live on after separating from her husband, wrote novels to add to her income. She remarked that though she received very little for *Millenium Hall* (1762) she had taken less than a month to write it and so had been paid about a guinea a day for her efforts. Sarah Fielding wrote to add to her small private income, but was still partially dependent on financial help from her brothers, and later from Elizabeth Montagu. Some of her novels were very profitable: *Familiar Letters between the Principal Characters in David Simple* (1747), sold at ten shillings a copy and had 500 subscribers. Elizabeth Griffith, daughter of a family connected with the Irish stage, worked for a time as an actress and turned to writing after her marriage. She and her husband published their courtship letters after the failure of his linen manufacture, and the success of the literary venture encouraged her to proceed with the translations, novels and plays which helped support a growing family. Women from various backgrounds and in various circumstances, then, turned to the novel for money.[27]

THE NEW IDEOLOGY OF FEMININITY

The expanding market for novels provided women with an opportunity that more and more of them exploited as the century wore on; but the picture is a more complex one than this account of supply and demand suggests. The woman novelist's rise has to be understood in terms of the underlying social developments that enabled women to take advantage of the new literary market. Central to the experience of all these writers was the changing role of women in late seventeenth- and eighteenth-century Britain, and the accompanying development of new ideas about femininity. In changing the way women lived and were regarded, and crucially, the authority they were allowed to assume, bourgeois society transformed people's notions of the woman writer.

In legal terms there was not much change in women's position during the century. A woman was still regarded basically as a chattel, under the authority first of her father and then her husband. In the propertied classes she was herself treated as part of the property—'given in with an estate' when she married, as one of Mary Wollstonecraft's heroines reflected.[28] Any legal restrictions on her husband's use of the wealth she brought were intended to protect her family's interests, not in recognition of her individual claim to it. In fact her very individuality, legally speaking, was gone. The married woman, as described by William Blackstone, was practically a legal nonentity: 'By marriage, the husband and wife are one person in law: that is, the very being or legal existence of the woman is suspended during the marriage, or at least is incorporated and consolidated into that of the husband: under whose wing, protection, and *cover*, she performs every thing.'[29] This meant that a married woman's activities were severely limited. She could not enter into contracts, could not sue or be sued, and had no legal entitlement to her own earnings. Her husband was supposed to support her and was held responsible for her debts, but he could repudiate this responsibility if she left him, as Eliza Haywood's husband did when she deserted him. In practice the woman was not always so helpless as these laws imply. Eliza Haywood seems to have effectively escaped Valentine Haywood's authority and had control of her earnings. Charlotte Smith, though she did not retrieve her dowry when she left her husband, managed to keep her publishers' payments under her control. These experiences were unusual but not singular; and for the previous century, the evidence suggests that married women were often traders, members of guilds or subjects of lawsuits.[30] It is not surprising, then, to find them in the eighteenth century entering the new trade of novel writing.

A single woman was considered in law to have her own separate existence, but she was supposed to be under her father's authority. It was the widow who held the most independent place a woman could have in society. Freed from masculine authority she could trade on her own account, in many cases taking over her late husband's business. During the eighteenth century, though, the traditionally independent and wilful widow lost much of her economic power. 'I may venture to say, that where there is one Widow that keeps on the trade now, after a husband's decease, there were ten, if not twenty, that did it [in former times]', reported Daniel Defoe in the 1720s. The reason he gave was the traders' aspirations to gentility: 'The tradesman is foolishly vain of making his wife a gentlewoman, and forsooth he will have her sit above in the parlour, and receive visits, and drink Tea, and entertain her neighbours, or take a coach and go abroad; But as to the business, she shall not stoop to touch it, he has Apprentices and journeymen, and there is no need of it'. In this case the widow was in no state to make her own living, though as Defoe insisted with some exasperation, 'WOMEN, when once they give themselves leave to stoop to their own circumstances, and think fit to rouze up themselves to their own relief, are not so helpless and shiftless creatures as some would make them appear in the world.'[31]

Womanly helplessness, though, was being encouraged. The single woman was also losing her economic strength. The word spinster, first used for unmarried women because spinning was such an important occupation among them, was losing its occupational reference.[32] A spinster was becoming an unmarried woman of no particular occupation, and this reflected a change in her real position. In the almost self-sufficient households of a previous era, there had always been a need for the unmarried woman's labour. During the eighteenth century, as trade expanded and commercial production gradually took over spinning, weaving, brewing, baking, soap and candle-making, and bleaching, her importance diminished. This was an effect felt in the prosperous middle and lower-middle trading classes, where the idle wife, as Defoe's remarks show, was becoming a man's status symbol. There was often very little for the middle-class daughter to do, and if she was left without enough money to support a life of genteel idleness her situation was pitiable. Unable or unwilling, in this increasingly class-conscious society, to become a domestic servant, what could she do? 'Few are the modes of earning a subsistence, and those very humiliating', reported Mary Wollstonecraft in the 1780s.[33] She herself had tried the two most usual yokes of lady's companion and governess and chafed bitterly under them. Other writers described the unmarried woman maintaining gentility but dependent on, and resented by, her more fortunate brother. A gentleman's daughter might find herself in poor lodgings, 'with difficulty living on the interest of two or three thousand pounds, reluctantly, and perhaps irregularly, paid to her by an avaricious or extravagant brother, who considers such payment as a heavy incumbrance on his paternal estate'.[34]

Such expressions of sympathy for the dependent woman's plight, together with some evidence of increasing concern for women's education, and a literature full of tributes to femininity, have led some historians to conclude that women's position was improving.[35] We need to distinguish, though, between their status in the home and their agency outside it. Alice Clark's research on women's work in the seventeenth century showed how expanded capitalist organization (intensified during the eighteenth century) reduced women's economic power. As the workplace became separated from the home, men, supported by a system of apprenticeship that excluded women, took over many jobs traditionally done by women in the home. The wife of an independent craftsman or trader might still share in his business, but as industries were organised on a larger scale more men were becoming wage-earning journeymen, whose wives had no share in their work.[36] Women were becoming more economically dependent on their husbands; and the concern expressed for women in so much eighteenth-century literature is evidence that their position in society was being perceived as a problem.

As women became more dependent on marriage for their livelihood and dignity, marriage itself seems to have become more difficult for them to achieve. The 1801 census revealed a surplus of women over men, and this situation had probably prevailed during much of the preceding century. Among the aristocracy, there was a shortage of husbands, exacerbated by the laws of primogeniture, which meant that younger sons might consider themselves unable to afford marriage—or, as they increasingly did, marry out of their class into the professions.[37] Lower down the social scale, men in trade were encouraged not to marry until they could afford to support a wife, once considered an economic asset, and now a burden.[38] No wonder getting married, and the problems facing a young woman without an inviting dowry, concerned so many eighteenth-century writers.

In sharp contrast to the growth of women's public role as professional writers, these changes in their role were all in the direction of making their experience more private and more domestic. The home, always the woman's place but once also the centre of family activity and source of the family's subsistence, was becoming cut off from the world of production and trade. Historical studies of women in medieval and Tudor times suggests that by the eighteenth century women had been forced to withdraw from many public activities.[39] Late in the century, feminist writers complained bitterly about this. They suggested that the growth of prostitution was to be blamed on the erosion of women's other economic opportunities. Men were becoming milliners, mantua-makers, and hairdressers, and had even taken control of that ancient female province, midwifery. The 'etiquette of the times' made trade out of the question for most middle-class women even if they had no fortune; and whereas sons were trained to professions, daughters were left idle. Exposing 'the fatal consequences of men traders engrossing women's occupations', Mary Anne Radcliffe demanded, 'What statute is there, which grants that men alone shall live, and women scarcely exist?[40] Women of rank should fight against the male takeover, argued Priscilla Wakefield. They 'should procure female instructors for their children; they should frequent no shops that are not served by women; they should wear no clothes that are not made by them'.[41] These strong feminist voices, emerging at the end of the century, should not make us take a rosy view of the period for fostering women's self-expression. The deteriorating situation they were complaining about existed: women's already restricted options were narrowing.

Accompanying the change in women's role was the rise of a new ideology of femininity. The separate 'woman's sphere' of Victorian times has received much attention, and the Evangelical movement has been shown to have influenced the glorification of woman's mission in the home in the period 1780–1830;[42] but the start of this development was further back. The increasing separation of home from workplace in the late seventeenth century and the eighteenth century laid the foundations for a new bourgeois ideology of femininity, according to which women were very separate, special creatures. It has been suggested that this view of womanhood replaced an older view, prevailing in the sixteenth and seventeenth centuries, in which sexual differences were perceived in hierarchical terms—women being considered essentially similar to men but inferior. In the eighteenth century, by contrast, women were more highly valued, but also more confined to a special feminine sphere, as guardians of the home and of moral and emotional values.[43] The contrast is probably not so complete as that implies: certainly the notion of specially feminine qualities was current long before our period, though what those qualities were, whether purity or lust, tenderness or heart-lessness, had never been settled. Nevertheless it is true that the eighteenth century saw a heightened interest in defining woman as a special being. Sexual differences received emphatic attention; and with their endless discussions of 'femalities' and 'feminalities', eighteenth-century writers were helping to construct a new definition of womanhood. The highly popular periodical writers Addison and Steele played no small part in this. One of Steele's pieces in *The Tatler* is typical of the new view:

> I am sure, I do not mean it an injury to women, when I say there
> is a sort of sex in souls. I am tender of offending them, and know it
> is hard not to do it on this subject; but I must go on to say, that
> the soul of a man and that of a woman are made very unlike,
> according to the employments for which they are designed. The
> ladies will please to observe, I say, our minds have different, not
> superior qualities to theirs. The virtues have respectively a
> masculine and a feminine cast.[44]

Women were not inferior, men gallantly assured them, just different; and the differences were explained to them at length. It seems that eighteenth-century women needed a good deal of educating into their 'inborn', 'natural' feminine qualities, for the 'conduct-book' or 'courtesy-book' for women proliferated. 'The Whole Duty of Man' was the Puritan concern of the seventeenth century, but the following age concentrated more on the special duty of woman. Typical of the female conduct-books is Dr James Fordyce's two-volume *Sermons To Young Women* (1765), which

Jane Austen's Mr Collins tried to read aloud to the Bennet girls in *Pride and Prejudice*.

The fictional clergyman's manners may well have been inspired by Dr Fordyce's style, which at times is worthy of Elizabeth Bennet's comic suitor. 'As for ourselves, indeed, we do not think it requires much fortitude to confess our having felt an early predilection for Good and Amiable Women', he confides to the reader of his *Character and Conduct of the Female Sex* (1776). 'It proceeded from an early observation of the modesty which always adorns their deportment, of the elegance and vivacity which often distinguish their conversation, and of that delightful interest which the tender affections, and attractive manners, found among the most valuable of the sex, are peculiarly adapted to create in hearts of the least feeling'.[45] The *Sermons* set out in considerable detail what a good and amiable woman is: obedient, modest, gentle and formed to be man's companion. Fordyce stresses that his is an advanced, even elevated, view of her function.

> To divert fancy, to gratify desire, and in general to be a sort of better servants, are all the purposes for which some suppose your sex designed. A most illiberal supposition! The least degree of refinement or candour will dispose us to regard them in a far higher point of light. They were manifestly intended to be the mothers and formers of a rational and immortal offspring; to be a kind of softer companions, who, by nameless delightful sympathies and endearments, might improve our pleasures and soothe our pains; to lighten the load of domestic cares, and thereby leave us more at leisure for rougher labours, or severer studies; and finally, to spread a certain grace and embellishment over human life.[46]

For Fordyce, women are clearly to be defined in relation to men, for whom they are created. Woman's place is the home and her centre of interest her family. Anything outside that is a male concern: 'war, commerce, politics, exercises of strength and dexterity, abstract philosophy, and all the abstruser sciences, are most properly the province of men' (*Sermons*, I, 272). Their completely different roles in life make men and women dependent on each other, and their male and female characteristics are benevolently provided to make this arrangement work. 'Was not such reciprocal aid a great part of Nature's intention in that mental and moral difference of sex, which she has marked by characters no less distinguishable than those that diversify their outward forms?' (I, 175). This difference, examined closely, hardly bears out his claim to have an elevated view of women. 'I scruple not to declare my opinion, that Nature appears to have formed the faculties of your sex for the most part with less vigour than those of ours', he pronounces (I,

271–2), adding that, by way of compensation, she has granted women a better perception of character (I, 282). This helps them to fulfil their aim in the world, which he tells them, 'chiefly is to read Men, in order to make yourselves agreeable and useful' (I, 273). A woman who can do this has no reason, in his view, to regret her exclusion from other kinds of business. Instead of power a woman has a special feminine influence, which she can exert to moderate masculine behaviour. On this subject Fordyce grows eloquent.

> The influence of the sexes is, no doubt, reciprocal; but I must ever be of opinion, that yours is the greatest. How often have I seen a company of men who were disposed to be riotous, checked all at once into decency by the accidental entrance of an amiable woman; while her good sense and obliging deportment charmed them into at least a temporary conviction, that there is nothing so beautiful as female excellence, nothing so delightful as female conversation in its best form! (I, 21)

In praising woman's influence Fordyce is not withheld by any consideration of the evil nature ascribed to women by a long tradition of misogynous literature. Not for him the accusations of inordinate female lust so common in earlier times. Churchmen had called woman 'an occasion of sin to man', and medieval poets had described her 'beastly lust ... furious appetite ... and ... foul delight', to be echoed centuries later by Restoration wits who called her 'infinitely vile, and fair'. Even in the eighteenth century there were still plenty of men who suspected, with Pope, that despite outward appearances of modesty, 'Ev'ry Woman is at Heart a Rake'.[47] With delicate indirectness, Fordyce manages to attack such ideas. Referring to the traditional argument that Eve's eating the apple shows that woman brought sin into the world, he contends that female frailty is not, as so many men have declared, a matter of female sexual desire:

> But what was it that exposed the woman to that snare by which she was seduced? Passions, it must be owned, extremely culpable in their nature, and fatal in their consequences; but not the passions for which her daughters have been indiscriminately blamed. In reality, the resolute spirit and persevering vigilance, with which great numbers of women preserve their honour, while so few men in comparison are restrained by the laws of continence, seem to me no slight proof that the former possess a degree of fortitude well worthy of praise. (II, 53)

His attitude is typical of his age. Woman is no longer accused of untrammelled sexuality but only of vanities and follies. Chaste, pious and modest, her effect on man is entirely beneficial, so long as she remembers to cultivate her feminine qualities and provide men with what they desire: 'soft features, and a flowing voice, a form not robust, and a demeanour delicate and gentle' (II, 225). In his final sermon, 'On Female Meekness', Fordyce sums up his advice to the good and amiable young woman: 'It is thine, thou fair form, to command by obeying, and by yielding to conquer' (II, 261).

Fordyce's pronouncements, and those of many other like-minded moralists, would not seem likely to foster a climate in which women could take on a public role as writers. Exhorted from all sides to be discreet and reserved, to withdraw from public notice, to shine only in domestic accomplishments and to influence only through domestic affections, surely a woman was divesting herself of all female graces by putting her written work up for sale? This question troubled Fordyce's female contemporaries, as we can see in Frances Brooke's novel *The Excursion* (1777), which tells the story of a young woman led away from the feminine role Fordyce describes by her literary ambitions.

Brooke's heroine, Maria Villiers, 'quick, impatient, sprightly, playful', hopes, unlike her gentle, conventional, sensible sister, to find happiness in 'the brilliant mazes of the world'.[48] Her wish to sample public life in London is linked to her desire for literary notice. On her ill-judged excursion to the metropolis without her family, she takes the epic poem, the novel and the tragedy she has written, believing that she can rely on these for her support if her money runs out. Although her own inclinations are as virtuous as Dr Fordyce would expect in a young girl, Maria is naive and thoughtless, and these qualities almost lead to sexual disaster. She arrives in town to find that her friend Mrs Herbert is away in Paris, and instead of returning to her uncle and guardian now that she has no woman of character to stay with, she remains unchaperoned in London, mixing with an untrustworthy titled lady and her somewhat disreputable friends. She falls in love with Lord Melvile and hopes to marry him, but he only means to seduce her. Short of money, Maria tries to get her tragedy produced but it is rejected unread by David Garrick (an incident which gives Brooke the opportunity for a satiric portrait of the famous actor–manager, who had rejected her own work in the past). Eventually Maria escapes Melvile's clutches, marries the much worthier Colonel Herbert, and settles down to a life of decent country retirement. 'I have been very indiscreet indeed, Louisa,' she confesses to her sister, 'but the inconveniences I have found from that indiscretion will make me a pattern of circumspection for the future' (*The Excursion*, II, 259).

Maria's desire for independence away from home and her ambition for literary fame are both aspects of the indiscretion that threatens to be so disastrous in its consequences. 'Infatuated girl! Why did she leave her household gods?' demands the narrator. 'Those household gods are alone the certain guardians of female honour' (II, 201). The heroine's good-natured literary friend Mr Hammond admires her work but advises her against writing for the theatre, 'a pursuit in which her sex, her delicacy of mind, her rectitude of heart, her honest pride, and perhaps her genius, were all strongly against her success' (II, 31). Maria settles in the end to a domestic life in which her writing will be an accomplishment, not her maintenance nor a means of bringing her into public notice.

Maria's adventures may suggest that a literary profession is unsuitable for an unprotected young woman, but Brooke's sympathies are certainly with her erring heroine. If Maria is indiscreet, it is because she has '*genius*, that emanation of the Divinity, that fatal gift of heaven, pleasing to others, ruinous to its possessor' (I, 38). Her tragedy shows that genius and receives Mr Hammond's praise; and it is left unclear whether a literary career is a bad idea because of its inherent unsuitability for a woman, or because of prejudice against women writers. (Garrick resented the accusation that he did not appreciate women playwrights, citing his support of Hannah Cowley, Elizabeth Griffith and Hannah More.)[49] Frances Brooke may present literary ambition as a dangerous thing, but she certainly appreciates its power, which is hardly surprising considering the evidence of her own career.

In the year that Brooke sent her ambitious heroine packing off to country seclusion she was in London, managing the Haymarket theatre with her friend the tragic actress Mary Ann Yates. This venture followed a varied career which began in the early 1750s, when Frances Moore left her Lincolnshire home and travelled to the capital—apparently, like Maria Villiers, in search of literary fame. Adopting the persona of 'Mary Singleton, Spinster', she wrote a periodical, *The Old Maid*, in 1755–6; and in 1756, shortly after her marriage to the Reverend John Brooke, she published her play, *Virginia, a Tragedy* along with some poems and translations. She does not seem to have spent much time in rural retirement in her husband's Norfolk parish. She spent some time in London, writing novels and translations, while her husband went to Canada as chaplain to the English garrison in Quebec. Later she followed him out there, returning in 1768 to publish her Canadian novel, *Emily Montague*, in 1769. In the 1780s she turned her attention again to writing plays, and her sex, delicacy of mind, rectitude of heart and so on did not prevent her from having a considerable success with *Rosina*, a comic opera which became one of the most popular after-pieces on the London stage, being acted 201 times between 1782 and 1800.[50] Brooke only retired to the country (to her son's house in Lincolnshire) in 1788 when she was 64. On her death the following year, the *European Magazine* printed biographical 'Anecdotes of Mrs. Frances Brooke', which showed that in her case literary pursuits had not destroyed womanly reputation. She was praised for being 'as remarkable for her gentleness and suavity of manners as for her literary talents'.[51]

In *The Excursion*, Brooke produced an impeccably 'moral' work by criticizing the kind of independent and ambitious behaviour she showed in her own life. Maria Villiers' story was 'very properly calculated to deter young ladies from launching out into the world ... without discretion', remarked the *Critical Review*.[52] It is one example of a trend very general in the later years of the century: women novelists were carving a public niche for themselves by recommending a private, domestic life for their heroines.

The dangers run by an imprudent young writing woman might make a very good plot for a novel, but the novelist herself was living proof that this vocation could now be followed by the most virtuous. The reason none of the reviewers thought to point out the discrepancy between Brooke's honourable public career and her recommendation of household gods as women's only protectors, was that writing, at the same time as it was being professionalized, was also being domesticated. There was not only the general change from a system dominated by private circulation and aristocratic patronage to a more open literary market, the world of Grub Street; but a simultaneous movement of certain kinds of writing especially associated with women—the familiar letter, the diary, the domestic conduct book—out of the private and into the public arena. The rapid growth of the novel, which drew on all these private modes, is the best example. This meant not only that women could make a living out of what were thought of as essentially feminine accomplishments, like writing pretty letters; but that the public world itself could be affected by the values introduced to it by these hitherto private modes of writing.

The novel was exactly suited to bridging the gap between women and the public world writers like Fordyce thought so alien to them. For a start, the novel could be written at home, and many a woman novelist made sure she told her readers that she had not neglected family duties to write. Sarah Emma Spencer made a bid for her readers' sympathy by telling them that her novel *Memoirs of the Miss Holmsbys* had been 'written by the bed-side of a sick husband, who has no other support than what my writings will produce'.[53] Charlotte Smith, reminding her readers of her children's dependence on her earnings, boasted: '*I* ... may safely say, that it was in the *observance*, not in the *breach* of duty, *I* became an Author'.[54] In fact, writing novels might be seen as the literate middle-class household's substitute for the declining home industries which had once enabled the housewife to contribute to the support of her family.

Then the novel's usual themes and preoccupations were, as detractors and admirers alike never tired of pointing out, largely those of women.

Women's experience was a major preoccupation for society in general,
and for the novelist in particular. Because of women's dependence on
marriage, and the pressure on women to attract a husband while living
up to newly strict ideas of feminine propriety, many eighteenth-century
writers were interested in defining types of feminine sexual behaviour.
The coquette, the prude and the modest woman were described and
compared with one another. Sexual danger became a major preoccupation of fiction. Brooke's Maria Villiers is an unusual heroine for
her literary pretensions but an entirely normal one for being the subject
of unwanted libertine advances. Heroines became heroines by dodging
seduction attempts, and their creators moralized over their experiences.
Eliza Haywood's novels typically warned 'how dangerous it is to trans-
gress, even the least Bounds of that Reserve which is enjoined by Virtue
for our Guard!'[55] Samuel Richardson's *Pamela* (1740) suggested that a
woman's 'virtue', defended against a man's seduction attempts, could be
'rewarded' by a marriage which enhanced her social status.

The novel usually dealt with women's experience in a domestic setting—the home being the world to which middle-class women were
increasingly confined, and also now being a world considered important
enough to write about. By 1769 the *Critical* reviewer, considering Maria
Susanna Cooper's novel *The Exemplary Mother*, could remark: 'The rep-
resentation of domestic life is a source of moral entertainment, perhaps,
the most instructive and congenial to the universal taste of mankind, of
all the various scenes with which the human drama presents us. It is
within the compass of that narrow sphere that the tender emotions of
the heart are exerted in their utmost sensibility.'[56] It is not surprising
that the novel that called forth this encomium should be a woman's.
The redefinition of womanhood included a reappraisal of women's proper
authority, and women were now seen as having a legitimate authority
within the private sphere: including domestic life, emotions, romance
and the young girl's moral welfare. When that private sphere became
the central concern of a literary genre, woman's authority extended to
that too.

The novel of domestic life not only provided women writers with a
subject they were likely to know about, then, but one they had a special
authority to deal with. According to the new ideology of womanhood,
women were special creatures with a special mode of expression. Eighteenth-century commentators, especially towards the end of the century,
were full of praise for women's didactic writing, their sentiments, their
knowledge of the heart, their knowledge of their own sex. Female characters, explained Henry Fielding in the preface to one of his sister Sarah's
novels, were much better 'when drawn by sensible writers of their own
Sex, who are on this Subject much more capable, than the ablest of
ours'. Reviewers considered that 'a woman only can enter justly into all

the scruples and refinements of female manners', and that 'we naturally expect the most lively and touching delineations of [the tender passion] from the female pen'.[57] Women's writing was encouraged along 'feminine' paths by this kind of expectation. Her supposed feminine skills gave the woman novelist a special role. She could write about women's particular problems and desires, largely for an audience of middle-class women looking not just for amusement in their idle hours but for fables that would lend attraction and meaning to the narrowed feminine sphere. Paradoxically, the very restriction of economic power and opportunities for independence for the majority of middle-class women had created earning power and a public career for the small minority of them who wrote novels.

WRITERS AS HEROINES: FOUNDATIONS FOR WOMEN'S
LITERARY AUTHORITY IN THE SEVENTEENTH CENTURY

The rise of the novel, then, provided ideological as well as financial encouragement for the growth of women's writing. A literary form enshrining the domestic, moral and sentimental values thought of as feminine allowed women a special literary authority. However, the novel was not the origin of that authority, but rather the occasion of its fullest development. The foundations for the eighteenth-century acceptance of the woman novelist were laid in the seventeenth century, when the appearance of a number of women writers prompted discussion of 'feminine' characteristics in writing and distinctions between proper and improper women writers.

Seventeenth-century women writers included a number of aristocrats dedicating their leisure hours to literary pursuits, and, less well known but also important, several middle-class women writing on household, medical and religious matters. The works of many poets, diarists and letter-writers remained private, while women's published writing ranged from romance, poetry and drama to non-fictional prose. The traditional notion of woman's proper silence was being challenged, then, and in particular there were feminist writers who, by their emphasis on women's intellectual capacities and the need for education, fostered a view that women's learning and women's writing were the instruments of struggle against male domination.[58] In the early eighteenth century the feminist Sarah Fyge Egerton rounded off her poem 'The Emulation', which complained that women were enslaved by the tyranny of custom, by calling on women to show their learning and to write: in this way they could claim 'Wit's Empire' even if they could have no other.[59]

Despite opposition to women writers, many of their readers were willing to allow this claim, on certain conditions. In fact, there was a tendency among both men and women to see women writers as heroines. This was encouraged by the fact that woman's voice as expressed in earlier literature (whether created by a female or by a male writer) was often the voice of the heroine of a love-story. Ovid's *Heroides*, with letters written by passionate and deserted heroines; the letters of the real twelfth-century nun Héloise; and the probably fictional Portuguese nun of *Les Lettres Portugaises* (1669), associated women's writing with a heroine's writing for seventeenth- and eighteenth-century readers.[60] Moreover, the long romances written in seventeenth-century France by writers like La Calprenède and Madeleine de Scudéry, which were extremely popular in England, contained many interpolated 'histories' recounted by the various heroines.[61] Thus long sections of narrative appeared to come in a woman's voice, and the heroines also wrote love-letters, providing models for the writers of the short epistolary novels which began appearing in the late 1600s. The *salon* society that formed the background to the French romances fostered identification of these writing heroines with real-life women, for the characters in romance were often idealized pictures of the author's friends. When women began to correspond with their friends using pseudonyms drawn from these romances, heroine and writer moved closer still.

In England the effect of all this was apparent in women who became publicly known by a romantic pseudonym. The most famous example is Katherine Philips (1632–64), who corresponded with her friends in verse and prose, using romantic names for them and herself: hers was Orinda. When her poems were published 'Orinda' became a celebrated writer, and one of the reasons people were ready to praise her was that she had become a kind of heroine to them.

Useful as the notion of 'heroine-writer' was in gaining acceptance for women's work, it had drawbacks for the development of their writing. A woman writer was expected to show a heroine's sensibility, to write in the spontaneous manner associated with a woman in love. She was also expected to live up to the ideals of conduct followed by the heroine of romance. A set of firm restrictions on women's writing, in fact, grew up along with the woman writer's fame and respectability.

The implications of this are explored more fully in the next two chapters. Here we just need to note the essential point that making a woman writer into a heroine linked her life and her writing together, so that the one was judged in terms of the other. To some extent critics of male writers made the same link: good literature, it was thought, could come only from morally good writers. But the greater freedom, especially the sexual freedom, allowed to men in real life made this much less of a restriction. We have already seen that a woman novelist like Eliza Haywood could be attacked on the basis of her sexual life. In a female writer, bawdy expressions could be taken as evidence of an unchaste, and therefore unacceptable, woman; while knowledge of sexual irregularity in her life was used to condemn her writing as immoral. On the other hand, a woman whose writing expressed the delicacy and morality that were seen as indications of her personal virtue received extravagant praise.

A variety of women writers took a hand in building 'Wit's Empire', but it was only when a few of these rose to fame that a general public idea of the writing woman began to take shape. Three women earned substantial fame as writers in the mid and late seventeenth century: Margaret Cavendish, Duchess of Newcastle (1623–73); Katherine Philips; and Aphra Behn (1640–89). Margaret Cavendish, an aristocrat devoted to literature, was a prolific writer of poetry, plays, 'sociable letters', fiction, biography, autobiography, and works on natural philosophy: most of her writings were published in the 1650s and 1660s. Katherine Philips, daughter of a London merchant and wife of a landowner in Wales, produced a volume of poetry and a translation of Corneille's *Pompey* before dying young of smallpox. Aphra Behn, after a colourful early life which included visiting the West Indies and spying for Charles II in Antwerp, supported herself by writing many successful plays, performed and published in the 1670s and 1680s. She also wrote fiction and poetry.[62] In the reception accorded these women, we can trace the beginnings of the reading public's acceptance of the woman writer. We will also witness the process by which women claimed their 'empire' in literature by taking earlier women writers as heroines to celebrate and examples to imitate.[63]

Margaret Cavendish, the oldest of the three writers and the first to publish, received much flattery because of her high rank and riches, but never wide public respect. She first drew public notice in London in the 1650s, first for her eccentric style of dress, and soon afterwards for her no less eccentric habit of writing. Her first book, *Poems, and Fancies* was published in 1653, and was quickly followed by others. Undoubtedly it was her most 'unfeminine' desire for fame that gave her a reputation for madness. Alternately apologizing for her ignorance and presumption, and promising her readers more, she thrust herself on public notice with the express desire of gaining the attention usually denied to women. Her volume of *Playes* (1662) contained no less than 14 prefaces, nine of them addresses 'To the Readers' apologizing for the various defects of her work: an insistent humility far removed from the 'proper' feminine modesty of silence. Like one of her own heroines, the woman warrior Lady Victoria, Margaret Cavendish insistently demanded: 'shall only men live by Fame, and women dy in Oblivion?'[64]

Margaret Cavendish rightly anticipated that she would be censured for publishing. Dorothy Osborne, whose own not negligible literary talents were expended on private correspondence, needed only to hear about *Poems, and Fancies* to be convinced of its author's madness. She commented, 'Sure, the poor woman is a little distracted ... to venture at writing books, and in verse too. If I should not sleep this fortnight I should not come to that.'[65] However, Cavendish's younger contemporary, Katherine Philips, was widely praised for her publications, and she did not depend on high rank for her recognition. She was well off, but certainly no aristocrat. Her greater success in 'living by fame' is partly explained by her light, graceful lyrics, which have much in common with the 'Cavalier' poetry of her time, and also partly by the fact that fame was not her goal.

Katherine Philips spent most of her time in Pembrokeshire, writing poetry and corresponding with her friends. She admitted to having 'an incorrigible inclination to that folly of riming', and in spite of 'intending the effects of that humour, only for my own amusement in a retir'd life', she became a famous writer.[66] Her translation of Corneille's *Pompey* was produced in Dublin in 1663—probably the first performance of a play written by an Englishwoman—and printed soon after. To this publication she agreed, though with reluctance. She drew the line, though, at publishing a volume of her own poetry. When an unauthorized ed'tion of her poems appeared early in 1664 she had it suppressed, and refused her friends' advice to look to her literary reputation and replace the faulty impression with an authorized and corrected edition. 'I am so little concern'd for the reputation of writing Sense, that provided the World would believe me innocent of any manner of knowledge, much less connivance at this Publication, I shall willingly compound never to trouble them with the true Copies', she wrote.[67] The true copies only appeared in 1667, three years after her sudden death from smallpox.

In the late 1660s, then, interest in women writers had been stimulated by two recent examples, who polarized public opinion between them. One was the Duchess of Newcastle —socially prominent, eccentric in manners and dress, a dabbler in science and philosophy as well as poetry, and a prolific writer who insistently made herself known to the public, making no secret of her huge and easily ridiculed ambitions: quirky, rebellious, and very much alive. The other was Katherine Philips—graceful, modest, retiring, author of a small volume of lyrics and a translated play which she only reluctantly made public, and the young victim of a tragic disease: gentle, properly feminine, and safely dead. While the Duchess became a byword for oddity, the 'matchless Orinda' went down in the record as the ideal woman writer.

Later women writers looked to Katherine Philips as their heroine: a justification for female effort and an example of female skill. The tradition was begun in a poem by an anonymous woman calling herself 'Philo-Philippa', which was published, along with other encomiums, in Philips' 1667 *Poems*. 'Philo-Philippa' declares:

> Let the male Poets their male *Phoebus* chuse,
> Thee I invoke, *Orinda*, for my Muse.

She gives a new twist to the legend of Phoebus (Apollo, god of poetry) who pursued the nymph Daphne until, to escape being ravished, she changed into a laurel tree (source of the poet's crown). Men have achieved their literary pre-eminence by force, but it naturally belongs to women:

> He could but force a Branch, *Daphne* her Tree
> Most freely offers to her Sex and thee ...
> And men no longer shall with ravish'd Bays
> Crown their forc'd Poems by as forc'd a praise.

That the successful woman poet, 'glory of our Sex, envy of men', was representative of and an example for feminine achievement was to become a commonplace; and the success was seen in terms of a takeover of the kingdom of wit. 'The rule of Day and Wit's now Feminine.'[68]

Men and women both continually used battle imagery in praise of women writers: literature was a 'field' women were 'invading'. When they were writing the traditional encomium poem in which extravagant praise was in order, men were ready enough to concede defeat; but the kind of victory they hailed for women tells us a great deal about the terms on which women's writing was to be accepted. Abraham Cowley's tribute to her, 'Upon Mrs. K. Philips her Poems', is especially worth examining. It fits into its light pindarics references to all the characteristics of the 'proper' woman writer as eighteenth-century, as well as seventeenth-century readers were to conceive of her.

First, woman's wit is related to her beauty, so that her conquest of man is defined from the start as part of a sexual game:

> We allow'd you beauty, and we did submit
> To all the tyrannies of it.
> Ah cruel Sex! will you depose us too in Wit?

That caveat entered, female victory can be celebrated. Orinda:

> Does man behind her in proud triumph draw,
> And cancel great *Apollo*'s Salick Law,

a reference to the French regulation against female monarchs to which Englishmen were fond of pointing as a proof of their own greater respect for women. Orinda's triumph, then, counts as all women's. Her poetic and physical beauties are then conflated:

Thy Numbers gentle, and thy Fancies high,
Those as thy Forehead smooth, these sparkling as thine Eye.

Yet despite all this a lingering belief in women's inferiority means that Katherine Philips has to be seen as more than womanly to be praised. Her writing becomes 'Angelical':

For, as in Angels, we
  Do in thy Verses see
Both improv'd Sexes eminently meet;
They are than Man more strong, and more than Woman sweet.

Next, Orinda is exalted by dispraising her female predecessors, who are not so virtuous as she.

They talk of *Sappho*, but, alas! the shame
Ill Manners soil the lustre of her fame.

Orinda, on the other hand, writes of honour and friendship, 'instructive subjects', and uses her power benevolently. 'At once she overcomes, enslaves, and betters men.' The final verse defines Orinda's victory— and the projected victory of all women over men—by implicit contrast to the aggression of the Amazons, women warriors of old:

The warlike *Amazonian* Train,
Which in *Elysium* now do peaceful reign,
And Wit's Mild Empire before Arms prefer,
Hope 'twill be settled in their Sex by her.[69]

These lines captured a spirit which we will see hovering over eighteenth-century literature. Women's victory in wit, not arms, could be granted because it could be made to fit in with their gentle femininity; and wit's mild empire, after invasion by the seventeenth-century women writers, was to be settled in their sex by the eighteenth-century women novelists.
  Katherine Philips' early death did not long foster the illusion that the world had seen the last of women's wit: by the 1680s new eulogists were exclaiming:

... now no more with sorrow be it said,
  Orinda's dead;
Since in her seat *Astraea* does Appear.[70]

Astraea was Aphra Behn, whose literary career began with the performance of her *The Forc'd Marriage* in 1670, and continued until her death in 1689. Fourteen plays, a volume of poems, translations, and a variety of original fictional works made her one of the most prolific and successful authors of the Restoration period; and there was no lack of recognition for her from fellow-writers like John Dryden, Nahum Tate, and Rochester, or from the poetasters who filled her prefaces with flattery. Men wrote of Behn in the same terms Cowley had used of Katherine Philips, praising the beauty of her face and writing, seeing a union of masculine and feminine qualities in her verse, exalting her as the glory of her sex and man's conqueror. (We can see already that while men were always conceding defeat in verse, they were going to expect the battle to be fought over and over again.) Sappho was invoked as the woman poet's prototype, and Orinda, too, had now reached this semi-mythical status. '*Greece* boasts one *Sappho*; two *Orinda's*, we', wrote Nahum Tate, counting Astraea as the second Orinda; while one J. Adams considered Sappho and Orinda 'but low types' of 'the excellent Madam Behn'.[71]

There were problems, though, with Astraea's succession to Orinda's honours. In social class, public success, and tone, she was very different from both Katherine Philips and the Duchess of Newcastle. Behn's biographers differ over her origin,[72] but, whether she was born into the gentry or not, her appearance in Restoration London as the widow of a man none of her biographers has been able to trace was not that of the typical gentlewoman. Independent in her life and her writing, she made her living from the Restoration stage, one of a new breed of professionals 'forced to write for Bread and not ashamed to owne it'.[73] Instead of the Duchess's awkward blend of arrogance and self-doubt, or Katherine Philips's modest retreat from public gaze, Behn showed a direct confidence in her work and anger against male prejudice: 'had the Plays I have writ come forth under any Mans Name, and never known to have been mine; I appeal to all unbyast Judges of Sense, if they had not said that Person had made as many good Comedies, as any one Man that has writ in our Age', she wrote.[74] She did not hesitate to provide her audience with the bawdy writing it desired, and so fuelled the arguments of those who thought writing for money implied depravity—a view that formed a possible stumbling-block for the eighteenth-century novelists, also professionals but catering for very different tastes.

Behn had plenty of detractors, and they were able to seize on the view that selling one's work was like selling onself to claim that '*Punk* and *Poetess* agree so pat./You cannot well be *this* and not be *that*'.[75] Behn was not a punk (prostitute) but she had lovers, and her affair with John Hoyle, a lawyer of libertine principles and bisexual practice, gave rise to sneers that he had paid for her favours by writing her plays for her.[76] In her 'loose' life and bawdy writing Behn differed crucially from recent famous women writers. 'Chaste' was an adjective almost automatically attached to Orinda, and whatever else might be said of Margaret Cavendish, no-one has challenged her claim that 'neither this present, nor any of the future ages can or will truly say that I am not Vertuous and Chast'.[77] So Behn, even more than the eccentric Duchess, was a problematic model for the aspiring woman writer, and because of her professional success, much harder to ignore. At the turn of the century Philips and Behn stood together in the public mind: the first gentle and genteel, irreproachable; the second a successful professional, and surely (as one of the best writers of fiction in England in her time) a better model for the eighteenth-century woman novelist, but also bawdy in her work, unchaste in her life. Women writers had a choice: Orinda versus Astraea.

The choice did not have to be made straight away. For some time Orinda and Astraea were added together, not set one against the other. Behn very soon had successors in the theatre. Mary Pix, Delariviere Manley and Catharine Trotter, the ones that bothered Chagrin the Critick, wrote for the stage during the 1690s, and after the turn of the century Susanna Centlivre emerged as a popular dramatist for the new era. Two of these women wrote a good deal in other genres: Trotter (later Cockburn) began as a precocious teenage writer of verse and fiction, and later wrote on philosophy, while Delariviere Manley incorporated political writing into her voluminous works of fiction. Like Behn, Manley began as a dramatist and turned to the novel later, a pattern that was reduplicated on a larger scale during the eighteenth century as the novel took over from the play as the most lucrative form of writing. Just as many early women novelists had roots in the theatre, the general idea of the professional woman writer had its roots in the image built up around the Restoration playwrights.

As the first group of professional women writers, Manley, Pix and Trotter made women's writing even more publicly visible. Sometimes nerve failed the early women writers and their work was either presented anonymously, in the hope of being taken for a man's,[78] or its female authorship was emphasized with apologies. Manley said she was convinced by the failure of her first play, *The Lost Lover*, in 1696, that 'Writing for the Stage is no way proper for a Woman', though she was busy planning the production of *The Royal Mischief* at the time.[79] Mary Pix was afraid that when Richard Minchall read her *Ibrahim*, dedicated to him, he would 'too soon find out the Woman, the imperfect Woman there.'[80] When they came to write about each other's work, though, self-doubt—or conventional authorial modesty—could be cast aside and the convention of the encomium poem took over, with much better results for their common cause. In praising each other, they conducted a deliberate advertizing campaign for women's writing.

Here, Aphra Behn was very useful to them. She was 'Wit's eldest

Sister',[81] and they united her with Katherine Philips as twin precursors. Manley hailed Trotter as the successor to '*Orinda*, and the Fair *Astrea*', and was herself described by Pix:

> Like *Sappho* Charming, like *Afra* Eloquent,
> Like chast *Orinda*, sweetly Innocent.[82]

The battle imagery we have seen in male praise of Philips sounded different coming from women proclaiming their joint assault on male dominance. Manley set the tone in her poem on Trotter's *Agnes de Castro* (1696), beginning:

> *Orinda*, and the Fair *Astrea* gone,
> Not one was found to fill the Vacant Throne:
> Aspiring Man had quite regain'd the Sway,
> Again had taught us humbly to Obey;
> Till you (Natures third start, in favour of our Kind)
> With stronger Arms, their Empire have disjoyn'd,
> And snatcht a Lawrel which they thought their Prize ...[83]

Not quite the gentle assault Cowley welcomed. Trotter returned the compliment in a poem prefixed to Manley's *Royal Mischief*:

> I knew my force too weak, and but assay'd
> The Borders of their Empire to invade,
> I incite a greater genius to my aid:
> The War begun you generously pursu'd ...[84]

The struggle for wit's empire was on, and the shades of both Orinda and Astraea could be invoked on the women's side.

At the same time, these writers were being used as the basis for constructing a definition of specially feminine qualities in writing, which was later to restrict women's empire and make it a mild one. Sappho's reputation as a poet of love had already begun to establish a precedent for the kind of writing expected from a woman, and the later association of women writers with romance heroines was reinforcing the notion that their subject was love. Behn had been hailed as a poet of love, one admirer claiming that no writer could rouse 'our softer Passions' like her,[85] and this tradition of praise continued unabated. 'Sure thy mind was meant the court of love', Catharine Trotter was told,[86] and 'Quote *Ovid* now no more ye amorous Swains', cried one of Delariviere Manley's admirers, for '*Delia*, than *Ovid* has more moving Strains'.[87] The soft passion became established as women's subject.

The women writers themselves helped to build up this definition. It enabled them to present their writing as an expression of, rather than

a rebellion against their femininity. Love was the centre of *The Royal
Mischief*, Manley explained, because 'in all Writings of this kind, some
particular Passion is describ'd, as a Woman I thought it Policy to begin
with the softest, and which is easiest to our Sex.'[88] By the turn of the
century they were claiming to offer a special subject matter aimed at
women: Mary Pix thought she could excuse the presumption of a mere
woman daring to imitate Shakespeare and write history plays by an
appeal to the women of the audience. What she was offering was not a
picture of valour but that other staple of the Restoration heroic play,
love. She wrote of herself:

> To please your martial men she must despair,
> And therefore Courts the favour of the fair:
> From huffing Hero's she hopes no relief,
> But trusts in *Catharine's* Love, and *Isabella's* grief.[89]

Her analysis was common to her time. Women were generally believed
to prefer tragedy to comedy because of the elevation of women in the
love-themes of heroic tragedies, and it was their taste that was being
considered, as 'pathetic tragedies' dealing less with affairs of state and
more with the heroine's love began to replace the heroic play. Pix's *Queen
Catharine* is one example of this trend, and her prologue shows she was
aware that as a woman writer she could exploit it, claiming a special
relationship with the female admirers of a new 'feminine' genre.

Exploiting 'feminine' qualities, though, led to special restrictions. Not
all ways of treating the soft passion were acceptable from women. At
the same time as they were credited with a natural ability to write of
love, they were criticized if their work was erotic ('warm') or bawdy.
Behn had protested against this double standard, mocking the ladies
who, she claimed, flocked to the men's plays to hear sexual innuendo,
but could not tolerate similar freedom in her work because they said
that *'from a Woman it was unnaturall'*.[90] Manley complained that critics of
The Royal Mischief had objected to 'the warmth of it, as they are pleas'd
to call it', and argued that warmth was necessary in a play about love.[91]
But as agitation for stage reform gained ground, protests against these
restrictions declined. Jeremy Collier's attack on the immorality of the
stage, published in 1698, had expressed many people's feelings, and a
few years later Addison's and Steele's drama criticism, published in the
Tatler and the *Spectator*, developed the taste for moral messages and
freedom from sexual references in drama. Women writers, like men,
followed the trend of the age. A Mr Hodgson's prologue to Pix's *False
Friend* (1699) told the audience that the performance was staged 'In
Hopes a Moral Play your Lives will Mend',[92] and Susanna Centlivre
claimed that her aim in *The Gamester* (1705) was 'to divert, without that

Vicious Strain which usually attends the Comick Muse, and according to the first intent of Plays, recommend Morality.'[93] The women's relation to this new emphasis on morality was different from the men's. If love was seen to be their natural subject, morality was soon to be seen as their natural mode. And as always the woman's personal life, specifically her sexual life, was brought into the question of her work's tendency. This was clear when John Hughes called Catharine Trotter 'the first of stage-reformers' for her moral plots and her clean language: 'Your *virgin* voice offends no *virgin* ear', he reassured her.[94]

By the beginning of the eighteenth century, then, a path was open for the woman writer, but it was full of pitfalls. There were common expectations about women's writing: their main subject would be love, their main interest in their female characters. The idea that women were naturally inclined to virtue, and could exert a salutary moral influence on men, was spreading; and so was the idea that it was through women's tender feelings and their ability to stimulate tender feelings in men, that this influence operated. Hence women writers who wished to claim a special place in literature because of their sex were constrained by the twin requirements of love and morality. The two could be mutually antagonistic. The theme of love could lead to warm, and therefore immoral writing; and on the other hand didacticism could kill romance, a danger that was to be apparent later, in some of the eighteenth-century novels. Women writers had the delicate task of balancing a 'feminine' sensitivity to love with an equally 'feminine' morality.

The women novelists of the eighteenth century inherited a role from the women dramatists of the seventeenth century, but their relationship with those professional predecessors was not always easy. The novel, even more than the pathetic tragedy, allowed for concentration on women's sensibility and women's dilemmas; but the novelists, even more than the earlier dramatists, were affected by the double requirement to delight with romantic love yet instruct according to the strictest of contemporary moral standards. As they tried to fulfil this requirement, they defined their female characters in accordance with the developing ideology of femininity, and though the terms they used changed in line with the century's increasing delicacy, their concerns were similar throughout. Women were defined by their sexuality: and so were women writers. A woman's writing and her life tended to be judged together on the same terms. The woman novelist's sexual behaviour was as much a subject for concern as her heroine's. Her main subject—female sexuality, as controlled by female chastity—was established by the early 1700s. Not only this subject matter but her attitude to it had to be carefully controlled by the ever more onerous demands of proper femininity. Male writers too, of course, were affected by the simultaneous demand for passion and morality so typical of the century: but women writers felt it as a demand on their entire selves, not just on their writings.

With these drawbacks, women's empire of wit was founded. It was an empire internally divided by the contradictory demands made by bourgeois society's ideals of femininity, and its attitude to the women who had first won it was deeply ambivalent. But its achievements are worth remembering in themselves and for the legacy they left to us. For as we watch the women novelists of the eighteenth century weighing passion against prudence, sexual attachment against female independence, desire against duty, and morality against romance, we will find them building, out of the contradictions of 'femininity', an identity for themselves as writers and a female tradition in literature.

NOTES

1. Review of *Poems on various Subjects and Occasions*, by Mrs Savage *Critical Review* **44** (1777), p. 151.
2. *New Lady's Magazine* **7** (1792), p. 12.
3. Several of them wrote fiction, however. Catharine Trotter's early work *Olinda's Adventures*, and Elizabeth Rowe's fictional *Letters* will be treated in later chapters. Most of Hannah More's tales, and her *Coelebs in Search of a Wife* (1809), came later in her career. Helen Maria Williams's one novel, *Julia*, appeared in 1790, but she was well known as a poet before this. For further details of these women's lives and writings see J. M. Todd, ed. *A Dictionary of British and American Women Writers, 1660–1800* (Totowa, New Jersey: Rowman and Allanheld, 1985), one recent attempt to counteract the tendency to forget about women writers.
4. *Monthly Review* **20** (1759), pp. 275–6.
5. Review of *The Adventures of Sylvia Hughes* (anon.) *Monthly Review* **23** (1760), p. 523.
6. *Monthly Review* **48** (1773), p. 154.
7. F. G. Black, *The Epistolary Novel in the Late Eighteenth Century: A Descriptive and Bibliographical Study* (Eugene: University of Oregon, 1940), p. 8. I feel that this estimate is a little high. When Black gives figures a slightly different picture emerges. Of 191 epistolary novels published between 1781 and 1790, 48 are known to be by women and 31 by men. A further 30 are 'By a Lady'. Of the remaining 82 he claims, 'a great majority bear unmistakeable internal evidence of feminine composition' (p. 8). His estimate, then, relies on always believing the 'By a Lady' claim, which is probably usually true but not an entirely reliable guide, and more dubiously on unargued assumptions about internal evidence of women's authorship. Black also finds that of 74 known epistolary novelists in 1781–90, 48 are women and 26 men. There is then good evidence for his claim of a 'preponderance of female authorship' in the later decades of the century, though this may well only apply to the epistolary novel.

8. Walter Scott, 'Charlotte Smith', in *Miscellaneous Prose Works* **IV** (Edinburgh: Cadell and Co., 1827), p. 62.

9. *The Dunciad Variorum* (1729) Book II, lines 155–6 and Book III, line 141; in James Sutherland, ed., *The Dunciad*, Vol. V of Pope's *Poems*, Twickenham, ed. (Methuen, 1943), p. 120, p. 162.

10. See *The Dunciad* and Book III, line 141; in James Sutherland, ed., *The Dunciad*, Vol. V of Pope's *Poems*, Twickenham, ed. (Methuen, 1943), p. 120, p. 162.

11. Anne Finch, *Poems*, ed. J. M. Murry (London: Jonathan Cape, 1928), 'The Introduction', p. 24.

12. Margaret Cavendish, *Poems, and Fancies* (London, 1653), 'To all Noble, and Worthy Ladies', sig. A3 r-v.

13. *A Comparison Between the Two Stages* (London, 1702), pp. 26–7.

14. Virginia Woolf, *To the Lighthouse* (1927; rpt Penguin, 1974), p. 57. Woolf wrote of the importance of eighteenth-century women writers in *A Room of One's Own* (1929): 'towards the end of the eighteenth century a change came about which, if I were rewriting history, I should describe more fully and think of greater importance than the Crusades or the wars of the Roses. The middle-class woman began to write'. (Panther, 1977, pp. 62–3).

15. The most important study of this is Ian Watt, *The Rise of the Novel: Studies in Defoe, Richardson and Fielding* (London: Chatto and Windus, 1957). See especially chapter 2, 'The Reading Public and the Rise of the Novel'.

16. James Pellor Malcolm, *Anecdotes of the Manners and Customs of London During the Eighteenth Century* (London: Longman, Hurst, Rees and Orme, 1808), p. 186.

17. The reviewer of the anonymous *Letters from Sophia to Mira: Containing the Adventures of a Lady* wrote that 'the number of *Authoresses* hath of late so considerably increased, that we are somewhat apprehensive lest our very Cook-wenches should be infected with the *Cacoethes Scribendi*, and think themselves above the vulgar employment of mixing a pudding, or rolling a pye crust'. *Monthly Review* **27** (1762), p. 472.

18. 'When a farmer's daughter sits down to *read* a novel, she certainly mispends [sic] her time, because she may employ it in such a manner as to be of real service to her family: when she sits down to *write* one, her friends can have no hopes of her.' Review of *Virtue in Distress; or the History of Miss Sally Pruen, and Miss Laura Spencer*, By a Farmer's Daughter in Gloucestershire, in *Critical Review* **33** (1772), p. 327.

19. Review of Helen Maria Williams, *Julia*, in *General Magazine and Impartial Review* **4** (1790), p. 162.

20. Susanna Centlivre, who supported the Whigs, is one writer whose political services would certainly have been rewarded with political preferment had she been a man. See J. W. Bowyer, *The Celebrated Mrs. Centlivre* (Durham, N.C.: Duke University Press, 1952), p. 154.

21. Biographical information about Haywood is taken from G. Whicher, *The Life and Romances of Mrs. Eliza Haywood* (New York, 1915; rpt Ann Arbor: University Microfilms, 1973).

22. *Love in Excess, Gulliver's Travels* and *Robinson Crusoe* were the three most popular works of fiction before the publication of *Pamela* in 1740. See John J. Richetti, *Popular Fiction Before Richardson: Narrative Patterns 1700–1739*

(Oxford: Clarendon Press, 1969), p. 179.

23. See Marcia Heinemann, 'Eliza Haywood's Career in the Theatre', *Notes and Queries* **218** (1973), pp. 9–13.

24. Biographical information about Charlotte Smith is taken from F.M.A. Hilbish, *Charlotte Smith, poet and novelist* (1749–1806) (Philadelphia: University of Pennsylvania, 1941) and R. P. Turner, 'Charlotte Smith (1749–1806): New Light on her Life and Literary Career', unpub. diss. University of Southern California, 1966.

25. Charlotte Smith, letter (to Nichols?) 28 December 1791, Bod. MS. Eng. Lett. c. 365, fol. 60.

26. Elizabeth Carter to Elizabeth Montagu, 30 June 1788; in *Letters from Mrs. Elizabeth Carter to Mrs. Montagu* (London: F. C. and J. Rivington, 1817), **III**, p. 295.

27. Biographical information on these writers is found in W. H. McBurney, 'Mrs. Mary Davys: Forerunner of Fielding', *PMLA* **74** (1959), pp. 348–55; W. M. Crittenden, introduction to *Millenium Hall* by Sarah Scott (New York: Bookman Associates, 1955); W. L. Cross, *The History of Henry Fielding* (New Haven: Yale University Press, 1918), Ruth L. Witthaus, 'Sarah Fielding, A Study of her Life and Writings', unpub. diss. Oxford, 1950; and D. H. Eshleman, *Elizabeth Griffith: A Biographical and Critical Study* (Philadelphia, 1949).

28. Mary Wollstonecraft, *Mary* (1788) in *Mary* and *The Wrongs of Woman* ed. Gary Kelly (Oxford: Oxford University Press, 1980), p. 28.

29. *Commentaries on the Laws of England* (1753) (Oxford, 1765), **I**, p. 430.

30. Blackstone's comments apply more to the law of Royal Courts, which could be circumvented by borough customs. See K. O'Donovan, 'The Male Appendage—Legal Definitions of Women', pp. 134-52 of Sandra Burman, ed, *Fit Work for Women* (London: Croom Helm Ltd, 1979). For details of married women's public roles see Alice Clark, *Working Life of Women in the Seventeenth Century* (1919; rpt London: Routledge and Kegan Paul, 1982).

31. *The Complete English Tradesman* (London: Charles Rivington, 1726), **I**, p. 352, p. 355, p. 367.

32. 'Spinster', originally a woman who spins, was used from the seventeenth century onwards as the legal designation for an unmarried woman, and later was used generally of unmarried women; *OED* first cites its use in sense 2b, 'a woman still unmarried', in 1719.

33. *Thoughts on the Education of Daughters* (London: J. Johnson, 1787), p. 69.

34. William Hayley, *A Philosophical, Historical and Moral Essay on Old Maids* (1786, quoted in Bridget Hill, *Eighteenth-Century Women: An Anthology* (London: George Allen and Unwin, 1984), p. 129.

35. For example, Peter Gay claims that in the eighteenth century, 'Especially in the middle ranges of Western European society, the father's power over his children and the husband's power over his wife markedly declined ... women and children secured new respect and new rights.' *The Enlightenment: an Interpretation*, **II**, *The Science of Freedom* (London: Wildwood House, 1973), p. 31 and p. 33. Lawrence Stone also argues that women's position improved in the century because of the development of stronger emotional bonds between husbands and wives in 'companionate marriage'. One piece of evidence he cites is changed public opinion about wife-beating. The

theory that a husband had the right to administer 'modest correction' to his wife was asserted in court in 1730, but when a judge repeated this in court in 1782 there was an outcry. See *T̨he Family, Sex and Marriage in England 1500–1800* (London: Weidenfeld and Nicolson, 1977), pp. 325–6. Jean E. Hunter, examining the opinions about women expressed in eighteenth-century issues of *The Gentleman's Magazine*, concludes that they show the signs of 'an era of continuing if gradual improvement in the status and position of women', a rosy view which ignores the fact that most of the support for female education which Hunter finds stressed its benefits for males, who would thereby gain better wives and mothers. See 'The Eighteenth-Century Englishwoman: According to the *Gentleman's Magazine*', in Paul Fritz and Richard Morton, eds, *Woman in the Eighteenth Century and Other Essays* (Toronto: Hakkert and Co., 1976), p. 88.

36. Alice Clark, *Working Life of Women in the Seventeenth Century*, Chapter 5, 'Crafts and Trades'. See especially pp. 196–7.

37. See H. J. Habakkuk, 'Marriage Settlements in the Eighteenth Century', *Transactions of the Royal Historical Society*, 4th ser. **32** (1950), pp. 15–30, esp. pp. 24–6.

38. Defoe advises a man 'not to marry, 'till by a frugal industrious management of his trade in the beginning, he has laid a foundation for maintaining a wife, and bringing up a family'. *The Complete English Tradesman*, I, p. 176.

39. For a discussion of women's work in medieval times see Eileen Power, *Medieval Women*, ed. M. M. Postan (Cambridge: Cambridge University Press, 1975). For a survey of Tudor women's roles in business see Pearl Hogrefe, *Tudor Women: Commoners and Queens* (Ames, Iowa, 1975).

40. Mary Anne Radcliffe, *The Female Advocate: or an Attempt to Recover the Rights of Women from Male Usurpation* (London: Vernor and Hood, 1799), pp. 17, 68–9.

41. Priscilla Wakefield, *Reflections on the Present Condition of the Female Sex; with Suggestions for its Improvement* (London: J. Johnson, and Darton and Harvey, 1798), p. 154.

42. For a discussion of the influence of Evangelical religion on conceptions of womanhood see Nancy Cott, 'Passionlessness: An Interpretation of Victorian Sexual Ideology, 1790-1850', *Signs: Journal of Women in Culture and Society* **4**, no. 2 (Winter, 1978), pp. 219–36.

43. See Ruth H. Bloch, 'Untangling the Roots of Modern Sex Roles: A Survey of Four Centuries of Change', in *Signs: Journal of Women in Culture and Society* **4** no. 2 (Winter, 1978), pp. 237–52.

44. *The Tatler* (no. 172, May 16, 1710) ed. George A. Aitken (London: Duckworth and Co., 1898), III, p. 304.

45. James Fordyce, *The Character and Conduct of the Female Sex, and the Advantages to be derived by Young Men from the Society of Virtuous Women. A Discourse, in three parts, delivered in Monkwell-Street Chapel, January 1, 1776* (London: T. Cadell, 1776), p. 36.

46. *Sermons to Young Women* (London: A. Millar and T. Cadell, J. Dodsley, and J. Payne, 1766), I,| pp. 207–8.

47. St Thomas Aquinas, *Summa Theologica*; anonymous medieval poem, 'Against Evil Women'; John Wilmot, Earl of Rochester, 'Ramble in St. James's

Park'; Alexander Pope, 'Epistle to a Lady'. The first three are quoted from Katharine M. Rogers, *The Troublesome Helpmate: A History of Misogyny in Literature* (Seattle and London: University of Washington Press, 1966), p. 66, p. 64 and p. 163.

48. Frances Brooke, *The Excursion* (London: T. Cadell, 1777), **I**, 12.

49. He wrote to Frances Cadogan on July 17, 1777:

> I hope You have seen how much I am abus'd in yr Friend Mrs Brook's new Novel? . . . she Even says, that I should reject a Play, if it should be a woman's—there's brutal Malignity for You—have not ye Ladies—Mesdames, *Griffith, Cowley* & *Cilesia* spoke of me before their Plays with an Over-Enthusiastick Encomium?—what says divine Hannah More?

The Letters of David Garrick, ed. D. M. Little and G.M. Kahrl, with P. de K. Wilson (London: Oxford University Press, 1963), **3**, p. 1172.

50. *The London Stage 1660–1800* (Carbondale: Southern Illinois Univ. Press, 1965–69), *Part 5, 1776–1800*, **I**, p. clxxii, p. 448.

51. *European Magazine* **15** (February 1789), p. 99. For further biographical information about Brooke see E. Phillips Poole's introduction to *The History of Lady Julia Mandeville* (London: Scholartis Press, 1930), and Lorraine McMullen, *An Odd Attempt in a Woman: The Literary Life of Frances Brooke* (Vancouver: University of British Columbia Press, 1983).

52. *Critical Review* **44** (1777), p. 63

53. Author's Preface, *Memoirs of the Miss Holmsbys*, quoted in *Monthly Review* **80** (1789), p. 169.

54. Charlotte Smith, *Desmond, a Novel* (Dublin, 1792), Preface, **I**, pp. iii–iv.

55. Eliza Haywood, *The Rash Resolve* (London, 1724), p. 56.

56. *Critical Review* **27**, (1769), p. 297.

57. Henry Fielding, Preface to *Familiar Letters Between the Principal Characters in David Simple* (London: A. Millar, 1747), **I**, p. xvii; *Critical Review* **13** (1762), p. 435; and *Monthly Review* **57** (1777), p. 174.

58. Historians have found women pamphleteers, writing in support of women's spiritual equality, among the radical religious sects in the English revolution; thus the challenge to established hierarchy included an attack on the idea of women's silence and subordination. See K. V. Thomas, 'Women and the Civil War Sects', *Past and Present* **13** (1958), pp. 42–62. Recent work suggests that the beginnings of modern feminist ideas were developed soon after the Civil War, but mainly by woman of Royalist and later Tory principles, especially Mary Astell. See Hilda L. Smith's study, *Reason's Disciples: Seventeenth-Century English Feminists* (Urbana, Chicago, London: University of Illinois Press, 1982).

59. *Poems on Several Occasions* (London, 1703), p. 109. For a discussion of Sarah Fyge's work see Jeslyn Medoff, 'New Light on Sarah Fyge (Field, Egerton)', *Tulsa Studies in Women's Literature* **I**, no. 2 (Fall 1982), pp. 155–75.

60. The letters of Héloise to Abelard were not published in England till 1713. After this they quickly gained wide currency through Pope's *Eloisa to Abelard* (1717). *Les Lettres Portugaises* were translated into English by Roger L'Estrange in 1678, and 10 English editions appeared before 1740. See

R. A. Day, *Told in Letters: Epistolary Fiction Before Richardson* (Ann Arbor: University of Michigan Press, 1966), pp. 33–8. For an account of the debate about the authenticity of the Portuguese nun, see *Lettres Portugaises Valentins et Autres Oeuvres de Guilleragues*, ed. F. Deloffre and J. Rougeot (Paris: Garnier, 1962), pp. v–xxiii. For a discussion of the significance of the attribution of the letters to a woman, see Nancy K. Miller, "I's' in Drag: The Sex of Recollection', *The Eighteenth Century* **22** (1981), pp. 47–67.

61. For a discussion of these romances and their reception in England see T. P. Haviland, *The roman de longue haleine on English soil* (Philadelphia, 1931).

62. Details of Margaret Cavendish's life are taken from Douglas Grant, *Margaret the First: A Biography of Margaret Cavendish Duchess of Newcastle 1623–1673* (London: Rupert Hart-Davis, 1957). Details of Katherine Philips's life are taken from Philip Souers, *The Matchless Orinda* (Cambridge: Harvard University Press, 1931). Two recent biographies of Behn, used for details of her life, are Maureen Duffy, *The Passionate Shepherdess: Aphra Behn 1640–89* (London: Jonathan Cape, 1977) and Angeline Goreau, *Reconstructing Aphra: A Social Biography of Aphra Behn* (Oxford: Oxford University Press, 1980).

63. The importance of 'female precursors' for women writers is argued in Sandra M. Gilbert and Susan Gubar's study, *The Madwoman in the Attic: The Woman Writer and the Nineteenth-Century Literary Imagination* (New Haven: Yale University Press, 1979). See especially chapter 2, 'Infection in the Sentence: The Woman Writer and the Anxiety of Authorship'.

64. Margaret Cavendish, 'Bell in Campo', Second Part, in *Playes* (London, 1662), p. 609.

65. *The Letters of Dorothy Osborne to Sir William Temple 1652–54*, ed. Kingsley Hart (Folio Society, 1968), p. 53.

66. Katherine Philips, letter to 'Poliarchus' (Sir Charles Cotterell) printed in *Poems By the most deservedly Admired Mrs. Katherine Philips The matchless Orinda* (London, 1667), sig. A2v.

67. Letter to 'Poliarchus', *Poems*, sig. A2r.

68. 'To the excellent *Orinda*', signed 'Philo-Philippa', *Poems*, sig. c2r.

69. 'Upon Mrs. *K. Philips* her Poems', *Poems*, sigs. b2v, c1r, c1v. This poem appeared in the 1668 collected edition of Cowley's poems as 'On *Orinda*'s Poems'.

70. '*To Madam* A. Behn *on the publication of her Poems*', signed F. N. W. Poem prefixed to Aphra Behn, *Poems Upon Several Occasions: With a Voyage to the Island of Love* (1684), rpt in *The Works of Aphra Behn*, ed. Montague Summers (London: William Heinemann, 1915), **VI**, p. 133.

71. 'To the Incomparable Author', signed N. Tate, in the introduction to Behn's *The Lover's Watch* (1686), rpt in *The Works of Aphra Behn*, **VI**, p. 7; and '*To the excellent Madam* Behn, *on her Poems*', signed J. Adams, in introduction to *Poems Upon Several Occasions*, in *Works*, **VI**, p. 120.

72. Both Duffy and Goreau discredit the long tradition that Behn was born Aphra Amis in Wye, Kent, and show that her maiden name was most probably Johnson. Duffy suggests as her parents Bartholomew Johnson, a yeoman, and Elizabeth Johnson, who was wetnurse to one child or more

of the Culpeppers, a substantial Canterbury family. Goreau inclines to the view that Behn's education shows that she was educated as a gentlewoman, and suggests that she was adopted into a gentry family and may even have been an illegitimate daughter of the wife of Lord Willoughby, Governor of the colony of Surinam, which Behn visited in her twenties and described in her novel *Oroonoko* (1688). Duffy's research into Kentish records is more thorough and I find her account in general more convincing, though the problem of just what status Behn had when she visited Surinam remains.

73. 'To the Reader', *Sir Patient Fancy* (1678), in *Works*, **IV**, p. 7.

74. Preface to *The Lucky Chance* (1687), in *Works*, **III**, p. 186.

75. Robert Gould, 'The Poetess, A Satyr', in *The Works of Mr. Robert Gould* (London: W. Lewis, 1709), **II**, p. 17. In the couplet quoted he is referring specifically to 'Ephelia' and 'Sappho'. 'Sappho' is identified as Aphra Behn by Maureen Duffy, *The Passionate Shepherdess*, p. 280.

76. Alexander Radcliffe, in 'The Ramble: An Anti-Heroick Poem' (1682), reported that,

> The censuring Age have thought it fit
> To damn a Woman, 'cause 'tis said,
> The Plays she vends she never made.
> But that a *Greys Inn* Lawyer does 'em,
> Who unto her was Friend in Bosom.

The woman is Aphra Behn, the lawyer, her lover John Hoyle. Radcliffe, however, does not include himself among Behn's detractors. A few lines later he includes her among 'the better sort' of writers, 'Damn'd only by the Ignorant'. See 'The Ramble' (London, 1682), pp. 6–7; included, with separate title page and pagination, in *The Works of Capt. Alex. Radcliffe In One Volume*. 3rd edn augmented (London: Richard Wellington, 1696).

77. '*The Blazing-World*', in *Observations Upon Experimental Philosophy* (London, 1666), **II**, p. 26.

78. Susanna Centlivre did this with her *The Stolen Heiress* in 1702, probably because of pressure from the players: see J. W. Bowyer, *The Celebrated Mrs. Centlivre* (Durham, N.C.: Duke University Press, 1952), p. 48.

79. *The Lost Lover: or, the Jealous Husband: A Comedy, As it is Acted at the Theatre Royal by His Majesty's Servants* (London, 1696), Preface, n.pag.

80. *Ibrahim, the Thirteenth Emperour of the Turks: A Tragedy, As it is Acted by His Majesties Servants* (London, 1696), Dedication, n.pag.

81. Anonymous, prologue to Behn's posthumously produced play *The Younger Brother* (1696); in *Works*, **IV**, p. 320.

82. D. Manley, 'To the Author of Agnes de Castro' in C. Trotter, *Agnes de Castro. A Tragedy, As it is Acted at the Theatre Royal, by His Majesty's Servants* (London, 1696); M. Pix, 'To Mrs. *Manley*, upon her Tragedy call'd *The Royal Mischief*, in D. Manley, *The Royal Mischief, A Tragedy, As it is Acted by His Majesties Servants* (London, 1696).

83. 'To the Author of Agnes de Castro', lines 1-7.

84. 'To Mrs. *Manley*. By the Author of *Agnes de Castro*', lines 7–11, in *The Royal Mischief*.

85. Prologue to *The Younger Brother, Works*, **IV**, p. 320.
86. P. Harman, 'To the Author, on her Tragedy, call'd Fatal Friendship', in *The Works of Mrs. Catharine Cockburn*, ed. Thomas Birch (London, 1751), **II**, p. 466.
87. From an anonymous poem 'To Mrs. *Manley*, on her Tragedy call'd *The Royal Mischief*, in D. Manley, *The Royal Mischief*.
88. D. Manley, 'To the Reader', in *The Royal Mischief*.
89. Prologue to *Queen Catharine: or, the Ruines of Love, A Tragedy, As it is Acted at the New Theatre in Little-Lincolns-Inn-Fields by His Majesty's Servants* (London, 1698).
90. 'To the Reader', *Sir Patient Fancy*, in Behn, *Works*, **IV**, p. 7.
91. D. Manley, 'To the Reader', *The Royal Mischief*.
92. Prologue to *The False Friend, Or, the Fate of Disobedience. A Tragedy: As it is Acted at the New-Theatre in Little-Lincolns-Inn-Fields* (London, 1699).
93. Dedication to George Earl of Huntingdon, in *The Gamester: A Comedy, As it is Acted at the New-Theatre in Lincolns-Inn-Fields, by Her Majesty's Servants* (London, 1705).
94. John Hughes, 'To the ingenious Author, on her Tragedy called, Fatal Friendship', in *The Works of Mrs. Catharine Cockburn*, **II**, p. 471.

2
Three Self-Portraits

What people thought about women writers changed with the times, and so did what women writers thought about themselves. Before the 1690s they were maverick figures, hesitant or bold according to individual temperament, with little sense of group identity despite the appeal back to Sappho and ancient female tradition. Delariviere Manley, Mary Pix and Catharine Trotter changed that, but some of the claims that they, especially Manley, made for women's special talents began to look more like accusations before very long. Once the belief in naturally chaste womanhood was established as a foundation of the bourgeois world view, the only way for a woman writer to be acceptable to herself and her society was to fit herself and her writing into the new mould.

Female literary authority was built up in various ways: one of the most intriguing, as well as most important ones was women writers' self-portraits. In autobiographies women explained why they thought themselves special, why they were learned and articulate. As often as not they apologized for this too, being conscious, with Margaret Cavendish, that readers might ask, 'why hath this Lady writ her own Life?',[1] or indeed why had she presumed to write at all? Perhaps the most interesting, because freer-ranging, self-portraits are those where the writer mingled fiction with autobiography, simultaneously projecting herself in fantasy and trying to justify herself to the world. The late seventeenth and early eighteenth centuries are rich in semi-auto-biographical fiction. This mode suited women because in it they could become their own heroines, and as we have seen the cultural association between heroine and woman writer was strong. Romanticized auto-biography, or fantastic fiction starring an idealized version of the author, provided a means not just of self-projection but of creating one's identity and authority as a woman writer.

Aphra Behn, Delariviere Manley and Jane Barker are three writers whose view of women's literary authority is expressed through fiction-alized self-portraits, and their three very different self-images can show us something of the historical change in the woman writer's cultural position. The contrast between Manley and Barker is a representative one. Barker, born in 1660, was a few years older than Manley, and she began writing earlier. Her first book, *Poetical Recreations*, appeared in 1688. Yet Manley, by the self-image she creates, represents the kind of woman writer the eighteenth century was to turn away from, while Barker represents the new, moral woman writer, acceptable to later generations. In the works of these two we can witness the process of a cultural shift. Aphra Behn's position is not so easily assessed. She stands somewhat apart from general trends, refusing to be accommodated within the boundaries her contemporaries were beginning to draw round the female author. It was because she appeared at a very early stage in this process that she was not much affected by it. Yet at the same time, depicting herself as narrator in her novels led her to examine the idea of a specifically female authority.

APHRA BEHN

Aphra Behn's comments on herself as a writer are sprinkled liberally in the prefaces to her plays. She had to struggle for recognition of her right to a professional role—hence her tart remarks that women were equally entitled to write bawdy, and that people would have admired her plays more if they had thought a man had written them. To someone so determined to be accepted on equal terms with men, a good deal of the praise she was given must have been more galling than gratifying. Her admirers were busy building her a reputation as a writer of love, praising her poems for being erotic, even suggesting that reading Behn was tantamount to being seduced by her. Thomas Creech's poem to her announced:

> ... thy Pen disarms us so,
> We yield our selves to the first beauteous Foe;
> The easie softness of thy thoughts surprise,
> And this new way Love steals into our Eyes; ...
> In the same trance with the young pair we lie,
> And in their amorous Ecstasies we die ... [2]

Using another common assumption about femininity, one eulogist saw her work as evidence of her delicate understanding of the mysteries of nature, women and love.

What Passions does your Poetry impart?
It shows th'unfathom'd thing a Woman's Heart,
Tells what Love is, his Nature and his Art,
Displays the several Scenes of Hopes and Fears,
Love's Smiles, his Sighs, his Laughing and his Tears.[3]

A posthumous edition of her poems was introduced with similar claims: 'The Passions, that of Love especially, she was Mistress of, and gave us such nice and tender Touches of them, that without her Name we might discover the Author.'[4] Behn was certainly not above exploiting this image of herself when it came to selling her poems and her translation of Balthazar de Bonnecourse's *La Monstre, The Lover's Watch: or, the Art of making love*. Love was her subject here, and the encomium poems printed at the beginning of these volumes served as advertisements of the fact. Moreover, it is certainly fair that she should be remembered as a poet of love, when we consider such deservedly celebrated lyrics as 'Love in Fantastic Triumph sate' and 'A Thousand Martyrs I have made'. To Behn, though, love was not an especially feminine subject, it was simply an important poetic theme; and it was as a poet, simply, that she wanted to be remembered. 'Poetry (my Talent)', she wrote in proud parentheses, deceptively casual.[5] In the preface to one of her comedies, *The Lucky Chance* (1687), she asked for a very different kind of recognition from the kind she got:

> All I ask, is the Priviledge for my Masculine Part the Poet in me, (if any such you will allow me) to tread in those successful Paths my Predecessors have so long thriv'd in, to take those Measures that both the Ancient and Modern Writers have set me, and by which they have pleas'd the World so well: If I must not, because of my Sex, have this Freedom, but that you will usurp all to your selves; I lay down my Quill ... for I am not content to write for a Third day only [i.e. just for money: playwrights took the proceeds of the third performance]. I value Fame as much as if I had been born a *Hero* ... [6]

Instead of placing herself in the tradition of Sappho and Orinda, Behn is appealing here to the precedent of all the 'Ancient and Modern Writers', mostly men, and defining her poetic talent as masculine. The freedom she is demanding here is the freedom to write without any special restraints because of her sex.

Behn tended to compromise her claim for the freedom to write as men wrote by simultaneously denying that she wrote bawdy plays as they did: 'they charge [*The Lucky Chance*] with the old never failing Scandal—That 'tis not fit for the Ladys: As if (if it were as they falsly give it out) the Ladys were oblig'd to hear Indecencys only from their Pens and Plays.'[7] However, the fact that her comedies were successful on the stage in the 1670s and 1680s indicates that she escaped the requirements of 'decency' soon to bear especially hard on women. Her success in Restoration comedy has been held against her by some recent critics who find her work *too* 'masculine': reproducing the attitudes of male libertines, so that the hero of her comedy *The Rover* (1677) is rewarded for his philandering by marriage to the chaste heroine, who (as it transpires in the sequel to the play) soon dies, leaving him free to rove once more.[8] Behn is not without general concern for her sex and for women's freedom, as her plays' treatment of arranged marriages and her heroines' criticisms of various masculine tyrannies demonstrate.[9] Still, it is outside the plays themselves that she supports women most thoroughly, through her claims for women's abilities as writers.

Her novels are particularly interesting from this point of view, because in them she tackles the problem of the woman writer's authority by creating an explicitly female narrator. Fiction formed a large part of Behn's output in her later years. First to be published was *Love Letters Between a Nobleman and his Sister*, in three volumes from 1784 to 1787. Based on the contemporary scandal of Lord Grey of Werke's elopement with his sister-in-law Lady Henrietta Berkeley, and containing much anti-Monmouth sentiment at the time of Monmouth's rebellion, it contained enough sexual and political intrigue to be very popular. Behn published several other works of fiction during her lifetime, the most important being *The Fair Jilt* (1688) and *Oroonoko* (1688), and there are several stories written probably about 1685 but not published until after her death.

Her experiments with narrative technique are notable. The first part of *Love Letters* is as the title suggests, epistolary, and the heroine's passionate letters have led to comparisons with the Portuguese nun, though here the man replies and the lovers are united. But emphasis on epistolary passion obscures the political and satirical slant of the work. Some of Silvia's letters to Philander are attempts to dissuade him from joining Monmouth in the Rye House Plot against Charles II. Philander's response shows that his adoration of Silvia is a cloak for political ambition. 'I design no more by this great enterprize, than to make thee some glorious thing', he tells her, but soon adds, 'in going on, Oh *Silvia*! When three Kingdoms shall lie unpossest, and be exposed, as it were, amongst the raffling Crowd, who knows but the chance may be mine, as well as any others ...?'[10]

In the second and third parts, Behn turned to third-person narration, which allowed her to develop more clearly her own ironic comments on Silvia and Philander. Her narrator undercuts any claim Silvia has to be a passionate heroine in the tradition of the Portuguese nun: Silvia has 'no other design on [Octavio, another admirer], bating the little Vanity of her Sex, which is an Ingredient so intermixt with the greatest Vertues of Womenkind, that those who endeavour to cure 'em of that disease, rob them of a very considerable pleasure ... whatever other Knowledge they want, they have still enough to set a price on Beauty.'[11] Generalizing from Silvia, the narrator comments on all female behaviour: Eve's 'love of Novelty and Knowledge has been intail'd upon her Daughters ever since, and I have known more Women rendred unhappy and miserable from this torment of Curiosity, which they bring upon themselves, than have ever been undone by less villainous Men.'[12] Such narrative comments seem to reiterate standard views of false womankind from a male perspective. The reason for this may be that Behn was modelling her narrative voice on that of Paul Scarron, whose *Comic Novels* were popular at this time in England as well as in his native France. Scarron's intrusive, sardonic and obviously masculine narrators place his work in a comic tradition later developed further by Le Sage and Fielding. Aphra Behn's story *The Court of the King of Bantam*, published posthumously in 1698, was said to have been written as 'a Trial of Skill, upon a Wager, to shew that she was able to write in the Style of the celebrated *Scarron*, in Imitation of whom 'tis writ',[13] and its facetious wit suggests that she must have won her bet. Already, though, Behn was moving away from the implicitly male viewpoint imitation of Scarron encouraged in her. The narrator of *The Court of the King of Bantam*, identified as a friend of the heroine, Philibella, rather than the more central male characters, might best be envisaged as a woman. In most of the other stories the narrator is clearly female.

In *The Unfortunate Happy Lady*, the narrator, describing the talk of a procuress and her girls, comments, 'our Sex seldom wants matter of Tattle'.[14] The narrator of *The History of the Nun: or, the Fair Vow-Breaker* (1689), confides to the reader that she was once encouraged to become a nun (*Works*, V, 265). Describing a duel between the heroine's rival lovers in *The Nun: or, The Perjur'd Beauty* (1698), the narrator exclaims, 'Ah! how wretched are our Sex, in being the unhappy Occasion of so many fatal Mischiefs, even between the dearest Friends!' (V, 341). In *The Unfortunate Bride: or, The Blind Lady a Beauty*, she tells us, ''tis the Humour of our Sex, to deny most eagerly those Grants to Lovers, for which most tenderly we sigh, so contradictory are we to our selves' (V, 404). In these stories the narrator identifies herself as a woman with the authority to make general statements about female nature—which are essentially the same as the stereotyped views she offered from a man's perspective in *Love Letters*.

There are times when Behn develops her narrative comments in the direction of that specifically feminine authority to comment on women's experience and on love, which her admirers were ready to grant her, but which in the prefaces to her plays she ignored so as to claim the same authority as men. In *The History of the Nun: or, the Fair Vow Breaker*, the narrator professes to offer new insights into love that are not available to most people:

> Love, like Reputation, once fled, never returns more. 'Tis impossible to love, and cease to love, (and love another) and yet return again to the first Passion, tho' the Person have all the Charms, or a thousand times more than it had, when it first conquer'd. This Mistery in Love, it may be, is not generally known, but nothing is more certain. (V, 313)

She also offers her experience as authority for advice on how to treat young women, explaining:

> I once was design'd an humble Votary in the House of Devotion, but fancying my self not endu'd with an obstinacy of Mind, great enough to secure me from the Efforts and Vanities of the World, I rather chose to deny my self that Content I could not certainly promise my self, than to languish (as I have seen some do) in a certain Affliction.

She adds that she now thinks it a mistake to prefer the 'false ungrateful World' to the peaceful cloister, but:

> nevertheless, I could wish, for the prevention of abundance of Mischiefs and Miseries, that Nunneries and Marriages were not to be enter'd into, 'till the Maid, so destin'd, were of a mature Age to make her own Choice; and that Parents would not make use of their justly assum'd Authority to compel their Children, neither to the one or the other. (V, 265)

Claiming a woman's right to advise and slanting her advice in the direction of young women's freedom to choose their destiny, Behn here is very close to many of the woman novelists of the eighteenth century.

Often Behn makes her narrator not simply a woman but specifically the self-portrait of a well-known author, referring in passing to her own works. In *The Dumb Virgin* she is so pleased with the hero's assumed name of Dangerfield that 'being since satisfied it was a Counterfeit, I us'd it in a Comedy of mine' (V, 429). In *Oroonoko* she mentions meeting 'Colonel *Martin*, a man of great Gallantry, Wit, and Goodness, and whom I have celebrated in a Character of my new Comedy, by his own Name, in Memory of so brave a Man' (V, 198).[15] The events of *The Fair Jilt* are said to have taken place in Antwerp, 'about the Time of my being sent thither by King *Charles*' (V, 98), referring to a spying mission she undertook in 1666 to obtain information from a former friend William Scot, son of one of the regicides. Clearly one purpose of references like this was to impress upon her readers the literal truth of her narratives, whose events she claimed to have witnessed; and recent research shows that *Oroonoko* and *The Fair Jilt*, at least, have their basis in truth.[16] Another reason for putting her self-portrait into her novels is to include in them her vindication of the woman writer's ability and authority.

This is most evident in *Oroonoko*, where the autobiographical element means that Behn's interest in the narrator's position develops into an examination of her own role as woman and as writer. This fascinating novel marks an important stage in the history of women's quest for literary authority. Writing before the full establishment of the convention that love is the woman writer's subject and a moral aim her excuse, Behn has a freedom denied to most of her eighteenth-century descendants. She ranges widely over different societies, to investigate the meaning of civilized values in a story beyond the scope of many more polished later novelists. *Oroonoko* is the story of an African prince tricked into boarding a slave vessel and taken to Surinam while it is under English occupation. Because of his royal bearing Oroonoko (or Caesar, as the English appropriate rename him) is treated with respect by the Cornish gentleman, Trefry, who becomes his master. In Surinam he meets his long-lost love, Imoinda, also a slave, and they marry and conceive a child. Unwilling to have his child born into slavery, Oroonoko foments and leads a slave rebellion, which is suppressed. He is cruelly beaten. Vowing revenge, he takes his wife into the forest and kills her to prevent her falling into his enemies' hands; but after her death he loses his resolution and remains by her body. When he is recaptured he inflicts horrible injuries on himself, and then on the orders of General Byam, Deputy Governor of Surinam, he is executed. The tale affords a picture of an exotic colony (lost to the Dutch by the time of *Oroonoko*'s publication), and shows the English in their relations with its native people and with the African slave-trade. Three very different cultures—the European, the native Surinam, and that of Coramantien, Oroonoko's African home—are compared to one another. Thus it is a novel of ideas as well as action, and the narrator's comments are crucial to the rendering of these.

She is a narrator of a type especially common in the early novel—herself a character within the tale, relating it with the authority of an eye-witness. Neither omniscient and outside the action, nor central to it, she provides her commentary on the events she narrates.[17] Having travelled out to Surinam, as we know Aphra Behn herself did, she meets the enslaved Oroonoko, hears the story of his past life and adventures, and either sees or hears of the rest of his story up to his dreadful end.

Trefry, she tells us, once intended to write the hero's life, but died before
he could do it, and so the task fell to her, which, she says modestly, is
a pity for Oroonoko. 'His Misfortune was, to fall in an obscure World,
that afforded only a Female Pen to celebrate his Fame' (V, 169). Yet
as events unfold we realize that her gender is an important part of her
authority: what she knows, and the comments she is able to make,
depend on it. The female pen is vindicated.

The scene is set for Oroonoko's story by the narrator's description of
Surinam. The Surinam natives represent 'an absolute *Idea* of the first
State of Innocence, before Man knew how to sin: And 'tis most evident
and plain, that simple Nature is the most harmless, inoffensive and
virtuous Mistress (V, 131). Civilization could only bring repression, and
'Religion would here but destroy that Tranquillity they possess by
Ignorance; and Laws would but teach 'em to know Offences, of which
now they have no Notion' (V, 132). Their simplicity contrasts markedly
with the duplicity shown by the white community throughout the story.

The story of Oroonoko's Coramantien life provides another contrast
to Europe. Here it is not so much a case of the noble savage against
civilization, as that of the truly civilized man against a decadent society.
The young prince Oroonoko embodies the Restoration's heroic ideal:
proud, honourable, superhuman in his prowess in battle, and 'as capable
of love, as 'twas possible for a brave and gallant Man to be; and in
saying that, I have named the highest Degree of Love: for sure great
Souls are most capable of that Passion' (V, 137). His wit, his judgement,
and his character all in all are as great 'as if his Education had been in
some *European* court' (V, 135). His experiences show those Europeans
whose highest values he has adopted in a very poor light. From the
captain who tricks him aboard the slave-ship, to Byam, Deputy-
Governor of Surinam, who tricks him into surrender after the slave
rebellion, they fail to live up to their own code of honour.

The contrast between the African prince and the English people is
used to expose what Behn saw as the recent betrayal of civilized values
by the English. Oroonoko, royal himself, echoes his creator's royalist
sentiments when he expresses horror at the execution of Charles I, 'with
all the Sense and Abhorrence of the Injustice imaginable' (V, 135). He
and his countrymen 'pay a most absolute Resignation to the Monarch,
especially when he is a Parent also' (V, 139), most unlike the English,
with Monmouth's plot against his father Charles II in their recent
history by the time Behn was writing Oroonoko's story. The Cora-
mantiens' attitudes to sexual relationships compare well with the Europeans', too. Oroonoko's early passion for Imoinda 'aimed at nothing but
Honour, if such a Distinction may be made in Love; and especially in
that Country, where Men take to themselves as many as they can
maintain; and where the only Crime and Sin against a Woman, is, to

turn her off, to abandon her to Want, Shame and Misery: such ill Morals are only practis'd in *Christian* countries' (V, 138–9).

As narrator, Behn has two assets which enable her to make Oroonoko's story serve this critique of her own society: her intimate acquaintance with and sympathy for the hero himself and her own identity as one of the Europeans, but not so completely at one with them that she cannot take a detached view of them.

Both these narrative assets are enhanced because of her social position and her sex. She has travelled out to Surinam with her father, who was to be Lieutenant-Governor of the colony, but died on the voyage. She lives in the best house on the plantation and has, she claims, 'none above me in that Country'.[18] She thus has status but no occupation, and no permanent stake in the colony; so she is well-placed to observe and comment freely. As a woman she can comment with authority on Oroonoko's gallantry and attractiveness. When she first saw him, she explains, he 'addressed himself to me, and some other Women, with the best Grace in the World' (V, 136). She gets to know him well because 'he liked the Company of us Women much above the Men' (V, 175). In fact 'we [women] had all the Liberty of Speech with him, especially my self, whom he call'd his *Great Mistress*; and indeed my Word would go a great Way with him' (V, 175–6). Thus she hears his story from his own lips and is able to report his noble sentiments.

The narrator also enters the action, exploiting Oroonoko's gallantry and his attachment to her in order to keep him under the control of the white settlers. Oroonoko is suspicious of their promises to set him free when the Lord Governor arrives, an attitude justified by his former experience of the Christian word of honour and by the narrator's comment that they 'fed him from Day to Day with Promises' (V, 175). The settlers, fearing a slave mutiny, ask the narrator to use her influence to persuade Oroonoko to wait till the Lord Governor makes his appearance. This she does, and it is hard to tell whether she does so in good faith or not. Her admiration for his heroic scorn of slavery sits oddly with her actions: 'I neither thought it convenient to trust him much out of our View, nor did the Country, who fear'd him', she reports (V, 177), relating how she and the other settlers surround Oroonoko with 'attendants' who are really spies. She encourages the royal slave to take several pleasant 'Diversions'—hunting tigers, fishing, visiting the Surinam Indians—the real purpose of which is to divert his thoughts from rebellion. She seems to be acting entirely, and with typical duplicity, as a European; but once the rebellion breaks out the narrator's ability to detach herself from her society's crimes becomes evident.

The whites, it now transpires, are split. Byam, 'a Fellow, whose Character is not fit to be mentioned with the worst of the Slaves' (V, 194), is for taking strong measures against the rebels, but 'they of the

better sort', including the narrator, believe that Oroonoko has been
badly treated and should not be harshly dealt with now (V, 193). Trefry
joins in the pursuit of the rebels, meaning to act as mediator; but, duped
by Byam's promises of leniency, he persuades Oroonoko to surrender,
and unwittingly leads him into a trap. The narrator now separates
herself from the Europeans responsible for Oroonoko's downfall. She
neither sides with Byam's cruelty nor shows Trefry's gullibility. If the
reader wonders why someone of her high social position did nothing to
protect Oroonoko from the vicious treatment he gets, the answer lies in
her sex. As a woman, she has had to flee from the scene of action:

> You must know, that when the News was brought on *Monday*
> Morning, that *Caesar* had betaken himself to the Woods, and
> carry'd with him all the *Negroes*, we were possess'd with extreme
> Fear, which no Persuasions could dissipate, that he would
> secure himself till Night, and then would come down and cut
> all our Throats. This Apprehension made all the Females of
> us fly down the River, to be secured; and while we were away,
> they acted this Cruelty; for I suppose I had Authority and
> Interest enough there, had I suspected any such Thing, to
> have prevented it. (V, 198)

The trust between the royal slave and his 'Great Mistress' has been
shattered by their racial differences, and yet her ignominious flight
reveals similarities in the positions of the European woman and the
enslaved African man. Like Oroonoko, who is given the outward respect
due to a prince but kept from real power, the narrator is under the
illusion that she has high status in the colony; but when it comes to a
crisis the men are the real rulers, and being the daughter of a man who
would have governed Surinam if he had lived does not help her. Ironically, she still seems to believe in her 'Authority and Interest' as she
tells a story which reveals how illusory these were.

The narrator's gender is now her alibi. It saves her from sharing the
guilt of her countrymen's treatment of the noble black prince, and, by
implication, from sharing in the general corruption of the European
society she criticizes. She is absent at other key moments too. She has
to leave the hero when she sees his self-inflicted wounds, being 'but
sickly, and very apt to fall into Fits of dangerous Illness upon any
extraordinary Melancholy' (V, 207). She is still away when he is
executed. Her mother and sister (scarcely mentioned in the story up to
this point) witness the event in her stead, but they are 'not suffer'd to
save him' (V, 208). Their position here is like the narrator's throughout:
a spectator, but because of her femininity, a helpless one.

This feminine position, though, is an appropriate one for a narrator.

On the fringes of her world, she is unable to act in the decisive scenes, but she observes, records, and eventually hands the story down to posterity. In *Oroonoko* the narrator's femininity is especially important because the similarities between the slave's and the woman's positions allow her her sympathetic insight into the hero's feelings at the same time as she creates a full sense of the difference of his race and culture. The limitations on women which Behn acknowledges, even exploits, within her narrative, do not apply to expression. As a character the narrator seems caught uneasily between admiration for her hero and allegiance to European civilization, but this means that she can present a picture of both sides. She ends with a flourish that implicitly asserts women's equal right to be recorders of events and interpreters of the world:

> Thus died this great Man, worthy of a better Fate, and
> a more sublime Wit than mine to write his Praise: Yet, I
> hope, the Reputation of my Pen is considerable enough to make
> his glorious Name to survive to all Ages, with that of the brave,
> the beautiful and the constant *Imoinda*. (V, 208)

The reputation of Aphra Behn's pen certainly was great at the time that *Oroonoko* was written, and she uses that reputation to present the female narrator as authoritative, disinterested and sympathetic, with as much authority as a male writer and also with special insights gained from her woman's position.

The marginality of the narrator's position is very important to Behn for another reason. It enables her to create her self-image as a writer, free from some of the restrictions on behaviour and feeling which operate on women as represented in the narrative. The contrast between the heroine, Imoinda, and the woman who writes her story is instructive. Imoinda is all that convention could desire of a noble hero's mate: beautiful, sensitive, ready to sacrifice all to preserve her chastity, capable of brave deeds in defence of her husband, and above all, devoted to him. Her qualities are best seen in her eagerness to die at his hands: when Oroonoko explains that he must kill her to preserve her honour, 'He found the heroick Wife faster pleading for Death, than he was to propose it' (V, 202). The narrator explains this attitude as part of exotic Coramantien custom: 'For Wives have a Respect for their Husbands equal to what any other People pay a Deity; and when a Man finds any Occasion to quit his Wife, if he love her, she dies by his Hand; if not, he sells her, or suffers some other to kill her' (V, 202). The killing of Imoinda shocks Oroonoko's European friends, but is presented as 'a Deed, (that however horrid it first appear'd to us all) when we had heard his Reasons, we thought it brave and just' (V, 201–2). Here an uneasy note creeps into the narrator's assessment of Coramantien, the place where natural honour and nobility are supposed to thrive. It has crept in before whenever women's position was considered. African polygamy is useful for the purposes of a satirical attack on European sexual hypocrisy, but Behn holds back from endorsing it as a real alternative by making Oroonoko vow to be true all his life to Imoinda alone; and the whole Coramantien episode shows that heroic society torn apart by the quarrel between Oroonoko and his grandfather the king over possession of the heroine. Writing *Oroonoko*, Behn was confronted with the problem of a woman's relation to the heroic ideal which she, along with other Restoration writers, endorsed. In some ways Behn identifies with her hero, but in the story of Oroonoko and his wife her position, as a woman, might be expected to be more analagous with Imoinda's, and that is an identification she does not want to make.

The female narrator Behn creates is important for *not* being the heroine. It is a pity that the autobiographical element of *Oroonoko* has caused so much criticism to centre on the truth or otherwise of the self-portrait within it, for Behn was deliberately not focusing on her own experience, and at a time when heroine and woman writer were coming to seem almost synonymous, she insisted on making a sharp distinction between them. If Imoinda, ideally lovely and noble, is Oroonoko's true mate, the narrator is his 'Great Mistress', sympathising with him, surviving him, recording his story, and assessing his significance. From the narrative stance Behn creates in this novel it is evident that for her being a writer was a way of escaping some of the limitations imposed on women.

Her prefaces claim a man's rights in writing, and her narratives claim something of a special authority as a woman, but without acknowledging any of the limitations on feminine expression that were later to come into force. Her double claim is well expressed in some lines she inserted into her translation of the sixth book of Cowley's Latin work, *Of Plants*. Here, unusually for her, she calls on the examples of Sappho and Orinda. The poet has been invoking Daphne, source of the poet's laurels, and then 'the Translatress in her own Person' addresses her:

> I, by a double Right, thy Bounties claim,
> Both from my Sex, and in *Apollo*'s Name:
> Let me with *Sappho* and *Orinda* be,
> Oh ever sacred Nymph, adorn'd by thee;
> And give my verses Immortality.[19]

Behn's confidence in her own authority as a woman writer is not matched in the century following her death.

DELARIVIERE MANLEY

Though later ages have tended to bracket Aphra Behn and Delariviere Manley together as erotic and immoral women writers, their self-portraits could hardly be more different from one another. Where Behn created for herself a role as detached and ironic observer, Manley made herself into a heroine. Where Behn tried to avoid the simple parallels between a woman's life and her writing made by her contemporaries Manley exploited that connection to the full and made it more difficult for women writers to avoid it in the future. Where Behn widened the woman writer's scope, Manley declared that love was the only subject for a woman. In moving from Behn to Manley we move from a declaration of independence to an attempt to found the woman writer's authority on her femininity, conceived of as eroticism.

Manley wrote two autobiographical narratives. The first is incorporated into the second volume of *The New Atalantis* (1709). Writing of herself under the slightly altered name of Delia, she describes her early, bigamous marriage to her cousin John Manley, with heavy emphasis on her own innocence throughout. Delia's story is told by herself, and its portrayal of Manley as the epitome of deceived innocence fits in with other pictures of seduction and treachery found in the work. *The New Atalantis* made Manley famous. It is a *roman à clef* containing scandalous allegations about various Whigs, the first Duke and Duchess of Marlborough in particular. Manley's method of attack is to accuse her targets of sexual intrigues, the stories of which are placed within an allegorical and moral framework. Astrea, goddess of justice, is travelling through Atalantis with her mother Virtue, both guided by the gossip-loving lady Intelligence. They witness and deplore the country's closely-linked political and moral corruptions. Atalantis is England under Queen Anne, or rather, from Manley's Tory viewpoint, under the illegitimate sway of Count Fortunatus (Marlborough) and his wife. Fortunatus is described as rising to power in his youth by seducing one of the mistresses of Sigismund the Second (Charles II). In order to marry Jeanita (Sarah, first Duchess of Marlborough), Fortunatus has to provide himself with an excuse for abandoning his Duchess. He does this by sending his friend Germanicus to keep one of his own assignments with his mistress, so giving himself an opportunity of finding them in bed together. The scene which follows is an example of Manley's 'warm' style. Germanicus is discovered in bed:

> his whole Person stood confess'd to the Eyes of the
> Amorous Dutchess, his Limbs were exactly form'd, his Skin
> shiningly white, and the Pleasure the Ladies graceful

entrance gave him, diffus'd Joy and Desire throughout all
his Form; his lovely Eyes seem'd to be closed, his Face turn'd
on one side (to favour the Deceit) was obscur'd by the Lace
depending from the *Pillows* on which he rested; the Dutchess,
who had about her all those *Desires*, she expected to employ
in the Embraces of the Count, was so blinded by 'em, that
at first she did not perceive the Mistake, so that giving her
Eyes, time to wander over Beauties so inviting, and which
encreased her Flame; with an amorous Sigh, she gently threw
her self on the Bed close to the desiring Youth ... [20]

The picture is comic as much as erotic, with the deliberate role-reversal
in the inviting posture of the seductive man, and the emphasis on sex
as trickery.[21] For Manley's first readers the main point of such scenes
was in discovering the identity of the protagonists and enjoying the
scandal about leading people at Court: this was the reason Lady Mary
Pierrepont (later Wortley Montagu) was eager to get a copy of *The New
Atalantis*.[22] Manley did not let her readers forget that the victims of her
allegations were the country's leaders, and *The New Atalantis* was probably the most effective attack on the Whigs published at this time,
undermining confidence in the ministry while it was vulnerable (a
Tory ministry succeeded in the following year).[23] When Manley was
imprisoned late in 1709, soon after the publication of the second volume
of her work, it was for her considerable political nuisance-value, certainly
not for her warm writing as such. Yet it is as an erotic writer rather
than a political propagandist that Manley has mostly been remembered,
and reviled.

One reason for this is to be found in Manley's second, and fuller
autobiography, *The Adventures of Rivella* (1714). Just as Delia and Rivella
are complementary echoes of the name Delariviere, so Rivella's story
fills in what was left out of Delia's—her life before and after the bigamous
marriage. The biggest difference between the two is that in *Rivella*,
Manley is concentrating on presenting herself as a writer; and the self-
portrait she gives had a powerful influence on the public conception of
women writers in her time. Partly because of Manley, woman writer
and erotic writer came to seem almost synonymous terms.

Rivella is autobiography disguised as biography, with the story of
Rivella's life and writings supposedly told by an old friend of hers,
Colonel Lovemore, to a visiting Frenchman, the Chevalier d'Aumont.
In the introductory section the Chevalier explains his curiosity about
Manley. He is fascinated by her amatory fiction:

I have not known any of the Moderns in [treating the subject
of love] come up to your famous Author of the *Atalantis*.
She has carried the Passion farther than could be readily

conceiv'd: Her *Germanicus on the Embroider'd Bugle Bed*,
naked out of the Bath:—Her *Young and innocent Charlot*,
transported with the powerful *Emotion of a just kindling
Flame, sinking with Delight and Shame upon the Bosom of her
Lover in the Gallery of Books*: Chevalier Tomaso *dying at the
Feet of Madam* de Bedamore, *and afterwards possessing Her in
that* Sylvan *Scene of Pleasure [in] the Garden*; are such
Representatives of Nature, that must warm the coldest Reader;
it raises high Ideas of the Dignity of Human Kind, and informs
us that we have in our Composition, wherewith to taste sublime
and transporting Joys: After perusing her Inchanting Descriptions,
which of us have not gone in Search of Raptures which she
every where tells us, as happy Mortals, we are capable of
tasting. But have we found them, *Chevalier,* answer'd his
friend? For my Part, I believe they are to be met with
no where else but in her own Embraces.[24]

This passage contains the essence of Manley's image of herself as an
erotic writer. The descriptions of sexual encounters d'Aumont mentions
are all from *The New Atalantis*. According to him they arouse sexual
desires in the reader, and this erotic function is glorified by the terms
he uses: in his view Manley's tales of sexual intrigue raise human dignity.
Moreover, Manley's talents as writer and lover are linked together.
Because Lovemore is supposed to cherish an unrequited passion for
Rivella-Manley, he is the ideal character to make this connection. Only
Rivella herself, he sighs, could satisfy the desires her writing arouses.
Her personal desirability and the erotic power of her writings serve to
reinforce one another.

This picture is not what we would expect from someone whose career
in fact proved that women writers, far from being confined to the
depiction of love, could directly influence public life. *The New Atalantis*
was not her only political satire: *Queen Zarah* (1705), her first attack on
the Marlboroughs, preceded it, and the two-volume *Memoirs of Europe*
followed in 1710. The latter was written after encouragement from
Harley, the Tory Prime Minister who came to power in 1710. Manley
was also noticed as a useful political hack by Swift, and she took over
from him as editor of *The Examiner*. Manley's contemporaries knew her
as a powerful Tory writer, well versed in court life and intrigues,
who attacked her opponents with scandal in which, as the Duchess of
Marlborough once admitted, there was an uncomfortable ingredient of
truth.[25]

In *The Adventures of Rivella*, though, Manley does her best to disclaim
any political role. She does not mention the *Memoirs of Europe* or the
work on *The Examiner*, and she describes *The New Atalantis* with emphasis
on its erotic rather than political qualities. Rivella does try to justify her

political writing, claiming patriotic motives for exposing people who wanted 'to enslave their Sovereign, and overturn the Constitution' (*The Adventures of Rivella*, p. 109), but Lovemore lays stress on her renunciation of politics: 'She now agrees with me, that Politicks is not the Business of a Woman, especially of one that can so well delight and entertain her Readers with more gentle pleasing Theams' (p. 117). Manley's repudiation of her political role and her consequent emphasis on the erotic was itself clearly prompted by political considerations. In 1714, when *Rivella* was written, the Tory party's rule had ended. There was no prospect of success for Manley as a political writer. The best she could do for herself was to announce her move away from politics and present herself as an erotic writer, hoping in this way to gain an audience for her plays and fiction.

As far as Manley's long-term reputation was concerned, this expedient was only too successful. Her importance as a Tory writer has been virtually ignored since her death, while the picture she painted of herself as amorous woman and erotic writer has adversely affected her standing in literary history up to the present time. She has been seen as a lying scandal-monger, particularly reprehensible for concentrating on the erotic, a theme made even worse by coming from a woman whose own sex life was known to violate accepted standards of behaviour. After the bigamous marriage, she had affairs first with Sir Thomas Skipworth, and then with John Tilly, warden of the Fleet Street prison. In her later years she lived with John Barber, a printer. These liaisons were well known in her time. It is hardly surprising that contemporaries gossiped about the sex life of a woman whose own fame was built on her accounts of other people's sexual adventures. It is less excusable that twentieth-century criticism of her should base its judgement of her on her love-affairs.

Disparaging references to Manley's life have often been substituted for criticism of her work. She figures as 'a thorough minx' in a book called *Rogues and Scoundrels*, and is included in another work of revealing title, *Five Queer Women*.[26] In a study of early women novelists, published in 1944, Bridget G. MacCarthy introduces her discussion of Manley by warning her readers that they are about to enter on 'noxious swamps. Here be crocodiles, here be stenches! Let us clench our teeth, hold our noses and advance.' For her, Manley was a 'football of fortune ... she was the sport of many, and she gathered mud all the way ... it was a swift descent from bad to worse ... from one protector to another'. Added to this she finds 'deliberate prurience' and 'unquotable indecency' in Manley's work.[27]

There have been attempts to defend Manley from this kind of treatment. Dolores Palomo attacks 'the repeated fusion of judgments about the woman with judgments about the work', which has led to the presentation of Manley as 'an immoral woman who (therefore) wrote immoral books'.[28] She pinpoints the flaw in critical accounts not only of Manley but of many other women writers; but it is worth pointing out that such judgments are only hostile versions of the assessment Manley invited her readers to make. Her own presentation of herself, in *Rivella*, is as a desirable and sexually experienced woman who (therefore) writes marvellously erotic books. The connection between life and writing cannot be ignored in Manley's case, because she used it herself to create an image which affected her own reputation, and the reputation of women writers in general.

A specific political setback, the Tory fall from power, made Manley concentrate her claims for her writing on its femininity. There were wider cultural reasons behind the different *kinds* of femininity she claimed for herself in different works. The story of Delia and *The Adventures of Rivella* offer wholly different interpretations of Manley's sexuality, and comparing the two shows us the two images of womanhood—and hence, of the woman writer—that were jostling for supremacy in the early eighteenth century.

The self-image of *Rivella* was not an innovatory one. Manley was appealing to, and helping to ratify, already prevalent beliefs about women and writing. The connection between love in life and writing had often been made earlier, including in people's reactions to Manley's plays. In *Rivella*, she quotes some lines from a poem written years before in praise of *The Royal Mischief* (1696), in which her writing had been seen as a revelation and a promise of its author's sexuality:

> While she by writing thus our wishes warms
> What worlds of love must circle in her arms?[29]

In the story of Delia, Manley had offered a very different picture of herself. The plot of this story, verifiable in outline from external sources, resembles that of the seduction tales typical of Manley and her contemporaries.[30] Some time after the death of her father, Manley married her cousin. The marriage proved invalid, as his first wife was still alive, and Delariviere Manley was left to make a living for herself, which she did first by being companion to the Duchess of Cleveland, and later by writing. She managed to gain a livelihood, but found it more difficult to retrieve a lost reputation; and Delia's story is her attempt to do this by representing herself as an innocent victim.

Why should it become important to Manley to put in a claim of sexual innocence at this stage in her career? The bigamous marriage had ended years ago, before 1694. In the intervening time she had apparently been content to be known as an amorous woman writer, and her other love-affairs were known to her public. It may be that in a work which accused many of her contemporaries of sexual peccadilloes she wanted to forestall similar attacks on herself; and the overall picture *The New Atalantis* paints, of virtuous people (usually women) persecuted by corrupt ones (usually men) in high places, made a virtuous author a necessity. Perhaps the most important reason lies in the appearance of *The New Atalantis* at a time when common assumptions about women were changing. Though later readers found the book infamously immoral because it depicted sexual encounters, many of its episodes laid emphasis on female innocence and chastity. Manley's fiction can be seen as the meeting-ground for two conceptions of womanhood: one of the passionate, sexual being as often depicted in Restoration drama, the other of the innocent, passionless, easily deceived creature gaining ascendancy in the early eighteenth century. The Duchess who is tricked into bed with Germanicus is one example of the earlier image in *The New Atalantis*. In *Rivella* Manley fell back on a similar conception for her own self-portrait, and made what capital there was still to be made of it, while the story of Delia in *The New Atalantis* was her attempt to portray herself as the new pure woman.

Astrea, Virtue and Intelligence overhear Delia telling her story to a nobleman. Once she has explained how she was left an orphan, completely under the control of one of her guardians, Don Marcus (alias John Manley, the writer's cousin and bigamous husband), her narrative unfolds in a pattern typical of many seduction tales. At first, the seducer appears harmless and amiable to his child-like victim, and next the heroine's reading of romances awakens false expectations of love. Trustful, and ready to be aroused, she is vulnerable to her seducer's trickery. Don Marcus tells Delia that his wife is dead, and declares himself her lover. This deception might be considered sufficient excuse for her eventual acceptance of his marriage proposal, but the narrative provides further justification. All elements of desire are eliminated from her decision to marry. The hints that romances may have aroused passion in her are now dropped, and instead the romance heroine's conventional cold disdain is attributed to her. She explains that she 'would not permit my Adorer so much as a Kiss from my Hand, without ten thousand times more Intreaty than anything of that nature cou'd be worth'.[31] The situation is resolved after she recovers from a dangerous fever. Don Marcus cares for her during her illness, thus giving her a pretext for acceptance without desire: 'having ever had a Gratitude in my Nature ... upon my Recovery I promis'd to marry him' (*New Atalantis*, II, 184). Don Marcus's first wife is still alive, though, and Delia is therefore 'marry'd, possess'd and ruin'd' (II, 185). Heroic and helpless, she can neither leave Don Marcus nor reconcile herself to living with him; and although she has lost her honour in the world's eyes, her own story insists on her essential, uncorrupted innocence.

Using the conventions of romance and seduction tale, then, Manley creates herself as wronged heroine. Yet her goddess of justice makes a surprisingly severe judgment of the seduced girl. Ignoring Delia's claims that she never loved Don Marcus, Astrea comments on her narrative as if it were a story of unbridled feminine passion:

> I am weary of being entertain'd with the Fopperies of the
> Fair; ... How is it possible to hinder the Women from
> *believing*, or the Men from *deceiving*? the *Penalty* must be
> *there*, and something of a quicker Sense (if possible) than that
> of Honour lost! since we see the tender Sex, with all their
> *Native-Timorousness*, *Modesty* and *Shame-fac'd* Education, when
> stung by Love, can trample under Foot the consideration of
> *Virtue* and *Glory*. (II, 192)

Coming after Delia's repeated declarations that she has never felt love, this seems an unfair comment, but taken together with the quickly suppressed hints of passion earlier in the narrative, it somewhat undermines Delia's version of herself. This may be Manley's unconscious acknowledgement that this account of her life exaggerates her claim to the innocence of ignorance. She certainly had no success in convincing her contemporaries of her purity.[32]

Her second self-portrait, in *The Adventures of Rivella*, can be understood as her reaction to 'Delia's' failure to convince. It is a deliberate attempt to valorise the image of amorous woman, because that of pure woman is denied to her. Early in 1714, Edmund Curll advertized an account of Manley's life by Charles Gildon. To prevent the appearance of a publication which would no doubt have made the most of her love-affairs, Manley offered to write her own account. With the threat of Gildon's biography hanging over her she had no choice but to admit to these affairs and present them as favourably as possible.[33] The picture she gives of her own writing is partly determined by this predicament.

The narrative of *Rivella* begins with the heroine's early love for a soldier stationed in her father's garrison. Her marriage is passed over and the story moves on to life after the break with John Manley, including her connection with Hilaria (the Duchess of Cleveland). Then comes the publication of her first play. Next comes her affair with Cleander (John Tilly), at which point a fair proportion of the narrative is devoted to describing Rivella's and Cleander's involvement in a legal dispute. Lastly, Rivella's imprisonment after the publication of *The New Atalantis*, and her resolve to abandon political writing, are described.

Throughout the narrative a favourable picture of Rivella as woman and as writer is built up. In the introductory dialogue, d'Aumont and Lovemore define Rivella in relation to two other women whom they both admire. One is Madame Dacier, who proves that 'Wit and Sense' in women are more powerful charms than beauty, for she is 'a Woman without either Youth or Beauty, yet who makes a Thousand Conquests' (*Rivella*, p. 2). The other is the Duchess of Mazarin, who also managed to charm men in her old age. Rivella, too, can attract men by the power of her intellect even though she 'is no longer young, and was never a Beauty' (p. 5). Where she differs is in her ability to express her eroticism in literary form. Lovemore claims that the Duchess of Mazarin was 'entirely Mistress of the Art of Love; and yet she has never given the World such Testimonies of it, as has *Rivella*, by her Writings' (p. 6). The power to translate her personal attractions into the medium of literature is Rivella's distinction.

Instead of trying to prove Rivella sexually pure, this narrative suggests that generosity and integrity, instead of chastity, should be criteria for judging a woman's character. Rivella's proud integrity is demonstrated when she leaves Hilaria's house, justly offended by false accusations that she is having an affair with Hilaria's son. Her generosity is shown in the affair with Cleander. He wants to marry her after his wife's death, but against her own desires she refuses, advising him to compensate for recent financial losses by marrying a rich widow. 'One must be a Woman of an exalted Soul to take the Part she did', comments Lovemore (p. 105). Rivella's generosity is emphasized again when Lovemore relates that she gave herself up to the authorities to save the printer and publisher of *The New Atalantis* from being jailed instead of her.

The narrative ends with a vision of Rivella drawn in the manner of one of the love-scenes she was making her trademark. Lovemore pictures her on 'a Bed nicely sheeted and strow'd with *Roses, Jessamins* or *Orange-Flowers* ... her Pillows neatly trim'd with Lace or Muslin, stuck round with *Junquils*, or other natural Garden Sweets' (p. 119). He invites d'Aumont to imagine the sensations of 'the happy Man, with whom she chose to repose her self, during the Heat of the Day, in a State of Sweetness and Tranquillity'. D'Aumont is eager not just to think about these joys but to experience them: '*Allon*'s let us go my dear *Lovemore*', he exclaims (p. 120). His desires are aroused by Rivella as the subject of this passage, and also by Manley as its author. This final paragraph of *Rivella*, like the book as a whole, is an advertisement not primarily for Rivella's personal attractions but for the aphrodisiac qualities of Manley's writing.

In *The Adventures of Rivella*, Manley took her reputation into her own hands and influenced the picture of herself and her writings which has been preserved since her time. Her self-portrait as amorous, erotic woman writer was accepted because it fitted her public's expectations. Her attempts to replace innocence with generosity and love of truth as salient womanly virtues were markedly less successful. The loss of innocence was remembered against her, while the virtues she laid claim to were not credited to her; and as her erotic scenes became morally indefensible to the later eighteenth century, Manley was remembered as a warning to other women of how not to write.

In the short term, though, her emphasis on the connection between female authorship and erotic writing provided other women writers with a special role. Her work was imitated by several women, and her name invoked as an example. Having deliberately set about to establish a particular notion of the woman writer, Manley lived to be hailed as an honoured precursor by female admirers and followers.

Mary Hearne was the most whole-hearted of her imitators as far as the role of erotic woman writer is concerned. She produced two short epistolary novels, *The Lover's Week* (1718) and *The Female Deserters* (1719). Both end, most unconventionally, with their heroines not only seduced but delighted to be so. *The Lover's Week* is dedicated to Manley, 'a Standard Name and Reputation', so as to help her make the impact she wants with her first publication. 'YOUR NAME prefix'd to any thing of LOVE, who have carry'd that Passion to the most elegant Heighth in your own Writings, is enough to protect any Author who attempts to follow in that mysterious Path', she tells Manley. Her claim to be following in the famous novelist's footsteps is backed up by a poem 'To the Fair and Ingenious Author of the LOVER's Week', signed Joseph Gay, which ascribes to her many of the qualities Manley had called her own in *Rivella*. It praises the combination of bodily and mental charms in a woman writer: 'In the same Mould when Sense and Beauty meet, /In Her full Charms the *Woman* shines compleat ...'. Mary Hearne's work, like Manley's, is supposed to arouse desire in the male reader. The projected reader of her novel is a 'gen'rous Youth', who imagines himself in the place of the heroine's lover, and: 'His Breast all Anguish, and his Eyes all Fire,/He shudders with a Tempest of Desire.' Like Manley's work before her, Hearne's novel is said to prove: 'That best a *Woman* knows to write of Love;/Nature instructs Her with expressive Powers ... ' and this literary skill is once again linked to the woman's sexual experience: she can 'well describe, what she concerts so well'. Joseph Gay ends this poem of praise by erotic suggestion with a request to Hearne to write more tales of love, a task she will accomplish, he implies, more by sex appeal than literary skill. In comparing her to Behn and Manley, he urges her to make the most of her superior charms, 'And whom in Beauty you outvy, outvy in Fame.'[34]

The most important heiress of Manley's writing role, however, is Eliza Haywood. Some of her works, like *Memoirs of a Certain Island* (1725) and *The Court of Carimania* (1727), are scandal novels in Manley's vein. Others were more simply fictional, and also focused on sexual affairs, if not quite so warmly as her predecessor's work. Haywood did not write her own life, nor did she make any of Manley's explicit connections between amorous woman and erotic writer, but she inherited a tradition of belief in the woman writer as expert on love, which she exploited to the full. The second part of *Love in Excess* was prefaced by a poem praising woman's intellectual powers and physical attractions together. The anonymous writer claims that until he read *Love in Excess* he did not believe either in the strength of women's souls or in the power of love, but he assures Haywood that 'A Convert, now, to both, I feel that Fire/ YOUR Words alone can paint! YOUR Looks inspire!'[35] As a prolific and popular writer of love tales in the 1720s, Haywood perpetuated a notion of the female writer which had its roots in a general cultural idea of womanhood, but owed much of its impact to Delariviere Manley. Manley, demonstrating in her own life a woman's ability to make her way in the masculine sphere of politics, was driven by political setbacks and by the scandal that surrounded her personal life to adopt a narrowly feminine persona as writer. She was to be remembered as Rivella; other women novelists were to model themselves on Rivella's image; and the memory of Rivella was to damn her and the women writers of her time in the eyes of a later, more moralistic generation.

JANE BARKER

Like Delariviere Manley, Jane Barker presented herself as her own heroine, but a very different kind of heroine. Virginity, instead of eroticism, was the keynote of her self-portrait. Autobiographical elements take a central place in Barker's work, none of her writings being free of them, and in fact much of what is known about her life comes from her own account. Born in Wiltsthorp, Lincolnshire, in 1660, she grew up in the country and was taught Latin and medicine by her brother, whose early death had a profound effect on her. Her family was royalist in the Civil War and later supported James II. Jane Barker converted to Catholicism, and in 1689 she followed James II into exile in France. She went blind by 1700, but continued to write. It seems to have been while she was in France that she wrote the account of her early life eventually published as *Love Intrigues: or the Amours of Bosvil and Galesia* in 1713, some years after her return to England. *Bosvil and Galesia*, like the later narratives which appeared in 1723 and 1726, uses material from the poetry she wrote much earlier, some of which was published as *Poetical Recreations* in 1688. Barker's career covers a long period, then, but one concern remained constant throughout: the creation of her self-portrait as woman and as writer.

Barker adopted two personae in different places in her writing, Fidelia and Galesia (sometimes spelt Galecia or Galaecia). Fidelia is the name she gives herself when proclaiming her fidelity—to Jacobitism and to her chosen faith—in a number of poems extant in the manuscript 'A Collection of Poems Refering to the Times' (*c.*1700).[36] It is in the person of Galesia, though, that she examines her literary vocation. Galesia appears many times in her work—not directly in the 1688 poems, but in the praise of them written by men from Cambridge colleges, whom Jane Barker had apparently got to know through her brother. This suggests that the pseudonym was originally acquired, like Katherine Philips's Orinda, in the course of correspondence with a circle of Platonic friends. In *Exilius: or, the Banished Roman*, an imitation of the French heroic romance begun early in life but not published until 1715, Galesia makes a brief appearance, transformed into a princess for the occasion. In *Bosvil and Galesia* Galesia is both narrator and heroine. In the later narratives, *A Patch-Work Screen for the Ladies* and its sequel *The Lining to the Patch-Work Screen*, Galesia's story continues, interspersed with a number of fictional tales. Because all three narratives use some of the early poems and attribute them to Galesia, it is clear that Galesia in the narratives is intended as a self-portrait of Jane Barker the writer. In contrast to Aphra Behn's insistence on her descent from masculine predecessors, Barker confines her claims to a place in the tradition of Orinda. In fact her poems often seem closely modelled on Cowley's odes, but she does not mention him as her inspiration or mentor. Like most women writers of her time, she sees her work as part of a feminine tradition, and in her case she emphasizes this because of her deep fears that writing is itself an unfeminine pursuit.

In her poems and her prose Galesia always shows herself concerned about her role as a woman. She is an intellectual woman who studies Latin and medicine, she is a practising healer, and she is a poet: so she is bound to seem unwomanly to many of her contemporaries, and this worries her. On the other hand she, unlike Delariviere Manley, can lay claim to that virtue most required of women, chastity. Barker did not marry, and her Galesia narratives were written at a time when it must have been clear that she never would do. So she emphasizes her identity as virginal spinster, and uses it to defend her literary life, just as Manley laid stress on her own sexual experience in order to portray herself as the writer Rivella.

In her Galesia narratives Barker not only provides herself with a romantic pseudonym, but wraps her life story in the conventions of romance. The first-person narrative of *Bosvil and Galesia* is prefaced by a short framing account, signed 'J.B.', introducing Galesia and the friend, Lucasia, who is supposed to be listening to her story. In *A Patch-Work Screen* and *The Lining*, Galesia is referred to in the third person, though within the narrative of *A Patch-Work Screen* Galesia tells her own story to a lady she meets. In each of these last two works there is an

introduction signed by Jane Barker, who claims to have met Galesia.
Thus Barker distances herself from her persona, freeing 'Galesia' to be
like a heroine of romance. By transforming the autobiographical story
she has to tell into the life of a romance-like heroine, she is able to
claim that Galesia's story is significant and to justify Galesia's actions
according to romance convention. Turning her own life story into what
she calls a 'diverting Novel',[37] she is offering her public the kind of work
it wants; and she is also protecting herself and liberating her imagination.

The first of the narratives, *Bosvil and Galesia*, is the story of a failed
courtship, told by Galesia to Lucasia years after the event. As a young
girl, Galesia loves her cousin Bosvil and believes he loves her, but her
maidenly decorum and his erratic behaviour—veering from enthusiastic
devotion to cold indifference—prevent them from reaching an understanding, and eventually he marries another woman. Galesia's narrative
is a subtle variation on an important theme in eighteenth-century narration—seduction, which, whether the heroine suffers or avoids it, is
nearly always central to her story.[38] In fact Bosvil neither seduces nor
attempts to seduce Galesia, but the idea of seduction haunts her and
provides her with a way of interpreting his enigmatic behaviour. Is his
clandestine and interrupted courtship a sign that he is unsure of his own
feelings, or of hers; or does it indicate a plan to seduce her? As she
recreates and analyses her youthful experiences in narrative, Galesia is
unable to decide.

Galesia accuses herself of a heroine's pride: flattered during her youth,
she thinks herself a 'goddess' to her lover, like a heroine of romance.
She keeps Bosvil at a distance, and her haughty behaviour, which makes
him think she cannot love him, is one explanation offered for the failure
of their relationship. On the other hand, her narrative shows that behind
a heroine's pride lies vulnerability. She has to conceal her feelings
because if a woman should 'betray [her] Weakness by a too ready
Compliance' with even an honourable proposal, her purity might be
questioned (*Bosvil and Galesia*, pp. 21–2). A young girl's reserve towards
her suitor is made necessary by the society she lives in: 'as the World
now rolls, we are under a Kind of Constraint to follow its Byass' (p.
10). The way the world rolls is implicitly criticized in the narrative. The
young Galesia acted like a proper heroine in being proud and punctilious;
yet this helped to deprive her of the virtuous heroine's proper destiny,
marriage.

Galesia's story, ending in neither of the usual alternatives—'ruin' or
marriage—open to the eighteenth-century heroine, seems an oddity to
those who do not take the autobiographical nature of the narrative
into account.[39] Barker has superimposed the literary convention of the
heroine's social and sexual initiation onto the story of her own single
life, attributing to herself as 'Galesia' the characteristics of heroines

whose destiny she does not share, in order to make the single life a new kind of heroine's destiny.

On the surface, Galesia's narrative is an explanation of her failure to marry; but underlying this is a tale of success, when the thwarted heroine of romance becomes a poet.

During the first of Bosvil's recurrent periods of coldness towards her, Galesia composes verses dedicating herself to poetry:

> Methinks these Shades, strange Thoughts suggest,
> Which heat my Head, and cool my Breast;
> And mind me of a Laurel Crest.
>
> Methinks I hear the Muses sing,
> And see 'em all dance in a Ring;
> And call upon me to take Wing.
>
> We will (say they) assist thy Flight,
> Till thou reach fair *ORINDA*'s Height,
> If thou can'st this World's Follies slight.
>
> We'll bring thee to our bright Abodes,
> Among the Heroes and the Gods,
> If thou and Wealth can be at Odds.
>
> Then gentle Maid cast off thy Chain,
> Which links thee to thy faithless Swain,
> And vow a Virgin to remain.
>
> Write, write thy Vow upon this Tree,
> By us it shall recorded be;
> And thou enjoy Eternity. (p. 14)[40]

The choice she is offered is clear: the hope of married life or the promise of literary achievement. By inscribing the verses on the tree as the muses suggest, Galesia has taken their offer: henceforth she (like so many women writers of her time) will try to emulate Orinda.

Here, then, is an alternative explanation for the heroinely pride that kept the lovers apart. Galesia actually preferred to remain unmarried and dedicate herself to poetry. Her other ambition, to be a healer, is mentioned immediately afterwards and linked to the literary aspirations in her description of herself as '*Apollo*'s Darling Daughter', Apollo being god of poetry and of medicine (p. 15). The sarcastic tone here expresses Galesia's typical uncertainty about the value of the choice she has made. On the one hand, she describes her intellectual life as merely a substitute for Bosvil's love: 'I, finding my self abandoned by *Bosvil*, and thinking it impossible ever to love again, resolved to espouse a Book, and spend my Days in Study' (p. 15). On the other hand, her readiness to make vows to the muses contrasts with her care never to promise anything to her lover, and even when her thoughts are in 'a Sea of Joy' at the thought of marrying Bosvil soon, her choice of poetry haunts her. In a dream she is made to climb a high mountain, evidently the poet's mountain, Parnassus, and she is warned by a mysterious 'angry Power' that:

> Since, since thou hast the Muses chose,
> *Hymen* and Fortune are thy Foes. (p. 33)

The opposition between poetry and love is intensified in the second edition of *Bosvil and Galesia*, in which, when Galesia climbs the mountain, Bosvil attempts to 'tumble [her] down', but is prevented by the angry power.[41] The sexual implication in this encounter befits Galesia's identification of poetry with chastity, and it suggests that the young Galesia's apparently unwarranted fears that Bosvil will try to seduce her arise from her unacknowledged dread that, if he marries her, he will seduce her away from her literary vocation.

Barker's later narratives continue to develop the picture of Galesia established here. The speaker of most of *A Patch-Work Screen for the Ladies* is Galesia after her return from France. She tells the story of her life after Bosvil's desertion, which contains further struggles between poetry and marriage. Once Bosvil has gone, Galesia devotes herself to the study of Orinda:

> I began to emulate her Wit, and aspired to imitate her
> Writings; in doing of which, I think, I deserved *Arachne*'s
> Fate, or at least to be transform'd into one of the lowest
> of *Mack-Fleckno*'s Followers: Her noble Genius being
> inimitable ... each line [of her poetry] was like a Ladder
> to climb, not only to *Parnassus*, but to Heaven: which I
> (poor Puzzle as I was!) had the Boldness to try to imitate,
> 'till I was dropped into a Labyrinth of Poetry, which has ever
> since interlac'd all the Actions of my Life.[42]

Galesia's praise of Orinda is mixed with typical self-mockery, but there is a sense of pride in having embraced the fate of a poet, whatever the effects on the rest of her life.

In *A Patch-Work Screen* Galesia's commitment to poetry and the single life is opposed by her mother, who tells her that marriage is 'the Business for which [she] came into the world' (p. 80). Fortunately, however, Galesia's numerous suitors justify her rejection of them by their evident unworthiness, and they soon disappear from the scene. One is hanged for robbery and another, who has led a profligate life, shoots himself. Galesia's rejection of sexual involvement receives further support from the reported experiences of the women she meets, including one who is suffering from a venereal disease after being seduced, and another who, marrying according to her father's wishes, was reduced to poverty and misery. Dutiful marriage and illicit sexuality seem equally to carry danger, and Galesia understandably celebrates 'A Virgin Life' in one of her poems, which explicitly links virginity with poetic achievement:

> Since, O good Heavens! you have bestow'd on me
> So great a Kindness for *Virginity*,
> Suffer me not to fall into the Powers
> Of Man's almost Omnipotent Amours.
> But let me in this happy State remain,
> And in chaste Verse my chaster Thoughts explain. (p. 90)

Galesia's verse opposes the common belief that to be a woman writer suggests sexual looseness. Not that Galesia receives any such accusation herself: it is her dedication to virginity that worries her mother. Nevertheless the continual insistence on the chastity of poetry in Barker's work suggests that the sexual reputation of some women writers disturbs her. One incident in *A Patch-Work Screen* seems to be an expression of her fears that poetry will unleash the dangers of sexuality. While she and her mother are lodging in London, Galesia escapes from the noisy world into 'a Closet in my Landlady's Back-Garret which I crept into, as if it had been a Cave on the Top of *Parnassus*' (p. 64). The closet is both a retreat from the world and a vantage-point from which she can survey it, giving free play to her intellect:

> Out of this Garret, there was a Door went out to the Leads; on
> which I us'd frequently to walk to take the Air ... Here I entertain'd
> my Thoughts, and indulg'd my solitary Fancy. Here I could behold
> the *Parliament-House*, *Westminster-Hall*, and the *Abbey*, and admir'd the
> Magnificence of their Structure, and still more, the Greatness of
> Mind in those who had been their Founders. (p. 67)

On one occasion, though, Galesia's thoughts are interrupted by 'a hasty Knocking on the Door of the Leads' (p. 73). She opens the door to find a distressed young woman, Belinda, whose story is a familiar one in eighteenth-century narrative: she has been seduced and abandoned, and is pregnant. She was fleeing across the roof-tops of London to avoid the parish officers when she found Galesia's garret. After this Galesia's mother forbids her to use her garret closet, in case, Galesia explains, she should 'encounter more Adventures, not only like this, but perhaps more pernicious' (p. 78). Galesia cannot find an innocent poetic retreat without having her peace shattered by the appearance of a seduced woman, and it seems that her intellectual interests, however pure in themselves, carry with them the danger of contact with impurity.

In *A Patch-Work Screen* Galesia is surrounded by various arguments against her vocation, but her bitter feeling that a learned woman may be 'at best but like a Forc'd Plant, that never has its due or proper Relish' (p. 11) are counteracted by the attitude of the lady to whom she relates the story. This appreciative listener praises Galesia's verses, and allays her fears that her writing is an unfeminine activity. She is working on a patch-work 'most curiously compos'd of rich Silks, and Silver and Gold Brocades: The whole Furniture was completed excepting a SCREEN' (Introduction, sig. a5r-a5v). Galesia is invited to contribute to this typically feminine endeavour, but her unconventional life has left her with no silks or brocades to offer. They open her trunks and boxes, but 'alas! they found nothing but Pieces of *Romances*, *Poems*, *Love-Letters*, and the like' (sig. a5v). However, the lady is happy to accept these pieces of writing as Galesia's version of silk patches, and it is from them that the screen is composed. Galesia's story of her writing career is thus set in a framework which justifies it by relating it to feminine accomplishments.

The Lining of the Patch-Work Screen is written to a similar plan. One side of the screen has been covered, and now the screen must be lined. Interpolated tales fill up much of the narrative. Galesia in this work is Jane Barker's self-portrait in her old age. She looks to the past for her inspiration, finding a lamentable moral decay in the literature of the present.

> Those honourable Romances of old *Arcadia*, *Cleopatra*, *Cassandra*, &c.
> discover a Genius of Vertue and Honour, which reign'd in the time
> of those Heroes, and Heroines, as well as in the Authors that report
> them; but the Stories of our Times are so black, that the Authors,
> can hardly escape being smutted, or defil'd in touching such
> Pitch.[43]

Praise is given, as usual, to Katherine Philips, long dead by this time, and not to any woman writing in the eighteenth century. In a dream within the narrative, a young man calling himself her 'good Genius' leads Galesia up Parnassus, where they find '*Orinda* seated on a Throne, as Queen of Female Writers, with a Golden Pen in her Hand for a Scepter, a Crown of Laurel on her Head' (*The Lining*, p. 174). Part of Cowley's poem 'Upon Mrs. K. Philips her Poems' is recited by 'a Bard' (p. 175). There is something wistful in the description of Galesia's appearance on this occasion. She arrives 'somewhat late; so that the grand Ceremonies were over', and sits inconspicuously 'in a Corner, where she might see and hear all that pass'd' (p. 174). This perhaps expresses Barker's feelings, late in her life, that she has survived into a new and uncongenial age, when the tributes to the poet she admires are over; and that she herself has failed in her ambition to 'reach fair *ORINDA*'s Height'.

Jane Barker's allegiance may have been to the past, but her auto-biographical narratives point to plots of the future. In her romance, *Exilius*, she concludes conventionally with the marriages of numerous pairs of lovers, but in the Galesia narratives her focus on her own life leads her to modify literary conventions. Various literary heroines contributed to the creation of Galesia, but the plots of fiction offered her no conclusion satisfactory to her author. While other writers were just beginning to experiment with the novel as the story of the heroine's journey to identity through marriage, Jane Barker was already offering an alternative pattern for the novel, with the creation of an unmarried heroine who achieves her identity through study, the practice of medicine, and writing.

Jane Barker, like Delariviere Manley, defined her authorial position by suggesting connections between her own character and situation and the kind of writing she produced. While Manley argued from her sexual life to her sexy writing, Jane Barker linked her virgin life to her pure and moral work. Manley's self-portrait encouraged others to adopt her image, whereas Barker, never so well-known a writer, was less influential in herself.[44] Yet she is the one who represents the winning side in the eighteenth-century debate about the woman writer. Choosing the famously pure Katherine Philips for her model, she rejected the other precursor with whom Philips had previously been associated—Aphra Behn. In *A Patch-Work Screen*, Galesia reports that a lady she met, 'asked me, if I lik'd Mrs. *Phillips*, or Mrs. *Behn* best? To whom I reply'd, with a blunt Indignation, that *they ought not to be nam'd together*' (p. 44). This is a very different attitude from that taken by Manley, Pix and Trotter in the 1690s. Whereas they saw both Philips and Behn as shining examples of the woman writer's power, Barker could only acknowledge Sappho and the chaste Orinda as her models, even though Behn's novels probably provided some material for her narratives.[45]

Jane Barker was never a best-selling novelist, but her Galesia narratives and *Exilius* did provide something for her support when she was spending her later years in England on a small income.[46] She was one of the earliest women novelists to unite the mercenary motive of the professional writer with a prominent display of the 'chaste Verse ... chaster Thoughts' associated with the leisured poetess; so she has a significant place in the history of women's writing. Her work, unlike Behn's and Manley's, would always remain respectable even to the later eighteenth-century reader. Her Galesia narratives give a fascinating picture of a woman wanting to be accepted as a writer, explaining what is unconventional about her life, anxiously insisting on her own purity. In her self-portrait we begin to see hints of something that will be much in evidence in the writing of other eighteenth-century women: the cost of becoming acceptable.

NOTES

1. Margaret Cavendish, 'A True Relation of the Birth, Breeding, and Life of Margaret Cavendish' (1656), in *The Lives of William Cavendishe, Duke of Newcastle, and of his wife, Margaret Duchess of Newcastle. Written by the Thrice Noble and Illustrious Princess, Margaret, Duchess of Newcastle*, ed. M. A. Lower (London: John Russell Smith, 1872), p. 309.

2. '*To the Authour, on her Voyage to the Island of Love*', signed T.C., in *The Works of Aphra Behn*, **VI**, p. 121. Maureen Duffy writes of Behn's friendship with Thomas Creech, and prints a letter of Behn's referring to her resentment of something he had done: Duffy suggests that Creech's concentration, in his poem, on the erotic side of Behn's writing had annoyed her. See Duffy, pp. 226–9.

3. Anonymous, '*To the Lovely Witty ASTRAEA, on her Excellent Poems*', in *Works*, **VI**, p. 123.

4. Charles Gildon, 'Epistle Dedicatory, To Simon Scroop, Esq; of Danby, in Yorkshire', in *All the Histories and Novels Written by the Late Ingenious Mrs. Behn, Entire in One Volume*, 3rd edn, with Additions (London: S. Briscoe, 1698), sig. A4v.

5. Dedication to Henry Pain of *The Fair Jilt*, *Works*, **V**, p. 70.

6. Preface to *The Lucky Chance*, *Works*, **III**, p. 187.

7. Preface to *The Lucky Chance*, *Works*, **III**, p. 185.

8. Katharine M. Rogers writes that '*The Rover* ... reveals a more masculine set of values than do the works of Etherege or Wycherley. ... [Behn's plays] afford a striking example of the callous attitudes which later sentimentalists rightly rejected as antifeminist'. *Feminism in Eighteenth-Century England* (Urbana, Chicago, London: University of Illinois Press, 1982), pp. 98–9.

9. For a discussion of the treatment of arranged marriage in Behn's comedies, claiming that she gives the 'clearest articulation' of this problem before the 1690s, see Robert L. Root, 'Aphra Behn, Arranged Marriage and Restoration Comedy', *Women and Literature* **5** no. 1 (Spring, 1977), pp. 3–14.

10. *Love-Letters Between a Nobleman And his Sister, Part* **I** (London: J. Hindmarsh and J. Tonson, 1693), pp. 103, 104, 105.

11. *Love-Letters from a Nobleman to his Sister: Mixt with the History of their Adventures. The Second Part, by the same Hand* (London: Jacob Tonson and Joseph Hindmarsh, 1693), pp. 124–5.

12. *Love-Letters*, Part **II**, p. 210.

13. 'Advertisement to the Reader', *All the Histories and Novels*, 3rd edn, sig. [A5v].

14. *The Unfortunate Happy Lady*, in *Works*, **V**, p. 43. Except for the three parts of *Love-Letters*, not included in Summers' edition, all quotations from Behn's

prose fiction are taken from Volume V of her *Works*, and further references to this are placed in brackets within the text.

15. A character named George Marteen is the hero of Behn's *Younger Brother*, posthumously produced in 1696. No Dangerfield appears in her plays, but it is possible she had intended to use the name. Montague Summers points out that the name Dangerfield appears in Sedley's *Bellamera*, and suggests that Behn 'gave' the name to Sedley: see *Works*, **V**, p. 523.

16. The truth or otherwise of Behn's narratives has been a source of controversy since Ernest Bernbaum claimed that she 'deliberately and circumstantially lied' in *Oroonoko*, and had never been to Surinam: see 'Mrs. Behn's Biography a Fiction', *PMLA* **28** (1913), p. 434. Her knowledge of the colony, however, is detailed, and not only Byam, but more obscure characters like Trefry had a real-life existence. A letter from Byam to Sir Robert Harley in March 1664 seems to refer to Behn's departure from the colony: see Duffy, pp. 38–40. Behn's use of Indian and African words is said to show authentic knowledge of both languages in B. Dhuicq, 'Further Evidence on Aphra Behn's Stay in Surinam', *Notes and Queries* **26** (1979), pp. 524 6. Behn also claimed to have brought back a feather-dress from Surinam, worn in a performance of Dryden's *The Indian Queen*; H. A. Hargreaves has investigated this and concludes that the statement is probably true. See 'New Evidence of the Realism of Mrs. Behn's *Oroonoko*', *Bulletin of the New York Public Library* **74** (1970), pp. 437–44. Behn's visit to Surinam is well established, then, but Oroonoko's existence is not. *The Fair Jilt* tells the story of Prince Tarquin's attempt, at his wife's instigation, to murder his sister-in-law, and of his narrow escape from the axe when his executioner fails to do his job properly. This story has usually been considered pure fiction, but Maureen Duffy has shown that a 'Prince Tarquino's' crime and the bungled execution were reported in newspapers of the day: see Duffy, pp. 72–3.

17. Franz K. Stanzel distinguishes this kind of 'teller-character', a 'narrative agent [which] dominated earlier novels', from the 'reflector-character' who is the focus of events in a narrative but does not comment on them. See 'Teller-Characters and Reflector-Characters in Narrative Theory', *Poetics Today*, **2** no. 2 (Winter, 1981), pp. 6–7.

18. This claim was made by Behn in the 'Epistle Dedicatory' of *Oroonoko* to Lord Maitland: see *Works*, **V**, p. 511.

19. 'Of Plants', in *The Works of Mr. Abraham Cowley*, 10th edn (London: Benjamin Motte, 1721), **III**, p. 440.

20. *Secret Memoirs and Manners Of several Persons of Quality, of Both Sexes. From The New Atalantis, An Island in the Mediteranean* (London, 1709), **I**, p. 34; rpt in *The Novels of Mary Delariviere Manley*, ed. Patricia Köster, 2 vols (Gainsville, Florida: Scholars' Facsimiles and Reprints, 1971).

21. The episode with Germanicus has been seen as evidence of Manley's prurience. Dolores Palomo argues that, on the contrary, it shows her 'ironic use of romance style' in the creation of a kind of mock-epic. I agree with her that the comic element of scenes like this have been ignored, but unlike Palomo, I find (as I argue in chapter 4) that elsewhere Manley seriously expresses sympathy for the victims of seduction. See Dolores Palomo, 'A

Woman Writer and the Scholars: A Review of Mary Manley's Reputation', *Women and Literature* **6** no. 1 (Spring, 1978), pp. 36–45.

22. She wrote to Mrs Frances Hewet on 12 November 1709: 'I am very glad you have the second part of the New Atalantis; if you have read it, will you be so good as to send it me, and in return I promise to get you the key to it. I know I can'. *The Complete Letters of Lady Mary Wortley Montagu*, ed. Robert Halsband. **I**, 1708–1720 (Oxford: Clarendon Press, 1965), p. 18.

23. A full treatment of the political effects of Manley's writing is to be found in G. B. Needham, 'Mary de la Riviere Manley, Tory Defender', *HLQ* **12** (1948–9), pp. 253–88. This article gave Manley's role in politics long-overdue recognition.

24. *The Adventures of Rivella; or, The History of the Author of the Atalantis* (London, 1714), p. 4. A facsimile reprint of this edition is in *The Novels*, ed. Köster, **II**.

25. Needham (pp. 261–2) quotes a letter from the Duchess of Marlborough to Queen Anne, vouching for the truth of 'some part' of Manley's allegations about Mrs Masham (a favourite of the Queen), whose 'famous amour with Mr. Chudd' appeared under disguise in the second volume of *The New Atalantis*.

26. See Philip R. Sergeant, *Rogues and Scoundrels* (London: Hutchinson and Co., 1924), Preface, p. 14; and Walter and Clare Jerrold, *Five Queer Women* (London: Brentano's Ltd, 1929).

27. B. G. MacCarthy, *Women Writers: Their Contribution to the English Novel 1621–1744* (Cork: Cork University Press, 1944), pp. 215, 217, 232.

28. Palomo, p. 38.

29. *The Adventures of Rivella*, p. 43. The lines are taken from an anonymous poem, 'To Mrs. *Manley*, on her Tragedy call'd *The Royal Mischief*', printed with that play in 1696.

30. For discussions of Manley's relationship with her cousin see P. B. Anderson, 'Mistress Delariviere Manley's Biography', *MP* **33** (1935–6), pp. 261–78, and Köster, Introduction to *The Novels*, **I**, pp. v–xxviii.

31. *The New Atalantis*, **II**, p. 184.

32. Delia's story does not coincide at all points with external evidence of Manley's life. Delia claims to have been under 14 at the time of her marriage. Manley's date of birth has never been established beyond dispute, but it is likely that she was born between 1667 and 1672 (Köster, p. vii; Anderson, p. 264). This would make her between 15 and 20 when her father died in 1687. Clearly the alteration in age (which may only be slight) is made to emphasize youth and innocence. Another small difference is in the story of the three guardians, for John Manley is not named as guardian in Manley's father's will, though it does name two executors—one of whom died soon after, while the other lived at a distance, as in Delia's story. It seems that John Manley was in effect Delariviere Manley's guardian, and may have been asked to act as such by her father (Köster, p. viii). Manley's claim that she believed her marriage to be valid would not be easy to prove or disprove. The case for her awareness of the bigamy is argued by Dolores

Diane Clark Duff in 'Materials Toward a Biography of Mary Delariviere Manley' (unpub. diss. Indiana University, 1965), pp. 58–70.

33. See Curll's introduction to an edition of *Rivella* published after her death, *Mrs. Manley's History Of Her Own Life and Times. Published from Her Original Manuscript. The Fourth Edition. With a Preface concerning the present Publication* (London: E. Curll and J. Pemberton, 1725), pp. iii–viii. See also Ralph Straus, *The Unspeakable Curll* (London: Chapman and Hall, 1927), p. 47.

34. Mary Hearne, Dedication to Mrs Manley, and Joseph Gay, 'To the Fair and Ingenious Author of the LOVER's Week', in *The Lover's Week: or, the Six Days Adventures of Philander and Amaryllis, Written by a Young Lady. The Second Edition* (London: E. Curll and R. Francklin, 1718).

35. 'By an Unknown Hand, To the most Ingenious Mrs. Haywood, on her Novel Entitled, Love in Excess', in *Love in Excess: or the Fatal Enquiry, A Novel. Part the Second* (London, [1719]).

36. The MS 'A Collection of Poems Refering to the Times' is in the British Library (Add. MS 21,621). Another MS copy of these poems comprises the first part of a three-part MS volume of Jane Barker's poems in the library of Magdalen College, Oxford (MS 343). The second part of this contains some unpublished poems, and some which are printed (with alterations) in her later narratives. The third part is a revised version of the poems published as *Poetical Recreations: Consisting of Original Poems, Songs, Odes, &c. With Several New Translations* (London: Benjamin Crayle, 1688).

37. See *Love Intrigues: Or, The History of the Amours of Bosvil and Galesia* (London: E. Curll and C. Crownfield, 1713), p. 2. The title page of both first and second editions of this work call it a novel.

38. Miller, *The Heroine's Text*, p. 4.

39. Patricia M. Spacks writes that 'One might expect *A Patch-Work Screen* to bring its heroine to a more satisfactory conclusion [than the one in the earlier narrative], educating her to achieve happiness in wedlock ... Galesia never manages to marry, the book ends *in medias res* ... the heroine's failure to unite herself to a man has come to seem oddly like a triumph.' *Imagining a Self: Autobiography and Novel in Eighteenth-Century England* (Cambridge, Mass.: Harvard University Press, 1976), pp. 66–7.

40. This poem is found in 'part the second' of Magdalen MS 343, and is given the title 'The contract with the muses writ on the bark of a shady ash-tree', in the list of contents to the volume.

41. *The Amours of Bosvil and Galesia, As related to Lucasia in St. Germain's Garden. A Novel*, 2nd edn, corrected (London: A. Bettesworth and E. Curll, 1719), p. 29.

42. *A Patch-Work Screen for the Ladies* (London: E. Curll and T. Payne, 1723), p. 3.

43. *The Lining of the Patch-Work Screen: Design'd for the Farther Entertainment of the Ladies* (London: A. Bettesworth, 1726), p. 129.

44. Some success for Barker's narratives may be inferred from the appearance of second editions of *Bosvil and Galesia* and *Exilius* together as *The Entertaining Novels of Mrs. Jane Barker* in 1719, and the further edition of *Entertaining*

Novels in 1736. Barker's name, however, rarely if ever appears in eighteenth-century discussions of the novel, while Manley's and Haywood's appear very frequently.

45. One of the interpolated stories in *The Lining of the Patch-Work Screen* appears to be modelled on Behn's *The History of the Nun: or, the Fair Vow-Breaker* (1689). See W. H. McBurney, 'Edmund Curll, Mrs. Jane Barker, and the English Novel', *PQ* **37** (1958), pp. 385–99.

46. Jane Barker is mentioned in a 1715 list of Roman Catholic nonjurors as holding an estate of £47-10s. annual value: see G. S. Gibbons, 'Mrs. Jane Barker', *Notes and Queries* ser. **XI**, no. 12 (1922), p. 278. Presumably she also benefited from the patronage of the Countess of Exeter, to whom she dedicated *Exilius*.

3
The Terms of Acceptance

When women writers were accepted it was on the basis of their femininity; and the kind of praise they received varied with their readers'
conceptions of that quality, so that to some people feminine writing
implied eroticism, to others, purity. From the reception of women writers
in the later years of the seventeenth century and the early years of the
eighteenth, it is clear that widespread approval was going to have its
drawbacks. Women's writing would have to confine itself within the
circle drawn by prevailing notions of the feminine, and women authors
would have to turn away from the examples of those precursors whose
femininity did not fit the fashionable definition.

This chapter is concerned with those elements of eighteenth-century
critical discussion which help explain why women's writing is welcomed,
and with the terms of the welcome as illustrated in women's literary
careers. Elizabeth Singer Rowe (1674–1737), Penelope Aubin (1679–
1731), Sarah Fielding (1710–68), and Fanny Burney (1752–1840) are
given special emphasis, because each was well known and highly praised,
and each one represents an important stage in the process of accepting
the woman novelist.

'TRUE FEMALE MERIT'

As the eighteenth century advanced the 'feminine' qualities of delicacy
and propriety became more generally important to bourgeois society.
Women writers, because they could be taken as representatives of these
central values, became more acceptable, but also more restricted.

Chastity in life and a corresponding morality in writing became the
necessary basis for a woman writer's reputation. The change in attitudes
to Aphra Behn, Delariviere Manley and Eliza Haywood—three writers
often grouped together in the eighteenth century—illustrates this. Early
in the century it was possible to take an alternative model to the chaste

Orinda: the 'amorous' woman writer, like Aphra Behn or Delariviere Manley. Eliza Haywood was praised as the successor of these two. In 1724 a poem prefaced to Haywood's *Secret Histories, Novels and Poems* called on any male reader who might be sceptical about women's talents to:

> Read, proud Usurper, read with conscious Shame,
> Pathetick Behn, or Manley's greater Name;
> Forget their Sex, and own when Haywood writ
> She clos'd the fair Triumvirate of wit.[1]

By 1751, Samuel Richardson was referring to the same three writers as examples of depravity. Commenting on women whose recent memoirs of their own unchaste lives had shocked him, he exclaimed:

> Mrs. Pilkington, Constantia Phillips, Lady V—, ... what a Set of
> Wretches, wishing to perpetuate their Infamy, have we,—to make
> the Behn's, the Manley's, and the Heywood's [sic], look white. From
> the same injured, disgraced, profaned Sex, let us be favoured with
> the Antidote to these Womens Poison![2]

Behn, Manley and Haywood were no longer a fair triumvirate, but a notorious trio.

Yet Richardson's attack on them is not an attack on women writers generally: on the contrary, it is on women he calls for examples of purer life and writing. By 1785, when Clara Reeve published one of the earliest historical accounts of the novel, *The Progress of Romance*, this call had been answered many times. Reeve found many women novelists of unexceptionable purity to praise. She even put in a word for Eliza Haywood, whose later work had detached her from the rest of the 'triumvirate':

> she repented of her faults, and employed the latter part of her life in
> expiating the offences of the former.—There is reason to believe that
> the examples of [Behn and Manley] seduced Mrs. *Heywood* [sic] into
> the same track ... [but she] had the singular good fortune to recover a
> lost reputation, and the yet greater honour to atone for her errors.[3]

Here, the change of tone in Haywood's work after the 1730s—a change no doubt made in response to a change in the literary market—is treated as a personal conversion, and the terms used are sexual ones. Haywood's later moral writing is taken to indicate recovery from a sexual fall. We can see the progress of Eliza Haywood's reputation as a paradigm for that of the eighteenth-century woman novelist generally: at first praised as amorous, then castigated as immoral, and finally accepted on new, and limiting, terms.

The new terms can be summed up as nature, morality and modesty. A 'natural' style that expressed feeling simply and apparently spontaneously, an evident moral aim, and a degree of diffidence, would all make a woman writer acceptable; and they were all, increasingly, expected automatically from women writers. At the same time these characteristics were gaining importance as general literary ideals. The moral utility of literature was an all-pervasive concern of eighteenth-century critics; modesty in the writer and his work was becoming an important term of praise; and simplicity and spontaneity in writing became greatly admired as the century progressed. What was happening, in fact, was that the properly 'feminine' and the properly 'literary' were both being re-defined along the same lines.

We can see this from the comments of various eighteenth-century writers on the 'wit' of their predecessors. The wit of Restoration dramatists and of metaphysical poets was under fire for immorality and over-elaboration respectively. 'Our witty and wicked triumvirate' was how the critic Joseph Warton described the Restoration playwrights Wycherley, Congreve and Vanbrugh.[4] Addison praised Sappho because 'she followed Nature in all her Thoughts, without descending to those little Points, Conceits and Turns of Wit with which many of our Modern Lyricks are so miserably infected.'[5] Instead of wit, modesty was praised: 'No, no Man shall be allowed the Advantages of Impudence ... nothing can attone for the Want of Modesty; without which Beauty is ungraceful, and Wit detestable', wrote Steele.[6] Modesty was requisite in literature as in general behaviour. Poetic conceits perhaps implied a degree of personal conceit in the writer, and a simple style was thought both more modest and more natural. The ideal, according to Addison, was 'that natural Way of writing, that beautiful Simplicity, which we so much admire in the Compositions of the Ancients'.[7] Properly feminine women writers were thought to fulfil this ideal. Addison took women—Sappho, and in another paper, Anne Boleyn—as his examples of natural simplicity in writing.[8] Modesty, too, though recommended to all, was seen as natural to women: the 'Characteristick of their Sex' as Steele put it.[9]

This conflation of literary and feminine virtues was particularly strong in the later years of the century, when sentimentalism predominated. The unification of feeling and morality which was at the heart of sentimental philosophy was also a characteristic of femininity as the eighteenth century defined it; and the true 'man of feeling' was therefore seen as 'feminine'. Sentimental writing was 'feminine' too. The tender feeling and delicacy of expression seen as the hallmarks of feminine writing also characterized sentimental writing in general, and so at the height of the sentimental movement, the most fashionable kind of writing coincided with the kind of writing expected of women.

All this encouraged women to write and meant that their work could be accepted and praised; but it had its drawbacks. However generally recommended the feminine virtues, they were interpreted differently in men and in women. The morality expected of a woman was stricter; her style was expected to be restricted to natural simplicity in a way a man's was not; and her modesty was of a very different order. When Steele contended that modesty was as important in a man as in a woman, he was careful to qualify this by distinguishing between modesty in men, 'a right judgment of what is proper for them to attempt', and the modesty of a woman, 'a certain agreeable fear in all she enters upon'[10]—agreeable, that is, of course, to the man who witnessed it, not to the woman who experienced it. Women's writing was bound to be affected once fear about all they did was considered desirable evidence of their worth; and the requirement for feminine modesty might even undo the effects of all other encouragements, and stop some women writing, or publishing, at all.

Moreover, it was acknowledged that the new literary and feminine virtues had their limitations, and women writers were strongly associated with these. This is evident in the ambivalence that even the sentimental age showed towards sentimentalism. The sentimental movement centralized women's writing and brought it public esteem, but sentimentalism, however popular, was always vulnerable to attack. The pursuit of sensation for its own sake, so that benevolent feeling failed to issue in charitable action, and excessive emotion was expended on trivial incidents, was an obvious danger, early pointed out. The dangers of sentimentalism, like its values, had particular relevance for women. Sentimental attitudes led to a glorification of weakness, not just in ideal heroes and heroines but in real women, whose beauty, according to Edmund Burke, 'is considerably owing to their weakness or delicacy, and is even enhanced by their timidity, a quality of mind analogous to it'.[11] The beauty of women's writing was thought of in the same way in the late eighteenth century. Never very far, even from the sentimental mind, was the idea that the delicate sensibility so well exemplified in femininity and feminine writing was an amiable *weakness*.

In fact, throughout our period praise of the 'feminine' literary qualities was given in such a way as to limit the woman writer's acceptable scope, and often to imply that for all its virtues her work was weak. We saw in Chapter 1 that ideas about feminine writing were formulated in response to early writing heroines, real and fictional. What appeared peculiarly feminine about their writing was the spontaneous expression of feeling: evidence of woman's 'nature'. The real writer Héloïse and the probably fictional Portuguese nun appealed to their readers in similar ways. Both were passionate women who had lost their lovers, and both wrote highly emotional letters to them from the chaste confines of a nunnery. The Portuguese nun's loosely structured, spontaneous writing was seen as a reflection of the feminine sensibility, and she was said to show women's ability to produce the charm of disorder by writing in passionate moments.[12] Such heroine–writers established a pattern of expectation from the writing woman—that she would be passionate and spontaneous, that her words would be personal and come direct from the heart. Clearly she was not taking over the masculine pen, instrument of rational discourse. It was more that her emotions overflowed onto paper.

If we look at comments on women novelists made by the periodical reviewers in the second half of the eighteenth century, we can see that 'natural', that is emotional and apparently spontaneous writing still drew praise. One anonymous novel, *The History of Miss Delia Stanhope*, reviewed in 1766, was judged to be a woman's because of its feminine virtues: 'From the ease of the language, the vivacity of spirit, the delicacy of sentiment, and the abundance of love and tenderness which we find in this novel, we hesitate not to pronounce, that a Lady wrote it'.[13] An anonymous woman's novel called *Constance* had the *Critical* reviewer beaming with approval. 'In this artless narrative, the incidents are numerous and striking, the situations interesting and pathetic, the morality unexceptionable'.[14] The somewhat equivocal compliment 'artless' was frequently applied to women's work, and praise of spontaneous creativity could easily shade into hints of a lack of control. Behind the reviewers' compliments there was often contempt for feminine writing, and sometimes this was made clear. One anonymous novel called *Laura and Augustus* (1784) was judged to be a woman's because it displayed that combination of feeling and morality demanded of women. 'If the young lady did not announce herself in the title, she would betray the author, by the warmth, the tenderness, and the unaffected modesty of her descriptions', explained the reviewer. The next sentence revealed the underside of compliment: 'She will excuse us for adding, .that she would betray herself, by a few inaccuracies in language, and a little improbability in some of the incidents'.[15] Another anonymous work, *The History of the Hon. Mrs. Rosemont and Sir Henry Cardigan*, was attributed to a woman 'from the freedom and vivacity with which it is written, and from several glaring deficiences [sic] even in common grammatical construction. This fault,' the reviewer continued, 'we have often observed in the compositions of ladies, who, notwithstanding, have acquired all the higher graces of language: and have almost instinctively caught at elegance without giving themselves the trouble of pursuing the strict forms of grammar'.[16] Instinctive elegance turns out to mean elementary error: natural feminine writing is apparently not so desirable after all.

There were critics who genuinely admired women's 'artlessness' though, and it is in their comments that we can best observe the terms on which women writers were accepted. Samuel Richardson offers some examples. In 1746 he wrote to his friend Sophia Westcomb asking her to write to him, after she had expressed reluctance to do so because she doubted her abilities. Private correspondence is all that Richardson is pressing for in this letter, but the argument could equally be applied to women who published their writing:

> It is the diffidence I wish to banish: the diffidence! which, in the right place, is so great a beauty in the charming sex;—but why the diffidence to such a one as I am!—a plain writer: a sincere well-wisher: an undesigning scribbler: who admire none but the natural and easy beauties of the pen; no carper: and one who has so just an opinion of the sex, that he knows, in an hundred instances, that the ladies who love the pen are qualified by genius and imagination to excell in the beauties of this sort of writing:—and that bashfulness, or diffidence of a person's own merits, are but other words for undoubted worthiness; and that such a lady cannot set pen to paper but a beauty must follow it; yet herself the last person that knows it.[17]

For Richardson, diffidence is linked to a special kind of literary talent, found especially in women. The 'natural and easy beauties of the pen' come only to those who do not know their own worth, and a modest woman cannot help but write well. This very praise reveals its own drawbacks, for in a sense the literary powers of the artless woman writer do not belong to her at all, being outside her control.

We can also see from Richardson's letter how, in order to present women's writing as acceptable, he has had to smooth over the internal contradictions in sexual ideology. He wants to banish the diffidence which is preventing his friend from writing, but at the same time this diffidence is necessary as proof that she *could* write. From this it would seem that no woman could manage to write well, for if she overcame her modesty sufficiently to write she would have thrown away the basis of her merit. Richardson overcomes this difficulty by offering his theory of the unconsciousness of the woman's writing: she will write without losing her modesty because she will produce beauties without knowing it. The bashfulness which tries to hide her talents will actually signal their presence.

The view Richardson expresses here was widely held in his time. One writer, Thomas Marriott, expressed the same paradox in a couplet of his poem *Female Conduct*, published in 1759:

> True female Merit strives, to be conceal'd
> And only by its blushes is reveal'd.[18]

Modest blushes were required of eighteenth-century women writers. Above all else, they were accepted on condition that they did not want to push themselves forward.

NATURAL, MORAL AND MODEST: ELIZABETH ROWE

The early eighteenth century found its ideals of feminine and literary virtue embodied in the life and work of Elizabeth Singer Rowe (1674–1737). A native of Somerset, she was the daughter of a Dissenting preacher, and received a pious education that laid the foundations of her religious outlook. She was writing verse by the age of 12, and by the early 1690s her poems were appearing in periodicals. Her *Poems on Several Occasions* was published in 1696. In 1710 she married Thomas Rowe, 13 years her junior, and went to live with him in London. His death in 1715 at the age of 28 prompted her return to Somerset, where she spent her life in rural retirement, religious meditation, charitable works, and writing.

Rowe was most celebrated for her religious and didactic fiction, which contributed to the early eighteenth-century moralizing of the novel. *Friendship in Death: or Letters from the Dead to the Living* (1728) was a series of letters supposedly written by the dead and delivered during brief returns to the world in order to comfort their friends' or relatives' grief, to tell them about the joys of the afterlife, and to leave warnings about impending moral dangers. In the same year the first part of *Letters Moral and Entertaining* (2nd part, 1731; 3rd part, 1732) appeared. This work was built on a similar plan, except that the letter-writers were still in this world, and sometimes a series of letters from one correspondent made for a more sustained narrative line.

Friendship in Death and *Letters Moral and Entertaining* appeared many times during the century, sometimes separately and sometimes together. At least 13 editions of Rowe's fiction appeared before 1800. Samuel Richardson, who was the printer for the 1740 and 1743 editions, admired Rowe's work, as did Samuel Johnson, which gives some indication of her respectable standing in the middle and late eighteenth century. After her death, her works were published in two volumes with an account of her life begun by her friend Henry Frome and completed by her brother-in-law, Theophilus Rowe. These volumes, which appeared in 1739, contained her letters to the Countess of Hertford as well as some family letters, and the feeling and piety expressed here added to her reputation, which remained high until into the next century. Elizabeth Rowe's work gave her readers all the nature, morality and modesty that they could desire, and with her example before them their acceptance of the idea of the virtuous woman writer was assured.

Elizabeth Rowe's 'exquisite wit, and beautiful imagination, were scarce any thing indebted to the assistance of art or labour', reported her biographer.[19] She was thought to have the spontaneity attributed to the famous Héloise; and the circumstances of publication and the reception of one of her poems suggests that her contemporaries thought of her as an eighteenth-century Héloise. In Pope's *Eloisa to Abelard*, published in the 1717 edition of his *Works*, Héloise's story was made famous. Pope conveys Eloisa's struggle to turn away from the sexual desires that can never again be fulfilled, and to translate her earthly passion into love of God. For Eloisa, writing is the means of directly conveying one's self to one's reader:

> Heav'n first taught letters for some wretch's aid,
> Some banish'd lover, or some captive maid;
> They live, they speak, they breathe what love inspires,
> Warm from the soul, and faithful to its fires.[20]

Yet this is obviously not the direct transmission of the self, because the poet mediates between the long-dead nun and the eighteenth-century reader. Something of the immediacy Pope's Eloisa writes of was offered to the public in 1720, when another edition of *Eloisa to Abelard* appeared together with an elegy for Thomas Rowe, 'Upon the Death of her Husband. By Mrs. Elizabeth Singer'. Here was an eighteenth-century Eloisa, who directly expressed her own passion in her own poetry. The poem addresses the 'gentle shade' of the departed husband:

> One moment listen to my grief, and take
> The softest vows that ever love can make.

Following the tradition of the heroic epistle and the letters of Eloise, the poet expresses sorrow for the loss of her lover, but whereas Eloisa's love was unsanctioned by marriage, Elizabeth Singer Rowe's is the devotion of a faithful wife. She vows to be true to the memory of her husband, keeping her love for him only:

> That sacred passion I to thee confine,
> My spotless faith shall be for ever thine.

Thomas Rowe's widow does not feel the conflict between heavenly vows and earthly desires expressed by Pope's Eloisa, because her love for her husband unites heavenly and earthly in a 'sacred passion'. Like Eloisa, she retires from the world, but not to a convent, out of compulsion. She goes to a country retreat, out of choice, and tells her lost husband:

> For thee, all thoughts of pleasure I forego,
> For thee, my tears shall never cease to flow;
> For thee at once I from the world retire,
> To feed in silent shades a hopeless fire.[21]

This voluntary devotion unites the ideas of strong passion and feminine virtue.

A poem 'On the Anniversary of her Husband's Death', printed in the *Gentleman's Magazine* in 1739, continues the mourning for 'Alexis', as she calls Thomas Rowe, and renews the promise of fidelity to his memory.[22] In a letter to her sister-in-law published in 1739 she vows: 'My constancy to the charming youth, and regard to his memory, shall be the pride and glory of my life.'[23] Her constancy certainly added to her fame, and it probably gave an added attraction to *Friendship in Death*, concerned as it is with bereavement and the hope of reunion in heaven. One letter from the dead to the living describes the joys of a love frustrated on earth and fulfilled in heaven. Delia writes to her friend Æmilia:

> The first gentle spirit that welcomed me to these happy mansions, was your charming brother ... That tender innocent passion I had long conceived for him, kindled at the first interview, and has taken eternal possession of my soul. ... In what figures of celestial eloquence shall I relate the loves of immortal spirits; or tell you the height, the extent, the fulness of their bliss!

Knowing that this was written by a widow longing to meet her husband again in heaven, Rowe's readers must have found this kind of writing a moving tribute to married love. In celebrating marriage, 'the most holy union that nature knows',[24] Elizabeth Rowe was in tune with eighteenth-century ideals far more than Jane Barker, who celebrated virginity. Rowe offered her readers exactly what they wanted in a woman writer: all Eloisa's sensibility, without any of Eloisa's guilt.

From the time her first poems were published, Rowe was hailed as the virtuous exception to the immoral rule governing women's wit. Her 1696 collection of *Poems on Several Occasions* included a preface by a woman called Elizabeth Johnson, who followed normal practice of the time in presenting women writers as female champions in the war between the sexes: 'we have ... *Sappho*'s, and *Behn*'s, and *Schurman*'s, and *Orinda*'s, who have *humbled* the most haughty of our Antagonists, and made 'em do Homage to our *Wit*, as well as our *Beauty*'. (Anna van

Schurman was a Dutch writer whose defence of women scholars was translated into English as *The Learned Maid* in 1659.) Despite this confident opening, Elizabeth Johnson is worried about women writers, because she considers that if men cannot rival the women's poetry they can still win the battle by seducing the poets. Men, she reports, tried 'to *Corrupt* that *Virtue* which they can no otherwise *overcome*: and sometimes they prevail'd'. The surest argument against women writer's enemies, she contends, is provided by the example of the uncorrupted woman poet: 'if some *Angels* fell, others remained in their *Innocence* and *Perfection-* ... *Angels Love*, but they love *Virtuously* and *Reasonably* ... And if all our *Poetesses* had done the same, I wonder what our Enemies cou'd have found out to have objected against us: However, here they are *silenc'd*'.[25]

If anything further was needed to establish Rowe's virtue it was her modesty, revealed both by the chastity of her language and the attempts to avoid fame which made her so different from the publicly visible professional playwright. Her early contributions to periodicals were anonymous, and so was her 1696 volume of poetry, 'by Philomela'. Elizabeth Johnson's preface assured the reader that the poems 'were actually Writ by *a young Lady* ... whose NAME had been prefix'd, had not her own *Modesty* absolutely forbidden it' (*Poems*, sig. A5r). Although a few years afterwards her maiden and her married names both became famous her life of seclusion from the world still provided evidence of a modest retreat from fame.

After Rowe's death, her friend the Countess of Hertford recalled her devotion to her dead husband, writing:

> Faithful to him, she from the world retir'd,
> Tho' by that world distinguish'd and admir'd.[26]

Thus Rowe's modest withdrawal from fame could be seen as another proof of her tender nature. The logical result of the importance of modesty is that a woman writer who tries to avoid fame is distinguished and admired—rewarded with the very praise she shuns.

Rowe's life was celebrated in several poems. One of her admirers was Elizabeth Carter (1717–1806), linguist and scholar, who praised her for having redeemed the virtue of the intellectual woman. In a poem written to mark Rowe's death she painted a gloomy picture of women's writing in previous times:

> OFT did intrigue its guilty arts unite,
> To blacken the records of female wit;

> The tuneful song lost ev'ry modest grace,
> And lawless freedoms triumph'd in their place.

Rowe, Carter claims, has mended matters by dedicating her female wit to religion and the moral improvement of her readers. Carter vows to take Rowe's religious and chaste writing as a model:

> Fix'd on my soul shall thy example grow,
> And be my genius and my guide below:
> To this I'll point my first, my noblest views,
> Thy spotless verse shall regulate my muse.[27]

Rowe, then, had become a new example to be followed by women writers worried about being classed with Behn, Manley and Haywood. Herself often compared to Orinda, she added to Orinda's purity two elements very important to eighteenth-century readers—a new emphasis on religious devotion and a new exaltation of married love.

Elizabeth Carter herself went on to become the representative virtuous woman of letters for a later generation. Like Orinda and Elizabeth Rowe before her, she was praised for chastity, her *Poems on Several Occasions* (1762) eliciting this response from the *Critical* reviewer:

> It has often been remarked ... that the female muse is seldom
> altogether chaste so could be wished, and that most of our lady-
> writers are rather deficient in point of morality. To the honour of
> Mrs. Carter it may be said, that there is scarce a line in this
> volume which doth not breathe the purest sentiments.[28]

Her translation of the Stoic philosopher Epictetus, published in 1758, proved to the *Monthly* reviewer that women were capable of intellectual work as well as purity:

> If women had the benefit of liberal instructions, if they were inured
> to study, and accustomed to learned conversation—in short, if they
> had the same opportunity of improvement with the men, there can
> be no doubt but that they would be equally capable of reaching any
> intellectual attainment.[29]

Women writers in general and learned women in particular were receiving new recognition by the 1750s. Catharine Trotter Cockburn's works were edited and published with an account of her life in 1751. Works celebrating eminent women writers began to appear: John Duncombe's *Feminiad: or Female Genius* in 1751; George Ballard's *Memoirs of Several Ladies of Great Britain* in 1752; and a collection of *Poems by Eminent Ladies* in 1755. Several women were included in Theophilus Cibber's *Lives of the Poets* (1753). With the exception of Cibber's work, which used early sources for its favourable accounts of Delariviere Manley and Aphra Behn, all these celebrations of female genius consistently stressed women's chastity and modesty. The preface to *Poems by Eminent Ladies* declared that 'genius often glows with equal warmth, and perhaps with more delicacy, in the breast of a female'.[30]

To prove their nature, morality and modesty, women writers by this time had to show an additional trait—domesticity. Johnson's praise of his old friend Elizabeth Carter because she 'could make a pudding, as well as translate Epictetus', illustrates this nicely: nobody had thought to enquire whether the matchless Orinda made puddings.[31] The eighteenth-century exaltation of family life is behind this new demand. The new ideal was a busy bourgeois woman who combined running a household with long hours of private study—someone like Richardson's second heroine, the famous Clarissa Harlowe. 'All that a woman *can* learn, she used to say ... above the useful knowledge proper to her sex, *let her learn* ... But then let her not give up for these, those *more necessary*, and therefore not *meaner*, employments which will qualify her to be a *good mistress* of a family, a *good wife*, and a *good mother*.' Elsewhere, Richardson took Elizabeth Carter as his example to demonstrate that this ideal could be found in real life.[32]

MORALIZING THE NOVEL: PENELOPE AUBIN

The public acceptance of the proper woman writer was not immediately granted to the woman novelist. In the early decades of the century the novel was still a 'low' genre, associated with immorality. Penelope Aubin (1679–1731) did much to change this, and she pointed the way forward for the moral novelists of the next generation.

Aubin was born in London, probably the daughter of an emigrant French officer.[33] She published some poetry in 1708 but began writing professionally in 1720, when financial losses, perhaps connected with her husband's death, made it necessary for her to earn a living. Towards the end of her life she was also a popular preacher, speaking in the York Buildings near Charing Cross. This was a logical extension of the preaching she had already done in her novels. Her first novel, *The Strange Adventures of the Count de Vinevil and His Family*, was published in 1721, and was quickly followed by several others: *The Life of Madam de Beaumont* (1721), *The Noble Slaves* (1722), *The Life and Amorous Adventures of Lucinda* (1722), *The Life of Charlotta du Pont* (1723), *The Life and Adventures of the Lady Lucy* (1726), and *The Life and Adventures of the Young Count Albertus* (1728).

Her works share some similarities with the travel narratives popular in the early eighteenth century. Shipwrecks, persecutions, imprisonments, escapes, separations and reunions follow in rapid and bewildering succession as her heroes and heroines move around the globe. Their experiences serve to test their virtue. Her heroines preserve their Christianity and their chastity in all circumstances, and the narrator points the moral: their 'Examples should convince us how possible it is for us to behave ourselves as we ought in our Conditions, since Ladies, whose Sex, and tender Manner of Breeding, render them much less able than Men to support such Hardships, bravely endured Shipwrecks, Want, Cold, Slavery, and every Ill that Human Nature could be tried withal'.[34]

Aubin's didactic fiction differs from Rowe's in using more elements from popular fiction of the time, and having a much more sustained (if breathless) flow of narrative: in short, she allows more romance into her moral lessons. In this way her fiction goes further than Rowe's towards making morality compatible with the novel tradition. She looked to Rowe, however, for her example. When Aubin's novels first appeared Rowe was well known as a religious writer, and Aubin seized on the famous name to add a lustre of virtue to her own endeavours. In 1723 she dedicated *The Life of Charlotta du Pont* 'To my much Honoured Friend Mrs. Rowe', whom she praised for 'Sense and Virtue', and 'all that is valuable in our Sex'.[35] The preface to a posthumous collection of Aubin's novels (1739) capitalized on this association with Rowe, claiming that the friendship between the two women could be inferred from 'the Tenor of both their Writings', both being religious and moral.[36] It is most unlikely that this alleged friendship ever existed, considering that Aubin's dedication refers to Thomas Rowe as if he is alive, eight years after the death that no reader of his widow's well-known elegy, let alone a personal friend of hers, could have remained unaware of. The dedication is no evidence of acquaintance between the two women, but strong evidence of the power of Rowe's name to guarantee the religious and virtuous character of any woman writer who could manage to appear associated with her.

Aubin looked to a religious woman poet rather than a novelist for her model (*Charlotta du Pont* was dedicated to Rowe before Rowe's fiction was published). Morality for her was the proper aim of fiction, and she found the society of her time in particular need of moral advice: 'the few that honour Virtue, and wish well to our Nation, ought to study to reclaim our Giddy Youth; and since Reprehensions fail, try to win them by Vertue, and by Methods where Delight and Instruction may go together'.[37] She declared herself opposed to contemporary trends in the novel, which she associated with an age of loose living generally, and with particular depravity among women writers. In her preface to *Charlotta du Pont* she explains that she has been encouraged 'to write more modishly, that is, less like a Christian, and in a Style careless and loose, as the Custom of the present Age is to live. But I leave that to the other female Authors my Contemporaries, whose Lives and Writings have, I fear, too great a resemblance' (*Collection*, III, vi).

She does not name these other female authors, but it is very probable she has Eliza Haywood in mind. Haywood's fiction was popular in the early 1720s, the time of Aubin's entry into fiction. This was the beginning of a decade of ideological struggle between the two kinds of novel, and of woman novelist, represented by these two prolific writers. Haywood moralizes, but her didactic tone is used to convey some very permissive comments on the inevitable effects of passion, whereas Aubin's work is intended to demonstrate that the passions can be controlled by virtue.[38]

Despite certain narrative crudities Aubin's novels, with their combination of fast-moving adventures and a plain didactic message, became very popular. Her example seems to have turned the tide in favour of moralized fiction, and her works were praised for not being like Haywood's. The preface to the 1739 collection of her novels contends that novels should be pure in style and manners, should punish the guilty characters, and should not allow the innocent to suffer. Unfortunately, the writer adds, most novels are not like this:

> And we are still more sorry to have Reason to say, That those of the *Sex*, who have generally wrote on these Subjects, have been far from preserving that Purity of Style and Manners, which is the greatest Glory of a fine Writer on any Subject; but, like the *fallen Angels*, having lost their own Innocence, seem, as one would think by their Writings, to make it their Study to corrupt the minds of others. ... Mrs. *AUBIN* had a far happier Manner of Thinking and Acting. (*Collection*, I, a2v–a3r)

It has been suggested that the author of this preface was Samuel Richardson,[39] who was soon afterwards to follow its precepts in his first novel, *Pamela: or, Virtue Rewarded*, published late in 1740. Certainly Penelope Aubin's determined efforts to moralize fiction provided Richardson with a precedent for his 'new species of writing', intended 'to promote the cause of religion and virtue'.[40]

RICHARDSON AND FIELDING: TWO TRADITIONS IN
THE NOVEL

Pamela had a crucial effect on the status of the novel. Its story, told in the heroine's own letters, of a young servant who preserves her virginity despite the repeated attacks of her master, Mr B, and marries him when he reforms, offered its readers a variety of attractions. There are the satisfactions of female virtue rewarded by true love with honour, and lower-class virtue rewarded by marriage into the gentry, as well as an insight into the mind and heart of an innocent yet feeling heroine. The combination of romantic wish-fulfilment and inflexible morality was very popular, and helped to rescue the very word *novel* from its association with lewd tales. Fiction became more respectable, and from the 1740s onwards more and more women novelists appeared on the scene with didactic works.

The women novelists after Richardson have usually been seen too simply as his imitators, ignoring their participation in a tradition of women's writing that begins much earlier. Richardson himself was following a long tradition of epistolary fiction, much of it written by women,[41] and his achievement owed much to cultural definitions of feminine writing and to the traditions established by women writers. Many women certainly did draw inspiration from *Pamela, Clarissa* (1748), and especially from the comedy of manners in *Sir Charles Grandison* (1751), but they were not thereby cut off from the women's tradition before them, which continued to exercise its influence both directly, and indirectly through Richardson. Richardson's importance for women novelists was not so much that he provided them with a model to imitate, as that he helped to create the climate in which they would be accepted.

Meanwhile Henry Fielding, Richardson's contemporary and rival, was also doing a great deal to raise the novel's reputation, but the tradition he followed was very different. We can sum up the differences between Richardson's and Fielding's novels under two heads, one technical, one moral, though the two are related. Johnson famously declared that the difference between them was like that 'between a man who knew how a watch was made, and a man who could tell the hour by looking on the dial-plate', pointing to the contrast between Richardson's technique of representing 'from the inside' his characters' states of mind and feeling, and Fielding's of representing character 'from the outside', with detached and ironic narration.[42] The difference in the two writers' moral visions is evident in the contrast between Fielding's comic and satiric realism and Richardson's creation of exemplary characters. Richardson hoped to have a good influence on his readers by depicting goodness. His Pamela, Clarissa and Sir Charles Grandison, though highly individualized and not quite unrealistically perfect, were clearly intended as good examples worthy of imitation. For Fielding, exemplary fiction was out of touch with reality. He deliberately made his Tom Jones lack the proper heroic qualities, arguing that imperfection made him human. He warned his readers:

not to condemn a character as a bad one, because it is not perfectly a good one. If thou dost delight in these models of perfection, there are books enow written to gratify thy taste; but as we have not, in the course of our conversation, ever happened to meet with any such person, we have not chosen to introduce any such here.[43]

Johnson, like Richardson, found pictures of vice morally suspect. For him, the problem with *Tom Jones* was not that its hero was not perfect, but that the reader was often invited to sympathize with him in his imperfections, which made Fielding one of those irresponsible writers who 'for the sake of following nature, so mingle good and bad qualities in their principal personages, that they are both equally conspicuous; and as we accompany them through their adventures with delight ... we lose the abhorrence of their faults'.[44]

For women novelists, the debate centred on Richardson's and Fielding's work was important because it not only divided the novel tradition into two distinct strands, but sexualized the division. Fielding's fiction was clearly masculine, Richardson's feminine, in eighteenth-century terms. Expounding his theory of the novel as 'comic-Epic-Poem in Prose',[45] Fielding gave the new form legitimacy by claiming a place for it within the classical tradition, which was outside the range of most women novelists of the time, and, it might be added, outside the unlearned Richardson's range too. He also treated subjects that were now being found indecent, and therefore out of bounds for moral and modest women writers. On the other hand, Richardson's concentration on female characters and on feeling, and his exemplary morality, meant that he wrote as women were ideally supposed to write.

It is not surprising, then, that Fielding's and Richardson's successors tended to divide along sexual lines, men being more likely to follow Fielding and Smollett, women being more likely to follow Richardson. This was not by any means a clear-cut distinction. Many women novelists, including Sarah Fielding and Fanny Burney, drew inspiration from Fielding. What happened was more that certain expectations about women's fiction developed: that it would be, like Richardson's, an examination of the feminine heart and a display of exemplary morality. This was in fact a crystallization of the notions about feminine writing that we have already observed being expressed in the late seventeenth century. Richardson's entry into the women's camp did not alter these definitions, but accorded new prominence and prestige to the fiction which fitted them.

MASCULINE APPROVAL AND SARAH FIELDING

Richardson and Fielding profoundly affected women novelists in another way, too—by approving of them. Fielding praised some women novelists. He did a great deal to boost his sister's writing career. He revised her first novel, *David Simple* (1744) for a second edition, to which he added a preface praising the work. He contributed five letters and a preface to her second work, *Familiar Letters Between the Principal Characters in David Simple* (1747), which he advertized in his journal, *The True Patriot*, in 1746. He reviewed Charlotte Lennox's second novel, *The Female Quixote* (1752) in *The Covent-Garden Journal*, praising its humour and its moral lesson taught through satire.[46] Richardson was even more enthusiastic about helping women novelists. His 'much-esteemed Sally Fielding, the author of David Simple', became acquainted with him some time before 1748, and he seems to have taken over from her brother as her chief patron.[47] He subscribed to her novels and encouraged others to do the same, and he printed several of her works: *The Governess, or Little Female Academy*, one of the earliest children's books, in 1749; *The Lives of Cleopatra and Octavia* in 1757; and *The History of the Countess of Dellwyn* in 1759. He was sometimes consulted about problems in her work, and sometimes made suggestions for alterations. Like Fielding, Richardson approved of Charlotte Lennox. To help her he gave her detailed criticism of the manuscript of *The Female Quixote*, and when the novel appeared he praised it to his correspondent Lady Bradshaigh, intimating his sympathy and respect for the author, who, he wrote, 'has genius ... has been unhappy'.[48] Johnson, too, was an influential supporter of some women novelists, including Charlotte Lennox, Frances Sheridan, Frances Brooke and Fanny Burney.

Of course, this was not the first time that eminent male writers had enjoyed themselves by offering gallant compliments to ladies of letters who remained flatteringly inferior. What was new in the 1740s and 1750s was the combination of this complimentary style with serious encouragement of the woman's professional writing career. For this reason, the mid-century marked a new stage in the acceptance of women writers. Some earlier women, like Aphra Behn, had fought their way to success and recognition, but by the middle of the eighteenth century, eminent men of letters were giving practical help and encouragement to obscure or unknown women aspiring to a literary career.

The novelist and critic Clara Reeve (1729–1807) gives us one indication of the encouraging effects of masculine approval on women with literary ambitions. In the preface to her first publication, *Original Poems on Several Occasions* (1769), she writes:

> I formerly believed, that I ought not to let myself be known for a
> scribbler, that my sex was an insuperable objection, that mankind
> in general were prejudiced against its pretensions to literary merit;
> but I am now convinced of the mistake, by daily examples to the
> contrary. I see many female writers favourably received, admitted
> into the rank of authors, and amply rewarded by the public; I have
> been encouraged by their success, to offer myself as candidate for
> the same advantages.[49]

The state of affairs Reeve outlines, had its drawbacks for women. If by
this time men, instead of employing gallant hyperbole to concede victory
over the empire of wit to a few splendid women, were more genuinely
welcoming women in general to the literary world, it was because women
were no longer considered a threat. Women writers, no longer seeing
themselves as men's antagonists, had dropped the battle imagery in
which their predecessors characterized their writing as an attack on
male domination. They were not boldly staking a claim to the field of
literature but modestly asking to be allowed to exercise their influence
in a special feminine sphere. While on the one hand it was useful for
the woman writer not to have to make her writing an attack, on the
other this severing of the link between women's writing and the defence
of womanhood had adverse effects on the development of feminist
thought in the century. Women's writing, in fact, seems to have been
limited in various ways by masculine approval, which many were so
anxious not to lose that they became very careful to write in the way
that men found acceptably feminine.

  We can see some of the effects of cultural acceptance in the career of
Sarah Fielding, who, as Henry Fieldings's sister and Richardson's friend,
had the advice and approbation of the two major novelists of her time.
Like many unmarried gentlewomen, Sarah Fielding suffered from the
problem of having too small an income to live independently and no
opportunity to earn wages. She tried what was becoming the obvious
solution—writing. *David Simple* (1744) was followed by the two-volume
Familiar Letters between the Principal Characters in David Simple in 1747, and
by *Volume the Last*, a sequel, in 1753. Her other publications included
several works of fiction, her book for children, and a translation of
Xenophon's *Memoirs of Socrates* (1762).

  Her first work, *David Simple*, is both sentimental and satirical. David
Simple is an early man of feeling, clearly to be admired for his simplicity
and goodness, though his naivety is mocked at times. His friend Camilla
(eventually his wife) and her brother Valentine are also the creations of
a sentimentalist, good-natured and trusting, and suffering because of it.
These gentle creatures seem to inhabit a different world from the
malicious Spatter, who imputes evil to everyone; yet characters like

Spatter are necessary to Sarah Fielding too, because they can make sharp reflections which, the reader suspects, have the author's judgement with them. For example, when David comments on a young woman's silence in company, Spatter explains that it is considered ill bred for a young unmarried woman to speak except when spoken to. 'I cannot tell the Meaning of it, unless it is a Plot laid by Parents to make their Daughters willing to accept any *Match* they provide for them, that they may have the *Privilege of speaking*'.[50]

Cynthia, the most interesting and vital of all the characters, has something of Spatter's function of satirical speaker of the author's bitterest apprehensions about human nature and society; but unlike Spatter she is also amiable. Her story gives a vivid glimpse of some of the problems encountered by an intellectual young woman in Sarah Fielding's time. She tells David:

> I loved reading, and had a great Desire of attaining Knowledge; but whenever I asked Questions of any kind whatsoever, I was always told, *Such Things were not proper for Girls of my Age to know*: If I was pleased with any Book above the most silly Story or Romance, it was taken from me. For *Miss must not enquire too far into things, it would turn her Brain; she had better mind her Needle-work, and such Things as were useful for Women: reading and poring on Books, would never get me a Husband*. (*David Simple*, p. 101)

Cynthia grows up into a vivacious and somewhat rebellious young woman. When a country gentleman condescendingly informs her, '*I like your Person, hear you have had a sober Education, think it time to have an* Heir to my Estate, *and am willing, if you consent to it, to make you my Wife*'— going on to give her a catalogue of her duties in that position—Cynthia, as she reports to David, 'made him a low Court'sey, and thanked him for the Honour he intended me; but I told him, I had no kind of Ambition to be his *upper Servant*' (p. 109). Refusing such a marriage has only led to the miserable life of a lady's companion, continually scorned and insulted. Wit, Cynthia decides, brings a woman no happiness. 'I am very certain, the Woman who is possessed of it, unless she can be so peculiarly happy as to live with People void of Envy, had better be without it' (p. 102).

Cynthia seems to speak from her author's experience of prejudice against women of learning. One of Sarah Fielding's letters to Richardson, written some years later, complained of a man who thought women unfit to correspond with literary men. She and one of the Collier sisters 'were at dinner with a *hic, haec, hoc* man, who said, well I do wonder Mr. Richardson will be troubled with such *silly women*'.[51] In the character of Cynthia Sarah Fielding denies that women are silly, endowing her creation with intelligence and a competence in dealing with the evils of the world that prevents her from ever really becoming its victim.

In Sarah Fielding's later work, the sharp, rebellious note often sounded in *David Simple* is muted. There is no explicit change of views, for in all her works Sarah Fielding consistently defends women's right to learning on the one hand, and endorses female subordination on the other; but there is a change of emphasis, a new and more anxious insistence on the respectability and submissiveness of the intelligent woman. There is less satirical wit and a more straightforward didacticism. This change was probably influenced by a general feeling among the circle she belonged to that a learned woman could be a respectable figure, but only on certain conditions. Like the novelists Frances Sheridan and Sarah Scott, both of them her acquaintances in later life, Sarah Fielding was a friend of Richardson and agreed with his views, expressed in *Clarissa*, of the compatibility of learning and womanly duties. Delighted to find an argument that made intellectual study acceptable in them, and a champion of their sex like Richardson to promote it, these women novelists of the mid-century sought to keep masculine approval by disclaiming any intention to overturn the sexual hierarchy.

Sarah Fielding, too, was anxious to keep approval for the learned woman by repudiating the views of earlier women writers that proof of women's intellectual abilities challenges male supremacy. This is especially clear in *The Lives of Cleopatra and Octavia* (1757), where the famous women of Shakespeare's *Antony and Cleopatra* and Dryden's *All For Love: or, The World Well Lost* are imagined resurrected from the dead to tell their histories. Shakespeare had made Cleopatra an enigmatic and compelling figure; Dryden had presented her more simply as a tragic heroine devoted to Antony; Sarah Fielding paints her as a thoroughgoing villain. Her Cleopatra does not love Antony at all, but manipulates him for her own ends by means of a cunning pretence of female weakness, as she flatters him with the notion that 'his own Wisdom must enable him to judge better than it was possible for a weak woman to do'.[52] Because Antony is so easily taken in by these wiles, a woman like Octavia, who uses her intelligence honestly, is at a disadvantage. All Sarah Fielding's sympathy in this work is given to Antony's wife, wronged, virtuous and, in this version, a woman of learning.

In this work, as in *David Simple*, Sarah Fielding criticizes men for misjudging women, but her defence of the learned woman is carefully qualified. Antony is not criticized because he fails to recognize women's rights but because he fails to recognize the ideal woman. In contrast to Cleopatra, 'an haughty, false, and intriguing Woman', the 'amiable and gentle Octavia' is 'an Example of all those Graces and Embellishments worthy the most refined Female Character. ... a sincere Friend, an affectionate Sister, a faithful Wife, and both a tender and instructive

Parent' (Dedication, n. pag.). The defence of the woman of learning has been modified from a feminist statement to an adjunct of conventional morality.

We can compare Sarah Fielding's presentation of the learned woman with Jane Barker's earlier in the century. Barker's Galesia is a self-portrait of a learned woman and writer as heroine: Sarah Fielding, constantly defending the intellectual woman, is also in a sense defending herself, but she does not dramatize herself within her narrative. Jane Barker, though in one sense a pre-eminently modest—i.e., chaste—writer, is immodest by comparison with Sarah Fielding because of her picture of herself as ambitious, rebellious Galesia. Through this persona she challenges the accepted feminine role, while Sarah Fielding denies that women's learning will have any effect on it.

THE DIFFIDENT SUCCESS: FANNY BURNEY

Sarah Fielding's career shows us one instance of a general trend in the mid-eighteenth century: as women writers' talents were more generally acknowledged they began to claim less for themselves. We might expect that when women novelists became more acceptable to the public, and especially to eminent men of letters, they would show increased confidence, whether individually or collectively. In fact, excuses and apprehensions became the order of the day for women novelists from the 1740s onwards. 'Perhaps the best Excuse that can be made for a Woman's venturing to write at all', explained Sarah Fielding at the beginning of *David Simple*, 'is that which really produced this Book; Distress in her Circumstances: which she could not so well remove by any other Means in her Power'.[53] Twenty-five years later, Elizabeth Griffith, an actress turned writer who had already made a name for herself with the publication of her courtship correspondence with her husband, offered her first novel, *The Delicate Distress*, to the public, 'with infinite timidity, and apprehension, as it is a species of writing, which I had never attempted before, from a consciousness of my deficiency in the principle article of such compositions, namely, invention'.[54] Although from a modern point of view this is a preface calculated to deter the reader, in an eighteenth-century context it could operate as an advertisement. The timidity Griffith expressed was just what her contemporaries required of her.

One famous writer deeply affected by her internalization of feminine diffidence was Fanny Burney. Joyce Hemlow's biography of Burney shows how greatly the fear of bringing disgrace on her family by her writing influenced her. One of the large family of gifted children born to the musician Charles Burney and his first wife, Fanny Burney began writing at an early age, but at fifteen she burned her story 'Carolyn Evelyn' together with a number of poems and plays. Many years later she explained that she was so impressed with ideas of the 'degradation' associated with works of fiction that she was ashamed of having written one herself. She went on writing, her diary (begun in 1768) becoming very important to her, but anything more ambitious than journals and letters became something to be indulged in secretly, as if forbidden. Because she was spending many of her days transcribing her father's *History of Music*, it was difficult for her to find time for what she later called 'an inclination at which I blushed', and much of *Evelina* was written in the quiet and secrecy of the night.[55]

The development of respectable female authorship did something to overcome her fears about writing. Without the climate created by Elizabeth Rowe and her female successors, it is doubtful whether someone so insistently proper as Fanny Burney would ever have published her works. Her meeting with Frances Brooke in 1774 perhaps dispelled some apprehensions, for she reported that 'the celebrated authoress of "Lady Julia Mandeville" ... is very well bred, and expresses herself with much modesty upon all subjects; which in an *authoress*, a woman of *known* understanding, is extremely pleasing'.[56] Not long afterwards she was planning to be an author herself, though she took precautions so as not to become known as one. She took her brothers and sisters into her confidence, and one brother and a cousin arranged for *Evelina* to be published anonymously.

Evelina, the daughter of the earlier heroine, Carolyn Evelyn, whose story was destroyed, enters London society as a naive young girl and describes it in letters to her guardian, Mr Villars. Thus the novel is part of the feminine tradition of expressing the heroine's sensibilities; and in Mr Villars' letters of advice it offers all the morality expected of a woman's novel. However, the humour of the world Evelina witnesses is as prominent as the moral lessons to be drawn from it. Unlike many of her female contemporaries, who were making delicacy and tenderness the hallmarks of their writing, Burney was also a skilful creator of comedy. Madame Duval, the heroine's grandmother, her relatives the Branghtons, vulgar 'cits' with whom Evelina goes to stay in Holborn, and people like foppish Mr Lovel and boorish Captain Mirvan, whom she meets during the course of her entrance into the world, provide opportunities for comic scenes. The pretensions of the Branghtons, who try to impress Evelina by taking her to the opera and other public places, and only succeed in revealing their lack of refinement every time they open their mouths, alternately amuse and embarrass her. Their friend Mr Smith, a would-be gentleman who thinks every woman is eager to marry him and tells Evelina, 'I assure you, there is nobody so likely to catch me at last as yourself', was a favourite character with Johnson.[57]

The *Critical Review*, delighted with *Evelina*, summed up its attractions as a combination of moral utility and comedy: 'It would have disgraced neither the head nor the heart of Richardson.—The father of a family, observing the knowledge of the world and the lessons of experience which it contains, will recommend it to his daughters; they will weep and (what is not so commonly the effect of novels) will laugh'. Johnson delighted Burney by praising her comic characters and declaring that there were things in her novel 'more than worthy of Fielding.' *Evelina*, in fact, was greeted as a new kind of novel, uniting the strengths of the two great novelists. Johnson said that both men would have felt themselves outclassed by her. 'Richardson would have been really afraid of her; there is merit in *Evelina* which he could not have borne. ... Harry Fielding, too, would have been afraid of her; there is nothing so delicately finished in all Harry Fielding's works, as in *Evelina*!'[58] Through Burney's fame, the whole notion of female authorship was raised to a new level of esteem. From this time on there was a woman novelist of undoubted high status, comparable to Richardson and Fielding, against whom to measure new writers.

After the success of *Evelina*, Burney began to write a play called 'The Witlings', despite her feeling that it would be safer to write no more for fear of losing her place in public esteem. Her reservations about developing her comic powers were shared by the men closest to her heart—her adored father and her friend Samuel Crisp, whose paternal concern for her was acknowledged in the affectionate nickname 'daddy'. Her correspondence with Crisp about 'The Witlings' reveals how much her comic powers seemed to her to threaten her feminine propriety. He warned her that comedy might not suit her prudery: 'in most of our successful comedies there are frequent lively freedoms ... [which] ladies of the strictest character ... perhaps would shy at being known to be the authors of'. Again, he wrote: 'I will never allow you to sacrifice a grain of female delicacy for all the wit of Congreve and Vanbrugh put together', and he tellingly described her new writing task as a process of restraining her natural energies: 'Do you remember, about a dozen years ago, how you used to dance Nancy Dawson [a hornpipe dance] on the grass plot, with your cap on the ground, and your long hair streaming down your back, one shoe off, and throwing about your head like a mad thing? Now you are to dance Nancy Dawson with fetters on; there is the difference'. Burney made no objection to the fetters, though she had already foreseen that a comedy so constricted would be in danger of being 'fairly slept off the stage'. 'I would a thousand times rather forfeit my character as a writer, than risk ridicule or censure as a female', she told Crisp.[59] When he and her father disapproved of 'The Witlings' she gave up all thoughts of performance and publication, sadly, but without complaint. After this, Burney's anxiety for paternal approval and her fear of public exposure led her on a search for correctness of language and sentiment that tended to kill her early vitality. The later novels, *Cecilia* (1782), *Camilla* (1796), and *The Wanderer* (1814) show more overt moralizing and less liveliness than her first, written when her anonymity 'afforded temporary security and made for uninhibited writing'.[60]

Burney's diffidence, even when she was a successful writer, forms a striking contrast to the confidence shown by Aphra Behn a hundred years earlier. Torn between her satirist's impulses and her timidity, Burney formulated an apology for her writing that stressed its femininity. *Evelina: or, A Young Lady's Entrance into the World* might seem 'a rather bold attempt and title, for a female whose knowledge of the world is very confined', but she explained: 'I have not pretended to show the world what it actually *is*, but what it *appears* to a girl of seventeen: and so far as that, surely any girl who is past seventeen may safely do?'[61] Playing down her own satire in favour of her creation of an innocent heroine, she almost denies her own artistry by implying that the creation of an Evelina springs simply from having been such a young girl. Burney's apology contains a formula for the novel of manners, and also suggests how restricted this opportunity for women could become if it was based on their writing only what could safely be attributed to any girl past 17. From Behn to Burney, women novelists discovered a special subject, but became confined to it; progressed from suffering 'censure as a female' to receiving tributes to their feminine modesty and morality; and exchanged the freedom of the outcast for the conformity of the lady accepted on carefully defined terms.

'NEAR THE THRONE'

By the late 1780s, Fanny Burney was a standard against whom new women novelists were measured. One reviewer complimented Charlotte Smith by remarking that her first novel showed 'little inferiority' to Burney's work.[62] Critics could now divide women novelists into two sorts, the writers of mere sentimental fiction, and those like Burney and Smith, who could also encompass life and manners, wit and satire, without losing the morality and modesty required of women. It was this tradition of weaving together the two strands in the novel that led to the greater achievements of early nineteenth-century women novelists: Maria Edgeworth and, pre-eminently, Jane Austen. These women could be acknowledged as exceptional, and at the same time, properly feminine. Over the years Jane Austen, who ironically deprecated herself as 'the most unlearned and uninformed female who ever dared to be an authoress',[63] has become at once the best-loved and most condescended-to of famous women writers, praised for creating a world that is seen as narrow, limited, and beautifully ordered—just what a woman's should be. Her work is not so limited as some of her admirers have supposed, but she was able, with the help of irony, to work unconfined within the women's tradition of the 'young lady's entrance into the world'.

An accepted female authorial position which afforded an opportunity to a writer of Austen's stature was a great gain for women. The terms of that acceptance, however, were a hindrance to many women writers. Some were simply limited in their scope. Others, like Charlotte Smith, protested about the restrictions on women novelists, expected to produce charming heroines and to avoid 'masculine' subjects like politics. Any refusal to conform to the terms of acceptance, though, led to bitter attacks on a woman writer. This is most clearly seen in relation to the woman who challenged the terms most directly: Mary Wollstonecraft.

In her *Vindication of the Rights of Woman* (1792), Wollstonecraft argues that the cultivation of what she calls a 'sexual character' in women, to the exclusion of reason, is degrading. The Christian who believes in the immortality of the human soul, the philosopher who pursues truth, must, she argues, apply the same standards to men and women: 'I here throw down my gauntlet, and deny the existence of sexual virtues, not excepting modesty. For man and woman, truth, if I understand the meaning of the word, must be the same'.[64] Wollstonecraft denies women all the special characteristics that have been attributed to them during the century. What has been praised as feminine sensibility and feminine modesty is not virtue, but the result of the false education that has rendered women 'more artificial, weak characters, than they would otherwise have been' (p. 103). Women are famed for gentleness: Wollstonecraft writes that gentleness has 'all the characteristics of grandeur' when it is coupled with strength, but not when it is a tactic adopted by women who have to be gentle because they are subordinate: 'smiling under the lash at which it dare not snarl' (p. 117). Modesty is a virtue she praises when it is 'a simplicity of character that leads us to form a just opinion of ourselves ... by no means incompatible with a lofty consciousness of our own dignity' (p. 227), and not the agreeable fear Steele liked to see in women. She rejects the 'chivalrous' argument that 'the sexes ought not to be compared; man was made to reason, woman to feel', pointing out that this relegates women to inferior status without admitting it, for 'what is sensibility? ... the most exquisitely polished instinct ... not a trace of the image of God' (pp. 154–5).

Wollstonecraft, then, exposes the belief in female inferiority hidden intact behind the rhetoric of appreciation for women's special abilities:

I wish to persuade women to endeavour to acquire strength, both of
mind and body, and to convince them that the soft phrases,
susceptibility of heart, delicacy of sentiment, and refinement of
taste, are almost synonymous with epithets of weakness, and that
those beings who are only the objects of pity, and that kind of love
which has been termed its sister, will soon become objects of
contempt. (pp. 81–2)

By criticizing all these 'mistaken notions of female excellence' (p. 83),
Wollstonecraft attacked the entire ideology of femininity that had been
developed during the century, and on the basis of which women writers
had been accorded acceptance and respectability. It is hardly surprising
that *A Vindication of the Rights of Woman* found only limited favour among
other women writers of the time. Its arguments were calculated to
undermine their hard-won position. Equally we can see why the work
was immediately attacked in the reviews. Wollstonecraft, claiming for
herself the discourse of reason which male admirers of women's writing
had expected to reserve for themselves, was breaking free of the terms
of acceptance. Her boldness swept male chivalry away and forced prejudice into the open. The public reception of *The Rights of Woman* plainly
demonstrates that women writers had been accepted only on condition
that they remained within a limited, feminine sphere, and did not disturb
men's dominance of the 'real' world outside it. 'Women we have often
eagerly placed *near* the throne of literature', wrote the *Critical* reviewer
of Wollstonecraft's work: but 'if they seize it, forgetful of our fondness,
we can hurl them from it.'[65] It is a declaration of power worthy to stand
as an epitaph on the century that accepted the woman writer.

NOTES

1. 'To Mrs. Eliza Haywood, on her Writings', in preface to Eliza Haywood,
   Secret Histories, Novels and Poems, 2nd edn (London: Dan Browne and S.
   Chapman, 1725), **I**, n. pag.
2. Letter to Sarah Chapone, 1750; in *Selected Letters of Samuel Richardson*, ed.
   John Carroll (Oxford: Clarendon Press, 1964), p. 173 n. 68.
3. *The Progress of Romance* (Colchester: W. Keymer, 1785), **I**, pp. 120–1.
4. Joseph Warton, *The Adventurer*, no. 105, 6 November 1753; quoted in John
   A. Vance, *Joseph and Thomas Warton* (Boston: Twayne Publishers, 1983), p.
   59.
5. *The Spectator* (no. 233, November 15, 1711), ed. D. F. Bond (Oxford:
   Clarendon Press, 1965), **II**, p. 366.
6. *The Spectator* (no. 20, March 23, 1711), ed. Bond, **I**, p. 88.
7. *The Spectator* (no. 62, May 11, 1711), ed. Bond, **I**, p. 268.
8. *The Spectator* (no. 397, June 5, 1712), ed. Bond, **III**, pp. 486–8.

9. *The Spectator* (no. 274, Jan. 14, 1712), ed. Bond, **II**, p. 568.
10. *Tatler* no. 52, ed. George A. Aitken (London: Duckworth and Co., 1898), **II**, p. 23.
11. Edmund Burke, *A Philosophical Enquiry into the Origin of our Ideas of the Sublime and Beautiful* (London: J. Dodsley, 1787), p. 219.
12. See Nancy K. Miller, ' "I's" in Drag: The Sex of Recollection', pp. 47–57.
13. *Monthly Review* **35** (1766), p. 485.
14. Review of *Constance*, in *Critical Review* **60** (1785), p. 394.
15. *Critical Review* **57** (1784), p. 233.
16. *Monthly Review* **64** (1781), p. 469.
17. Letter to Sophia Westcomb, 1746, in *Selected Letters of Samuel Richardson*, p. 66.
18. Thomas Marriott, *Female Conduct: being an Essay on the Art of Pleasing. To be practised by the Fair Sex, Before, and After Marriage. A Poem, in Two Books* (London: W. Owen, 1759), p. 60.
19. 'The Life of Mrs. Elizabeth Rowe' (1739) rpt in *Friendship in Death: In Twenty Letters from the Dead to the Living. To which are added, Letters Moral and Entertaining, in Prose and Verse* (Edinburgh: William Gray, 1755), p. xxix.
20. 'Eloisa to Abelard', lines 51–5, in *Poems of Alexander Pope*, ed. J. Butt (Twickenham 1-volume edn, London: Methuen and Co., 1975), p. 253.
21. *Eloisa to Abelard. Written by Mr. Pope. The Second Edition* (London: Bernard Lintot, 1720), p. 52.
22. *Gentleman's Magazine* **9** (May, 1739), p. 98.
23. Letter XV in *Miscellaneous Works In Prose and Verse of Mrs. Elizabeth Rowe* (London, 1739), **II**, p. 200.
24. *Friendship in Death*, p. 14.
25. Preface to the Reader, in *Poems on Several Occasions. Written by Philomela* (London, 1696), A3v–A5r.
26. 'Verses to the Memory of Mrs. Rowe. By a Friend', in *Miscellaneous Works*, **I**, p. cix.
27. 'On the Death of Mrs. Rowe' [by Elizabeth Carter] in *Miscellaneous Works*, **I**, p. cx–cxii.
28. *Critical Review* **13** (1762), p. 181.
29. *Monthly Review* **18** (1758), p. 588.
30. *Poems by Eminent Ladies*, quoted in Myra Reynolds, *The Learned Lady in England 1650–1760* (Boston and New York: Houghton Mifflin, 1920), p. 365.
31. *The Works of Samuel Johnson*, LL. D. (London, 1787), **XI**, p. 205.
32. *Clarissa* (London: Everyman, 1978), **IV**, p. 496; and see Richardson's letter to Lady Bradshaigh, 1751, in *Selected Letters of Samuel Richardson*, pp. 177–8.
33. For biographical details of Aubin, see W. H. McBurney, 'Mrs. Penelope Aubin and the Early Eighteenth-Century Novel', *HLQ* **20** (1956–7), pp. 245–67.
34. *Charlotta du Pont*, in *A Collection of Entertaining Histories and Novels ... By Mrs. Penelope Aubin* (London, 1739), **III**, p. 228.
35. Dedication to *Charlotta du Pont*, in *A Collection*, **III**, p. iii.
36. Preface to *A Collection*, **I**, A4v.

37. *The Strange Adventures of the Count de Vinevil and his Family* (London, 1721), p. 6.
38. See John J. Richetti, *Popular Fiction Before Richardson*, pp. 219–29, for a comparison of Aubin's 'positively exemplary Christian "realism"' with Haywood's 'erotic cautionary tales' (p. 219).
39. See Wolfgang Zach, 'Mrs. Aubin and Richardson's Earliest Literary Manifesto', *English Studies* **62** (1981), pp. 271–85.
40. Letter to Aaron Hill, 1744, in *Selected Letters of Samuel Richardson*, p. 41.
41. For a discussion of Richardson's relation to the women novelists before him see Margaret Doody, *A Natural Passion: A Study of the Novels of Samuel Richardson* (Oxford: Clarendon Press, 1974).
42. Boswell's *Life of Johnson*, ed. R. W. Chapman, corr. J. D. Fleeman (London: Oxford University Press, 1976), p. 389.
43. *Tom Jones*, Book X, ch. i (Harmondsworth: Penguin Books, 1976), p. 468.
44. *Rambler* no. 4, 31 March 1750, *The Yale Edition of the Works of Samuel Johnson*, ed. W. J. Bate and Albrecht B. Strauss (New Haven and London: Yale University Press, 1969), **III**, p. 23.
45. Preface to *Joseph Andrews* (London: Oxford University Press, 1978), p. 4.
46. See *Covent Garden Journal* no. 24, March 24, 1752; ed. G. E. Jensen (New Haven: Yale University Press, 1915), **I**, p. 282.
47. See letter to Sarah Fielding, 7 December 1756, in *Correspondence of Samuel Richardson*, ed. A. L. Barbauld (London: Richard Phillips, 1804), **II**, p. 101. For an account of Richardson's printing of several of Sarah Fielding's works, see W. M. Sale, *Samuel Richardson: Master Printer* (New York: Cornell University Press, 1950), pp. 113–14.
48. *Selected Letters of Samuel Richardson*, p. 223.
49. *Original Poems on Several Occasions. By C.R.* (London, 1769), p. xi.
50. *David Simple*, ed. M. Kelsall (London: Oxford University Press, 1969), p. 87.
51. Sarah Fielding to Richardson, 8 January 1749, *Correspondence*, **II**, p. 59.
52. *The Lives of Cleopatra and Octavia* (London, 1757), p. 45.
53. *The Adventures of David Simple* [first edn] (London, 1744), **I**, pp. iii–iv.
54. *The Delicate Distress, A Novel, In Letters, by Frances.* **I** and **II** of *Two Novels. In Letters. By the Authors of Henry and Frances* [i.e., Elizabeth and Richard Griffith] (London, 1769), **I**, p. vii.
55. See Burney's Dedication to *The Wanderer* (London, 1814), **I**, pp. xx–xxi. See Joyce Hemlow, *The History of Fanny Burney* (Oxford: Clarendon, 1958) for a discussion of Burney's attitude to authorship.
56. Letter to Mr Crisp, 20 February 1774, in *The Early Diary of Frances Burney 1768–1778*, ed. Annie Raine Ellis (London: George Bell and Sons, 1907), **I**, p. 283.
57. See *Evelina*, ed. Edward A. Bloom (London: Oxford University Press, 1970), p. 224. For Johnson's comment on Mr Smith, 'Harry Fielding never drew so good a character!', see *Diary and Letters of Madame d'Arblay (1778–1840)*, ed. Austin Dobson (London, 1904), **I**, p. 72.
58. *Critical Review* **46** (1778), pp. 202–3; and *Diary and Letters of Madame d'Arblay*, **I**, p. 90, p. 95.
59. See *Diary and Letters of Madame d'Arblay*, **I**, p. 150, pp. 164–5, and p. 162.

60. Hemlow, p. 139.

61. *Diary and Letters of Madame d'Arblay*, I, p. 22.

62. *Critical Review* **65** (1788), p. 530.

63. *Jane Austen's Letters*, ed. R. W. Chapman (Oxford: Oxford University Press, 1979), p. 443.

64. *A Vindication of the Rights of Woman*, ed. M. Kramnick (Harmondsworth: Penguin Books, 1978), p. 139.

65. *Critical Review*, 2nd ser. **5** (1792), p. 132.

PART 2
Heroines by Women Novelists

4
Seduced Heroines:
The Tradition of Protest

INTRODUCTION: TRADITIONS IN WOMEN'S NOVELS

Part One has outlined the process by which women novelists gained their accepted authority, at the price of agreeing to keep within the feminine sphere. Despite all the limitations implied by this, some important achievements in the novel emerged from the new situation, and these will form the subject of the remaining chapters. Women novelists, as we have already seen, tended to concentrate on depicting their own sex. Though their novels belonged to traditions in whose creation men shared—the epistolary, the sentimental, the novel of manners, the Gothic—we should remember that throughout the century their work had some distinctive attributes arising from the woman writer's special position. What women shared was basically the need to respond both to women's position in society and to the special role allotted the female writer, based on that position.

The women novelists' responses can be divided into three main kinds. They could protest against society's treatment of women, a response which often involved, to some extent, questioning the role of the respectable woman writer. They could accept the authority offered them as the teachers of young girls, and make their novels didactic treatments of the heroine's progress. This response often (but not always) meant that their advice to women was that they should conform to the accepted feminine role. The third possibility was that they could try to escape from the need either to conform or protest through a fantasy that transformed the feminine position.

These responses might be mixed in any one writer and in any one novel, but each kind of response did have its own most characteristic expression, so that it is possible to trace three traditions within women's fictional writing during the century. They overlap and influence one another, but are nevertheless sufficiently distinct to justify being discussed under three headings. Protest surfaces in many novels, but most strongly at the beginning and the end of the century. Conformity gave rise to the most continuously sustained of the women's traditions, the novel of the heroine's education. The desire to escape informs the romance tradition, which has so strong an influence on the developing novel and leads to the fantasies of women's Gothic. The traditions that follow from these latter two responses will be the subjects of the last two chapters. In this chapter, we will examine the tradition of protest.

FEMINISM AND THE NOVEL: THE SEDUCTION THEME

At the beginning of our period, with women's writing itself seen as a challenge to the feminine role, protest about male views of women seemed a natural part of the woman writer's concern. Around 1700, there was a strong tradition of nonfictional feminist prose. Feminists concentrated particularly on the issue of education, contending that male and female minds were naturally equal and that with education women could rival men in learning. The anonymous *Essay in Defence of the Female Sex* (1696) probably written by a woman called Judith Drake, used the Lockean argument 'that there are no innate *Idea's*' to contend that 'all Souls are equal, and alike, and ... consequently there is no such distinction, as Male and Female Souls'. In her *Serious Proposal to the Ladies* (1694), Mary Astell made practical suggestions for improving women's education, and in *Reflections upon Marriage* (1700), she described matrimony as the institution of male tyranny: 'Let the business be carried as Prudently as it can be on the Woman's side, a reasonable Man can't deny that she has by much the harder bargain. Because she puts her self entirely into her Husband's Power, and if the Matrimonial Yoke be grievous, neither Law nor Custom afford her that redress which a Man obtains.'[1] Mary Chudleigh, a friend of Astell's, also attacked marriage.

Despite occasional publications like the pseudonymous 'Sophia's' *Woman Not Inferior to Man* (1739), and the intermittent feminism of Lady Mary Wortley Montagu's periodical, *The Nonsense of Common-Sense* (1737–8),[2] the tradition of feminist polemic was, on the whole, submerged during the eighteenth century. It surfaced again in the final decade, which saw the publication not only of Wollstonecraft's *Vindication of the Rights of Woman*, but Mary Hays's *Appeal to the Men of Great Britain in Behalf of Women* (1798), Priscilla Wakefield's *Reflections on the Present Condition of the Female Sex* (1798), Anne Frances Randall's *Letter to the*

Women of England, on the Injustice of Mental Subordination (1799), and Mary Anne Radcliffe's *The Female Advocate* (1799).

Within women's fiction we can trace something of a similar progress of feminist thought. In the early decades of the century attacks on the male view of women and on the feminine role appeared in novels as they had in women's pamphlets. We saw in Chapter 2 that such protests were important in Jane Barker's autobiographical fiction, and here we will see how they pervaded the work of Delariviere Manley and Eliza Haywood. In the middle of the century, as women writers gained their respectable position, the tone of their work changed. Feminist protest did not entirely disappear, for though few works of feminist polemic *per se* were written in this period, questions about women's role were still raised within the novel. However, they were raised in such a way as to leave a distinct impression that the challenge to male authority was temporarily muted. Towards the end of the century, amid the ferment of radical ideas at the time of the French Revolution, feminism re-emerged to become a prominent part of the political discourse. At this time the novel was used by writers on both sides of the political debate to promulgate their ideas, and among the radical novelists feminist ideas were often given a central place.

Throughout the century, the tradition of protest, whether in the feminist pamphlets or in the novel, dealt with many aspects of women's lives, including their education, and their position as daughters and wives. There was one kind of protest, however, that the novelists were particularly well equipped to make, and which this chapter therefore takes as its central theme. This was the attack on the sexual mores of a society that overlooked promiscuity in men but severely punished women for any breach of chastity.

This double standard was reinforced during the eighteenth century by the idealization of a supposedly natural feminine purity. So strong was this ideal by the nineteenth century that it was commonly held that normal women had no sexual desires at all. In the eighteenth century this idea had not yet entirely obscured people's consciousness of the reason for imposing a double standard, which was that it helped keep women in subjection as pieces of family property. The daughter's virginity was an asset to be handed over to a financially and socially suitable husband, and the wife's fidelity ensured that property passed only to legitimate sons. Eighteenth-century men were quite unequivocal that this was why a wife's adultery was worse than a husband's. Boswell reports Johnson's comment on adultery: 'Confusion of progeny constitutes the essence of the crime; and therefore a woman who breaks her marriage vows is much more criminal than a man who does it'.[3]

The pure woman, for the eighteenth century, was one who never disturbed her usefulness as male property by any unruly desires of her own. The novel's role in the spread of this ideology was a double-edged one. It was in the novel that the ideal of pure femininity was most memorably expressed and popularly disseminated. The heroines who most caught the eighteenth-century imagination—Richardson's Pamela and Clarissa, Burney's Evelina, Radcliffe's Emily St Aubert (in *The Mysteries of Udolpho*)—were pure women resisting assaults on their virginity or on its psychological equivalent, their delicacy of mind. At the same time women's sexual desires could not be ignored in the novel, though they might be dealt with only in euphemisms. The plot of the feminocentric novel was predicated on the heroine's desires, which were usually to escape an unwanted suitor and to marry the man of her choice. It was the novel's focus on sexuality that made it capable of producing a distinctive contribution to the feminist debate.

In eighteenth-century conduct books for women, we see the doctrine of women's special purity being used to reinforce their position as men's property. In his *Father's Legacy to his Daughters*, John Gregory told his daughters that he would never try to force them into marriage, but the analysis he gave of women's lack of sexual desire implied that a positive choice in the matter of a marriage partner was not necessary to them. Women, he wrote, were not troubled with any sexual desires, 'at least in this part of the world' (he was obviously not going to answer for the more volatile constitutions of Mediterranean ladies). This natural deficiency would seem to be a great help when men wanted to choose wives and parents wanted to organize their daughters' marriages. Gregory informed his offspring that 'What is commonly called love among you is rather gratitude, and a partiality to the man who prefers you to the rest of your sex; and such a man you often marry, with little of either personal esteem or affection.' How could it matter that women were not allowed any choice about their sexual partner, when benevolent Nature had so wisely given them 'a greater flexibility of taste on this subject' than men?[4]

Voices were raised against this kind of sophistry. Mary Granville (later Delany) was one woman whose experience led her to detest prevailing marriage customs. At the age of seventeen she was cajoled into marrying Alexander Pendarves, an 'ugly and disagreeable' man of nearly 60. Her relations wanted the marriage because Pendarves had money and there was no other provision for Mary. Looking back many years and a happier second marriage later, Mary Delany criticized her society's use of women as objects of exchange on the marriage market. 'Why must women be *driven to the necessity* of marrying? a state that should always be a matter of *choice*!' she demanded.[5]

Choice in love and marriage was a cause more often defended like this, in women's memoirs and letters, than in published arguments. This central question in women's lives was decreed to belong to the sphere of private experience. Feminist polemics were on the whole more concerned with arguments for intellectual equality and support for female education than with revision of the prevailing view of love and marriage. Even Astell, critical of male dominance within marriage, still bowed to the convention that a girl's marriage should be arranged by her parents. In her *Serious Proposal to the Ladies* she envisaged a college where women could find an alternative to marriage in piety and learning, but she expected that many of its inmates would eventually leave to get married. The problem of finding a husband in the strict seclusion of the female academy would be easily solved. The parents would choose suitable mates, and the daughters could have no objection to this, for 'She who has none but innocent affections, [is] easily able to fix them where Duty requires'.[6] The assumption that duty should channel women's feelings into whatever was convenient for their rulers was often questioned in the letters and diaries where women recorded their discontents, but it was attacked most frequently, perhaps most effectively, in the novel.

Feminocentric novels often explicitly supported the ideology of female purity, but because they made the heroine's affections centrally important, they implicitly gave the lie to Gregory's breezy view of female malleability. For example, in his second novel, *Clarissa* (1748), Richardson exposed the hypocrisy involved in using female chastity to further family ambition. The heroine, pure daughter of the wealthy Harlowe family, has always been loved for her virtues, until these clash with the family's dynastic ambitions. For various selfish motives, her elder brother and sister oppose the aristocrat Lovelace's courtship of Clarissa, while she herself resists it because she disapproves of his libertine life. Then all her family press her to marry Solmes, a rich miser whose wealth, settled on her family, will help the Harlowes to realise their ambition of entering the peerage. To this end they are ready to use Clarissa's virtue against her. Like John Gregory's daughters and Mary Astell's projected students, Clarissa is told that a pure woman can marry any man her family may choose. When she refuses to marry Solmes it is taken as evidence of her unruly sexual desires for Lovelace: 'Such extraordinary antipathies to a particular person must be owing to extraordinary prepossessions in another's favour!' exclaims her mother. When Clarissa denies that she desires Lovelace, or any other man, the immediate demand is, 'since *your heart is free* let your duty govern it'—duty, of course, meaning obedience to her parents' wish that she marry Solmes.[7] Unless she agrees to this, they consider her purity sullied; yet it is, of course, that very purity which makes her reject Solmes, who is both physically and morally repugnant. In *Clarissa* the conflict between the pure woman and the society that exploits women's purity eventually leads to tragedy. Many other novels, like Richardson's, dealt with the problem of the pure woman's desires. By exposing the contradictions within the ideology of femininity, novels publicized the complaints made more privately by women like Delany in their letters, and constituted a kind of public forum for discussing the private sphere of love and marriage.

Established marriage customs were most persistently questioned in novels of seduction. The seduction theme, the story of the woman whose forbidden feelings overrode her chaste duty, with usually tragic effects, fascinated eighteenth-century readers, and seduction or its threat figured largely in the novel. The examples best known today are by men. Defoe's Moll Flanders embarked on her life of crime after being a seduced innocent. Richardson's Pamela avoided seduction and achieved a happy ending, while his Lovelace reacted to the failure of his seduction techniques by raping Clarissa, and turning their story into a tragedy. In *The Vicar of Wakefield* (1766), Goldsmith created pathos around the figure of seduced Olivia Primrose, and Henry Mackenzie united a fallen woman with her heartbroken father in *The Man of Feeling*. Women novelists, however, were the first ones to develop the seduction tale. Manley in *The New Atalantis*, and Haywood in her 1720s novels, established the novel of seduction which later writers drew on. In their work especially, but also in many of their successors', the novel with a seduced heroine became a vehicle for feminism.

It was able to do this because seduction was the obvious point where the ideal of love and marrige based on feminine purity broke down. The seducer deliberately attacked female purity, and then left his victim at the mercy of a society which ostracized her for losing her virginity. Such a plot could lend itself to a novelist's feminist interpretations. The lover's infidelity gave rise to general comments about man's untrustworthy nature, which could soon turn into criticism of masculine authority. The man's ability to get away with sexual misdemeanours (very few seducers in novels were punished) contrasted with the dire consequences awaiting the seduced woman, who was nearly always abandoned by her lover and rejected by society, sometimes with an illegitimate child she could not support. Her 'ruin' often led to her death. The seduction novel, therefore, could make a strong attack on the double standard which demanded chastity of women, but not of men.

At its most trenchant, the novel of seduction could reveal the contradictions at the heart of the bourgeois ideology of femininity. But that is not to say that it was without contradictions of its own. Positing a myth of female innocence and male guilt to explain seduction, it helped reinforce the ideology of femininity as purity at the same time as attacking those who demanded purity of women and not of men. Moreover, the seduction novel depended for its effect on an essentially sentimental view of innocence as weakness. In the typical seduction tale it was apparent that the heroine was seduced precisely *because* she was pure and innocent, and therefore unguarded: it was virtue that made her likely to fall.[8] This paradoxical notion is illustrated in one of Eliza Haywood's novels when a male character writes to the 'ruined' heroine:

> most adorable *Cleomelia*, you are too lovely to be guilty, and if seduc'd by your own heavenly Innocence, and the Force of a Passion, whose Effects too well I know, to believe the perjur'd *Gasper*, let him who alone merits it bear all the blame; his be the Infamy, my *Cleomelia* is clear.[9]

Eighteenth-century narratives are full of unfortunate females who, like Cleomelia, are seduced by their own heavenly innocence.

By idealizing the heroine as an innocent victim of men and fate, the novel of seduction sometimes reinforced rather than challenged the oppressive ideology of femininity. Ruin could be portrayed as an inevitably tragic destiny rather than an assailable social wrong. Haywood and Manley, for example, have been described as creators of a 'myth of persecuted innocence' which has ultimately conservative implications because it suggests that women can be nothing but victims.[10] However, there is more to the ethos of the seduction tale than this. In close and uneasy relationship to the picture of woman as victim, we find attacks on the social code which makes her one. Although Haywood was much given to narrative pronouncements about the inevitability of love, man's bad behaviour, and women's acceptance of both, and Manley's 'warm' descriptions of heroines about to be seduced were meant to titillate the male reader, a connection between feminist protest and the seduction novel remained. At their best these bold, 'immoral' women novelists could attack prevailing sexual mores more effectively than the respectable early writers of feminist polemic, who were weakest on this subject; and more trenchantly, too, than the respectable women novelists who succeeded Haywood and Manley in the middle years of the century.

DELARIVIERE MANLEY'S STORY OF CHARLOT (1709)

Manley's *New Atalantis*, as Chapter 2 showed, made its attack on the Whigs by accusing them of sexual irregularities. Seduction, in fact, figures largely in the work. We have already seen that Manley presented herself as man's victim in the autobiographical story of Delia, which is a typical seduction tale, stressing the victim's entire innocence and unconsciousness of sexuality, and the man's deceitfulness and selfish opportunism. Delia concludes on a note of protest against the double standard of sexual morality, demanding of her male listener, 'Why are your Sex so partially distinguish'd? Why is it in your Powers, after accumulated Crimes, to regain Opinion? when ours, tho' oftentimes guilty, but in appearance, are irretrievably lost?' (*New Atalantis*, II, 190–1).

One episode in the first volume of *The New Atalantis*, concerning the story of Charlot, takes this seduction theme and makes of it a far-reaching feminist critique of prevailing mores. As in Delia's story, the heroine is seduced by her guardian, 'ruin'd by him that ought to have been her Protector!' (I, 72). Then, like all men in seduction tales, her guardian tires of Charlot after conquest. He marries another woman and leaves the heroine heartbroken. Again as in Delia's story, Manley attacks the convention that makes seduction equal ruin for women. Her goddess of Justice complains: 'Men may regain their Reputations, tho' after a Complication of Vices, *Cowardice, Robbery, Adultery, Bribery*, and *Murder*, but a Woman once departed from the Road of Virtue, is made incapable of a return; Sorrow and Scorn overtake her, and ... the World suffers her to perish loath'd, and unlamented' (I, 83–4).

For Manley's first readers her stories of seduction had an extra point, lost on us, because they were based on real events in the contemporary court: they could be read, not as romantic tales, but as revelations of real men's treachery. The story of Charlot was based on a real intrigue.[11] In Manley's hands, this story of a woman betrayed becomes a fable about men's general betrayal of women. It is not just that the Duke, as Charlot's guardian, ought to have protected her, but that all men in the male-dominated society Manley depicts, stand as women's guardians, and exploit instead of looking after them. Related to this point is Manley's attack on the ideology of femininity which was used to explain and excuse the double standard. This was possible in the story of Charlot in a way that it was not in Manley's story of herself as Delia, when she was defending her own sexual conduct. It is in the story of Charlot that we find the freedom of the early, 'immoral' woman writer put to good effect. Manley does not base her defence of Charlot on a belief in woman's essential purity. Elsewhere in *The New Atalantis* she expresses the opinion that chastity, being opposed by nature, is not an innate virtue, and even that it is 'not strictly numbred among the Virtues' at all.[12] This attitude transforms the seduction tale. Though Charlot's story depends on the idea of female innocence, Manley does not idealize that innocence. Nor does she feel the need (as she does in the story of Delia) to deny that sexual desire is an element in her heroine's downfall. Instead, she shows the dangers to women in an ideal of undesiring womanhood. This does not appear so explicitly as it was to do in the work of Wollstonecraft, many years later; but the feminist critique, though implicit in Manley's work, is nevertheless there. As she traces the process of seduction by analysing the feelings of both seducer and victim, the ideal of female innocence is put into question.

Charlot's innocence is not essential femininity but the artificial construct of her restrictive education. Charlot's father dies leaving her to the care of the Duke, who means his son to marry her. If she is to be part of his family she must remain pure, and the Duke not only forbids external stimuli to the passions—novels, plays, romances, and love poetry—but does his best to curb her natural intelligence, which has a tendency to 'break out in dangerous Sparkles' (I, 53). He tells her 'that whatever carried her beyond the knowledge of her Duty: carried her too far; all other Embellishments of the Mind were more dangerous than useful, and to be avoided as her Ruin' (I, 54). Clearly, development of Charlot's mind would mean development of her passions too. The Duke's 'strongest Battery was united against *Love*, that invader of the *Heart*; he show'd her how shameful it was, for a young Lady ever so much as to think of any tenderness for a Lover, 'till he was become her Husband; that true Piety and Duty would instruct her in all that was necessary for a good Wife to feel of that dangerous Passion' (I, 54). Evidently he fears threats to Charlot's chastity not for her sake but because they would involve threat to her subordination in the family, specifically the 'Duty' which is meant to make her accept his son for her husband. The Duke's dislike of women who can rule men by charming them underlines this equation between sexual innocence and subordination. Women, he notes, try to gain power through their sexuality, because other kinds of power are denied them: 'they would by the Charms of their Beauty, and their sweet insinuating way of Conversation, assume that native Empire over Mankind, which seems to be politically deny'd them, because the way to Authority and Glory is stop'd up' (I, 55). It is notable that he considers it natural for women to have power, and thinks their powerlessness in society artificially induced. It means that he has an important reason for preventing his ward from assuming her 'native Empire' over men. By keeping Charlot innocent—that is, ignorant of the power of her own sexuality—he intends to keep her under his own control.

This is a bold exposé of the realities of women's situation, usually obscured by idealization of their purity. Manley goes further by adding that this carefully created female innocence is itself the trigger for men's desires to destroy it. During an evening's entertainment consisting of singing and acting such stories from classical literature as the Duke considers morally safe, Charlot impersonates Diana. Her appearance as the goddess of chastity arouses the Duke's desires, and it is because she fits the part so well that he is prompted to attack the innocence that attracts him. He enters on a scheme of re-education. Instead of keeping her secluded from the world as before, he takes her to live at court, where she takes part in '*Balls, Assemblies, Opera's, Comedies, Cards*, and *Visits*, every thing that might enervate the Mind, and fit it for the soft play and impression of Love' (I, 61). He encourages her to read the formerly forbidden works of Ovid, Petrarch, and Tibellus, famous for descriptions of love. Once she is 'prepar'd to softness' by her reading, he kisses her, and she finds 'new and unfelt Desires' awakening in her at this treatment (I, 64). He declares his love, and then leaves her, longing for his return, with only books explaining 'the Nature, Manner, and Raptures of Enjoyment' as her companions (I, 67). Her reading warns her of men's inconstancy as well as teaching her about love, and she refuses further kisses; but she agrees to spend a few days at his villa while he is away, and is at his mercy when he returns unexpectedly and ravishes her. She soon forgives him, and becomes his mistress, but this does not mean that she becomes one of the powerful women who rule through their charms. She truly loves him, and is incapable of regulating her favours according to his treatment of her, as a new friend, a widowed Countess, advises. Because of this the Duke soon loses interest in her and marries the Countess, who knows better how to dominate a man by feminine wiles.

Many writers of seduction tales detailed the pernicious effects of public life and the literature of love on the innocent female; but few had Manley's insight into these diversions as strategies created by masculine society for manoeuvring women into seduceable positions. The stress on the Duke's control over Charlot is important. He is a substitute for her father. She even calls him 'papa', and her embraces, given with daughterly affection, arouse his quasi-incestuous desires.[13]

There is more to this than an erotic novelist's attempt to titillate her readers. The Duke's fatherly relation to Charlot is analogous to the general relation of men to women under patriarchy—figures of authority controlling their lives. The father, or male in authority, betrays the trust placed in him by the woman who, in her male-created innocence, accepts her place as daughter. In the midst of the rhetoric of seduction-as-ruin which has led to the mistaken notion that Manley glorifies female innocence and weakness, there is a sharp analysis and indictment of men's rule.

ELIZA HAYWOOD'S *THE BRITISH RECLUSE* (1722)

Eliza Haywood is Manley's successor in this respect, as in others: she too attacks men's treatment of women in her tales of seduction. Because, like Manley and unlike the new 'respectable' women novelists, she places her protests within erotic love-stories, they have been ignored or belittled by her critics. John Richetti writes that Haywood had the 'public personality of feminist champion', but implies that this was undeserved: he sees her feminist arguments as 'degraded', merely 'moralistic covering for erotic fantasy'.[14] Certainly the frequent narrative pronouncements, in *Love in Excess*, about the inescapable power of love, especially over weak women, debar her from the cogent analysis of the politics of seduction, which is Manley's strength as a feminist. However, she does belong to the women's tradition of protest, not only because, like Manley, she deplores the social convention that a woman can never regain lost honour, but because in one of her novels, *The British Recluse*, she produces a radical revision of the idea of woman as victim, sketching the possibility of escape, through female friendship, from the seduced woman's fate of heartbreak and usually early death.

The British Recluse is the story of two heroines—Cleomira, the recluse herself, and Belinda, who meets her at the inn where she is living in hiding from the world. The two women immediately strike up a friendship and exchange confidences. Cleomira explains that, after being seduced and abandoned by her lover, Lysander, she had a stillborn child. Her mother died of grief at her daughter's ruin. Cleomira attempted suicide, and on recovery resolved to forget Lysander, who had felt no compunction when he heard of her supposed death. She now condemns her former self as 'meanly Soul'd' for having been in love with such a man.[15]

Belinda, too, is '*For ever lost to Peace by* LOVE' (*The British Recluse*, p. 12) but has escaped actual seduction. She only has folly to mourn, while the recluse feels shame, disgrace and guilt. Yet it is Cleomira who is now the wiser woman. She has more presence of mind than Belinda and proves her intelligence by reading 'the best Authors' (p. 7). This is because, though no older in years, she is older in experience. She has learned to reject men and love, while Belinda is still in love with Sir Thomas Courtal, the man who tried to seduce her. Belinda needs to learn from Cleomira's experience, and she begins to do so after the story's climactic revelation. Some details in Belinda's narrative make Cleomira realize that her 'Lysander' and Belinda's 'Courtal' are in fact the same man, 'the too lovely, faithless, *Bellamy*' (p. 135). This is the secret connection which explains, in retrospect, the immediate attraction between the two heroines: they are truly 'Companions in Affliction', betrayed by the same lover (p. 136).

This wildly improbable coincidence adds greatly to the story's moral point, which is also a feminist point. Lysander/Courtal/Bellamy, the seducer of practically every women he meets, is not meant as a realistic character in the way Belinda and Cleomira are. He is a representative of man as seducer. To fall in love with him is to take up the position of woman as victim, but to survive the experience and renounce him is to reject that position and gain wisdom. The experience of 'ruin' here, almost uniquely in eighteenth-century narrative, is not the end of a woman's hopes, but a calamity that can teach her to live more wisely and independently in future. The story ends with Belinda and Cleomira retiring from society to live in the country, where there is a hope that they will be happy together.

THE NEW MORAL NOVEL: SARAH FIELDING'S *THE COUNTESS OF DELLWYN* (1759)

Manley and Haywood both used the seduction tale for feminist social criticism. Manley directed her attack at the masculine manipulaton of the ideology of innocence, while Haywood depicted an alternative to the seduced woman's dependence on her lover and her eventual despair. Later women novelists also used the scenario of seduction and betrayal to carry their criticisms of society's treatment of women; but because of the different position of the woman novelist later in the century, their novels of seduction carried very different messages.

In one way, the tradition of protest in women's novels expanded during the second half of the century. The incorporation of wide-ranging discussions of society and morality into the love-story, always a tendency in the epistolary novel and increasingly common in all kinds of novel after Richardson, meant that women's role was more often explicitly discussed. Novels carried attacks on contemporary marriage customs, particularly on the parents' authority over the daughter's choice of husband, and on the wife's subjection to her husband. There were arguments for recognizing women's educational capacities, for better education for women, even an early call for votes for women.[16] Yet some of the strengths of earlier women writers were no longer found. Manley and Haywood acknowledged the existence of sexual desires in women, without presenting them (as male writers tended to do) as grotesque. Being beyond the respectable pale themselves, they were free to do so. Later women novelists defended their own respectability by banishing all hints of sexual desire in their heroines. Moreover, as the idealization of womanhood gained ground, novelists based their arguments for a better deal for women on a belief in essential female purity. The feminist analysis of the ideology of femininity which distinguished Manley's work was lost.

The new morality of women novelists meant that, for a period stretching from about the 1720s to the 1760s, their sympathy for the seduced woman was much reduced. Penelope Aubin's *Charlotta du Pont*, published the year after *The British Recluse*, contains an early example of severe judgment on the fallen woman. The pure heroine is contrasted to her persecuting stepmother Dorinda, whose wickedness dates from her 'ruin'

years ago. Even though she was given money to help her return to a
virtuous life, Dorinda went of her own accord into a brothel, for 'alas!
Youth once vitiated is rarely reformed, and Woman, who whilst virtuous
is an Angel, ruined and abandoned by the Man she loves, becomes a
Devil.'[17] Frances Sheridan's *Memoirs of Miss Sidney Bidulph*, published in
1761, expanded on the point made by Aubin almost forty years before.
In this novel, the heroine and her mother make the mistake of feeling
too much sympathy for Miss Burchell, who has been seduced by the
heroine's suitor, Orlando Faulkland. They see her as an injured innocent,
but she returns treachery for their kindness. Sidney persuades Faulkland
to marry Miss Burchell in reparation of the wrongs he has done her,
but the seduced woman turns into an unfeeling wife and an adulteress.
In these novels, the woman who felt sexual desire was shown to be a
devil. The prevalence of this view meant that the seduced heroine, to
retain any authorial sympathy, must feel no desire for her seducer.
Haywood's Cleomelia might have been 'seduc'd by [her] own heavenly
Innocence, and the Force of ... Passion', but later in the century these
two could no longer be allowed to co-exist. Innocence had to include
passionlessness.

As we saw in Chapter 3, Sarah Fielding's work was strongly marked
by the woman novelist's new need to conform. One of her novels, *The
Countess of Dellwyn* (1759), is a good example of women's treatment of
the seduction theme in the new moral climate. The tradition of women's
protest runs through this work, but is compromised by the moralism of
the author's outlook.

The Countess of Dellwyn is an unusual seduction novel, because its
seduced heroine is a married woman. This reflects the age's increasing
interest in the problems of marriage. The second volume of *Pamela*
(1741), the second volume of Mary Collyer's novel *Felicia to Charlot*
(1744), and Henry Fielding's *Amelia* (1751) had already made the
problems of life *after* marriage central. In these three works, an important
question is the heroine's adjustment to the results of her husband's pre-
marital sexual lapses, or to his infidelity after marriage. In *The Countess
of Dellwyn*, however, it is the wife's infidelity that is portrayed. Sarah
Fielding was not the first novelist to write the story of a wife's adultery—
Behn, Manley and Haywood had all done this earlier; but she was the
first of the new 'moral' women writers to make this a central subject,
and the first novelist to combine the story of a woman's adultery with
a detailed study of the marital relationship that it destroys.

Sarah Fielding attributes her Countess's downfall to the mistaken
concept of marriage upheld by her father and her husband, both backed
by all the force of society's conventions. Lord Dellwyn, having ruined
his health with debauchery in youth, suddenly decides at 63 'that to
live soberly, with a virtuous young Wife, might possibly render him

more solid Happiness, than he had ever hitherto enjoyed',[18] and proposes to Miss Lucum. Her father, an unsuccessful politician who now hopes for preferment from a rich and influential son-in-law, threatens to turn her out of the house if she refuses the match, 'being perfectly convinced that if his Daughter would not be a Countess, it was very reasonable that she should be abandoned to any Misfortunes or Miseries whatsoever' (*The Countess of Dellwyn*, I, 31). Miss Lucum eventually agrees to a union she first called 'Prostitution' (I, 30), because she wants to live the life of a fine town lady. The marriage, not surprisingly, turns the couple into 'a haughty, discontented, extravagant Wife; and ... a morose, covetous, and disappointed Husband' (I, 153).

When Lady Dellwyn has an affair with the practised seducer Clermont, she is cast off by her husband, her father, and fashionable society—all of them to blame for her situation. Lord Dellwyn, disappointed in what the narrator ironically terms 'his *reasonable* Hopes of purchasing the affections of a young Beauty by his Pomp and Title' (I, 149), has no mercy on her. Mr Lucum, who ought to have 'reflected that his own Ambition had been the first Cause of his Daughter's Ruin', tells Lord Dellwyn to be as severe as he likes towards his wife if only he will remain a patron to his wife's father. Lord Dellwyn sues for divorce, and Clermont flees the country to avoid being fined for seduction. Lady Dellwyn becomes an outcast from society.

In this story everyone seems to be to blame, and Sarah Fielding's satiric vision sweeps over the whole of society. The mercenary concept of marriage is seen as a force corrupting all kinds of human relationships. Lady Dellwyn's adulterous amour has none of the dignity of a fatal passion. It is vanity, 'her first and last Seducer', not love, that makes her enjoy Clermont's admiration and eventually yield to him (II, 205). Sarah Fielding's attitude to her heroine's motivation is somewhat ambivalent. On the one hand, Lady Dellwyn is the less excusable and her affair more sordid because she does not love her seducer. She is a contemptible figure when shown 'bewailing the fatal Effects of a too tender Passion' she has never even felt (II, 207). On the other hand, it appears that vanity is less of a crime than sexual desire, and Lady Dellwyn preserves a kind of innocence because she has no passion. The remnants of her original virtue ensure that she gets no pleasure from her liaison, being constantly aware of her guilt. 'She could not film over the Odium of her own Actions, by applying to them the Words Gallantry, Intriguing, Coquetting, with many other softening Terms, ... which have been imported to *England*' (II, 50–1). Once she is cut off from husband, father, and lover, she becomes the target for men's immoral suggestions, and 'As Vanity was the only Vice that had ever actuated Lady *Dellwyn*'s mind, she felt something that bore a near Resemblance to the Indignation of Virtue itself at [an] insolent Proposal' (II, 210). Sarah Fielding adapts the seduction-tale convention of the victim's innocence. Lady Dellwyn is not innocent, but nor is she so guilty as the fashionable people around her; and that is why society singles her out for special punishment.

Unlike Manley and Haywood, Sarah Fielding does not extend sympathy to her seduced heroine. Her cool, detached, ironical narrative allows none of the sympathetic identification with the victim found when the heroine tells her own tale. This cool tone suits the didactic purpose of analysing the errors which lead the Countess to fall a prey to the world's snares. Her moral scheme is evident at all times—perhaps excessively so. Clermont, for example, seems to seduce women for the sake of providing his creator with examples in support of her warnings rather than because of his own desires:

> [He] never failed endeavouring to succeed with Ladies he liked, who
> had sacrificed willingly their Youth and Beauty to the Gratification
> of Vanity and Ambition; ... To those young Women, who, in
> marrying for interested considerations, had regard only to the
> obeying of Parents and Guardians, Lord *Clermont* seldom made any
> Addresses; apprehending that they might be actuated by Principles
> which could not possibly incline them to satisfy his Inclinations. (II, 40)

Here we see the limitations of Sarah Fielding's attack on contemporary marriage customs. Marrying for money and title, it seems, is acceptable if the motive is filial obedience. This rather spoils her attack on Mr Lucum, who would have liked such obedience in his own daughter.

Sarah Fielding's scathing satirical attacks on society are considerably weakened by many other instances of praise for obedience and subordination in women. After clearly showing why Lord Dellwyn has never deserved his wife's respect, the novelist goes on to scold her for not giving it to him, because wives ought to respect husbands in all circumstances. Her former contempt is the reason he is quick to divorce her after her affair, and Sarah Fielding draws the moral that 'Lady *Dellwyn* was a memorable Instance of the great Imprudence a Woman is guilty of, when she fails in due Respect to her Husband. If he deserves such a Treatment, the Contempt justly returns redoubled on her own Head for consenting to be the Wife of a Man she despises' (II, 161).

Though Sarah Fielding acknowledges the difficulties her female characters face in society, she does not let this affect her judgment of their conduct. This is seen in her treatment of Miss Weare, who becomes companion to the outcast Lady Dellwyn because she has no other way of making a living. An orphan, she has squandered her small inheritance on keeping up genteel appearances in the hope of getting a husband.

Having failed, she must now descend to the servant class or live with
Lady Dellwyn. Because she chooses Lady Dellwyn, people assume that
she too is an immoral woman, and Sarah Fielding points out how unfair
this is: 'the Reputations of more Women have suffered by keeping
Company with the infamous Part of their own Sex, than from any real
Guilt or Imprudence with the other' (II, 220). Yet she shows no sympathy for Miss Weare, commenting only that 'she chose rather the
Venture of blasting her Character, than the more disagreeable Alternative of relinquishing her Rank' (II, 220–1). Thus the novelist makes
trenchant criticisms of the way a woman's reputation is handled in a
world that judges, falsely, by appearances; yet blames her female characters if they do not manage to maintain the appearance of virtue. This
self-contradictory treatment of female virtue and reputation is found in
many eighteenth-century women novelists, including Fanny Burney. It
shows one of the limitations placed by moral respectability and a didactic
role on the women novelists' feminist criticisms of society.

   In *The Countess of Dellwyn* Sarah Fielding is a satirist painting a dark
picture of a society where marriage has become an exchange of old
men's wealth for young women's beauty. Her ironic gaze is turned on a
set of fashionable people bent on material gain and superficial pleasures.
Her heroine's acceptance of their values is her real downfall—seduction
is only the consequence. Though her moral stance precludes this writer
from her predecessors' defence of female desire and their sympathetic
treatment of the seduced heroine, it means that she attacks, from a
different direction, the society that makes women saleable commodities,
and she gives a chilling account of a heroine led to ruin by only the
pathetic pretence of love.

FATAL SENSIBILITY: ELIZABETH GRIFFITH'S *HISTORY OF LADY BARTON* (1771)

When sentimentalism swept into the novel in the 1760s, with it came
a new wave of sympathy for the seduced woman. Many writers, to
whom Manley and Haywood were bywords for immorality, showered
far more pity than they had done on the woman seduced and betrayed.
The difference was that as well as pitying her they marginalized her. In
the typical Haywood novel it is the heroine who is seduced, and the
narrative focuses on her experience. In the typical woman's novel in the
second half of the century, there may be a seduced woman but the
heroine herself remains pure. Sarah Fielding could still focus on the
seduced woman, because as a satirist she did not intend any sympathetic
identification with her heroine. More sentimental novelists tended to
idealize the heroine as the representative of all that was special, and

specially virtuous, in woman. Her purity could therefore not be compromised in any way, and if the trials of seduction were to be depicted they were relegated to a minor character who served as a foil to the heroine.

Women novelists, especially, needed to believe in the incorruptibility of the pure heroine. Richardson's *Clarissa* had suggested that only the example of a woman whose inner purity withstood all trials could prove that female virtue really existed; and for the woman novelist, its existence was a precondition of her writing. Only by showing it in her own life and that of her heroine could she claim the right to teach virtue in her novels, and only by teaching virtue could she claim authority at all. So from Manley's feminist analysis of men's creation and exploitation of women's innocence, women novelists turned to idealization of innate female purity.

Women novelists embraced sentimentalism while carefully avoiding the moral dangers of a creed that tended to put individual feelings above social duty. The most sentimental of their novels are full of warnings about 'French authors; blending sense into sentiment, and leading us into the worst romance, that of a heated imagination'. It was never forgotten that 'Impassion'd sentiment, is even dangerous', especially to female chastity.[19] At the same time, that belief in the vulnerability of innocence so basic to the ethos of the seduction tale, remained in evidence, and in fact was strengthened by sentimental ideas. The very novel which provides these warnings of sentiment's dangers, *The Errors of Innocence* (1786) by the novelist and schoolmistress Harriet Lee (1757–1851), offers in its title a ready-made excuse for the heroine's mistakes. But her mistakes are not those of a Charlot or a Cleomelia. Harriet Lee's heroine, Sophia Vernon, is not literally seduced by her innocence, like a Haywood heroine. Instead she is tricked into marriage with a man she cannot love, but pities because she believes him to be dying. His sudden recovery after the death-bed wedding shows to what misery compassion can lead. The heroine's friend, Lady Helen, writes to her, 'my dear, my too noble and generous friend, where has your caution slept? What fatal sensibility, what treacherous benevolence, has sacrificed you to villainy and art!' (*The Errors of Innocence*, I, 263).

The heroine's virtues have led to her misery, but not to guilt. Feminine sensibility is fatal, but not to the heroine's purity. Only in minor characters can the paradox of innocence leading to ruin appear. In 1769, the hero of Frances Brooke's *Emily Montague* reflects on women's vulnerability: 'Virtuous less from reasoning and fixed principle, than from elegance, and a lovely delicacy of mind; naturally tender ... the helpless sex are too easily seduced.'[20] However, the ideal sentimental heroine has a special way of avoiding the dangers of her delicacy and tenderness. In her, sensibility is so pure and refined a force that its spontaneous manifestations are completely in accord with the strictest

code of decorum. Emily Montague herself demonstrates this when she
speculates, from the safety of her happy betrothal to the hero, about
what would have happened if she had already been married when she
met him:

> My heart burns with the love of virtue, I am tremblingly alive to
> fame: what bitterness then must have been my portion had I first
> seen you when the wife of another!
>
> Such is the powerful sympathy that unites us, that I fear, that
> virtue, that strong sense of honor and fame, so powerful in minds
> most turned to tenderness, would only have served to make more
> poignant the pangs of hopeless, despairing love. (*Emily Montague*,
> IV, 5)

Here, the terms of passion are applied to the proprieties: concern for
her virtue and fame (i.e., reputation for chastity), rather than love,
induces burnings and tremblings in this heroine. Emily Montague is
above all a heroine of sensibility, yet her sensibility is all directed
towards virtue. The moral code, far from being a check on sensibility,
is actually its object.

This sentimental equation of virtue with feeling made unseduceable
heroines like Emily Montague and Sophia Vernon more common in
women's novels in the later decades of the century; but if seduction was
moved from the centre-stage of the novel it was often evident in its
margins. The 'lives' and 'histories' of minor characters, interpolated into
so many novels, were not really digressions or evidence of a poor grasp
of narrative structure. They were important as contrasts to the main
story and as repositories for all the problematic feminine weaknesses
purged from the picture of the ideal heroine.

Elizabeth Griffith's three novels, *The Delicate Distress* (1769), *The
History of Lady Barton* (1771) and *The Story of Lady Juliana Harley* (1773),
are all concerned with the sentimental idealization of womanhood. *Lady
Barton* shows how the cult of the pure heroine altered the seduction
novel. Like *The Countess of Dellwyn*, it is an attack on fashionable and
mercenary marriage customs. Lady Barton, like the Countess of Dellwyn,
has married a man she cannot love, and like the Countess she is partly
to blame for her situation. She agreed to marry because she was flattered
by Sir William Barton's constant attentions. She only learns what love
is when, after her marriage, she meets Lord Lucan. Her desperate cries
of protest against the bonds of marriage always return her to the same
point: her initial responsibility and the impossibility of escape:

> If passion is involuntary it cannot be criminal ... Flattering
> sophistry! Alas! I would deceive myself, but cannot! Have I not
> vowed, even at the altar vowed, to love another? Yet how can that

vow be binding, which promises what is not in our power, even at
the time we make it? But grant it were, the contract sure is mutual;
and when one fails, the other should be free.

Wretched Louisa! strive no more to varnish o'er thy faults—Thou
wert a criminal, in the first act, who wedded without love; and all
the miseries which proceed from thence, too justly are thy due.²¹

Unlike the Countess of Dellwyn, Louisa Barton is portrayed so as to
gain the reader's sympathy. This is partly because of the epistolary
method. Instead of the third-person narrative and ironical tone of Sarah
Fielding's novel, in *The History of Lady Barton* we have direct access to
the heroine's feelings through her correspondence with her sister. Moreover, that correspondence reveals that she is really in love with Lord
Lucan, unlike the Countess who errs from vanity. Most important of
all, Lady Barton for all her mistakes is a pure heroine. She remains
faithful to her husband.

The novel thus depicts one of the most affecting situations to the
sentimental mind, the situation of 'a married woman, of sensibility and
honor, who dislikes her husband' (*Emily Montague*, III, 29). It is a
common situation in sentimental novels. Sophia Vernon in *The Errors of
Innocence* suffers it, but she is eventually released by the deaths of her
husband and her true love's wife. The heroine of Charlotte Smith's novel
Desmond (1792) has similar sufferings and a similar release. For Lady
Barton, however, there is no convenient widowhood, and her love leads
to tragedy when the villainous Colonel Walter leads Sir William to
suspect his wife's virtue. Lord Lucan kills the slanderer in a duel, and
Lady Barton dies soon afterwards of 'the gentlest of decays', apparently
brought on by her predicament (*Lady Barton*, III, 294).

Lady Barton's tragic story is placed in relief by the contrasting stories
of three other women in the novel. The first is her sister and correspondent Fanny Cleveland, who responds sympathetically but firmly
to the heroine's complaints about the power of husbands, and advocates
wifely submission. She is duly rewarded at the end of the story with a
happy marriage. The author's sympathies, however, remain with her
rebellious heroine, chafing under the yoke of marriage to a misogynist
who thinks 'that women should be treated like state criminals, and
utterly debarred the use of pen and ink ... that those who are fond of
scribling [sic], are never good for any thing else; that female friendship
is a jest' (I, 2). The very form of the novel—in letters between two
women who demonstrate their worth and their mutual love through
their writing—belies Sir William and supports his wife's angry resistance.

The stories of the two other women, Olivia d'Alemberg and Maria
Colville, introduce the theme of seduction into the novel. Olivia d'Alemberg claims that she is 'ruined' because of her clandestine marriage with

Colonel Walter, who keeps her as a virtual prisoner while refusing to acknowledge her as his wife. Maria Colville's 'ruin' is more complete. Like Lady Barton, she marries one man and loves another, but unlike the heroine she yields to her passion for her lover. The different fates of these two women neatly reflect their different degrees of sexual transgression. Olivia d'Alemberg, innocent if foolish victim of male treachery, escapes to Fanny Cleveland's house with Lady Barton's help. Maria Colville's affair ends with her lover's death and her own retreat into a convent: she dies soon afterwards. When Lady Barton hears Maria's story, her comment spells out its moral: 'Maria was certainly more wretched than I am, by the addition of one circumstance'—namely, the guilt of adultery (III, 248–9).

Unlike Sarah Fielding, Elizabeth Griffith indicates that she has every sympathy with her seduced woman. Maria's mother is made to blame herself for encouraging her daughter's mercenary match. 'I respected the opinions of the world, more than the philosophy of nature', she admits (III, 106–7). The adulterous lovers, who were ideally suited according to 'the philosophy of nature', and who were parted by underhand means before Maria's marriage, are both presented as victims. However, Griffith gives the story of the seduced woman only a marginal position in the novel. She is a warning to the heroine, instead of being the heroine herself.

Elizabeth Griffith, like many of the women who wrote sentimental novels in the late eighteenth century, was self-consciously a champion of her own sex. In her letters to her future husband she contended that 'Souls are not of different genders: Therefore, in the metaphysical nature of the question, your sex has, originally, no advantage over our's'. Differences in male and female intelligence she ascribed to differences in education, writing 'it is as unfair to censure us for the weakness of our understandings as it would be to blame the Chinese women for little feet; for neither is owing to the imperfection of nature, but to the constraint of custom'.[22] In her last novel, *Lady Juliana Harley*, she puts similar arguments into the letters of her hero and his friend. In *Lady Barton*, Griffith's feminist consciousness is evident in her sympathetic portrayal of the heroine's dilemma when she finds she loves Lord Lucan (who has a high opinion of women) and not her tyrannical woman-hating husband. Yet her sentimental idealization of feminine purity prevents her from carrying her feminist arguments very far. Her defence of women is based on her insistence on woman's virtue; and to prove her virtue the heroine must not only remain faithful to her husband but obedient to him; must stifle her feelings of rebelliousness; and finally, must fade gracefully away into early death. The argument that women's natural virtue proved their right to a better position in society tended to rebound very rapidly on the woman who professed it. Virtue involved not only chastity, but by implication, submissiveness and self-abnegation. True feminine sensibility, according to the heroine of *The Errors of Innocence*, meant a sensibility for *others*, never for oneself, and was thus to be distinguished from the potentially more dangerous quality, 'feeling'. 'By sensibility I understand a certain tender sympathy of disposition, which tho' originally deriv'd from the passions, is meliorated into somewhat gentler and more pleasing than those, whilst feeling is that quick sense of insult or injury which is exerted rather for ourselves than for others'. No wonder that Janetta Sutherland, a character described as having 'a good deal of feeling, [but] little sensibility', becomes the villainess of this novel (*The Errors of Innocence*, I, 46). She rebels against her husband's authority, and commits adultery. This is the dire consequence of having feeling for herself. The ideal heroine with her pure sensibility proved that women deserved more rights: but she would never claim them.

RADICALISM AND THE NOVEL OF SEDUCTION

By the end of the 1780s, women novelists were beginning a new feminist revision of the seduction tale. Women's criticisms of the sentimental ideal of woman's passionless purity were developed, paradoxically, within the sentimental tradition. Because one aspect of sentimentalism had always been its championing of the individual's impulses against the inflexible rules of society, its premises could lead to the support of sexual freedom, which was why sentimental women novelists like Frances Brooke and Harriet Lee took care to give their heroines a sensibility inclined towards strict morality, and to warn against the dangers of impassioned sentiment. During the 1780s, as the more subversive aspects of sentimentalism gained some ground in England, amid a generally liberal political climate in which the individual's right to personal liberty was much discussed, some women novelists offered a different sentimental message. Charlotte Smith, whose sympathy with radical political ideas is evident in many of her novels, offered a reconsideration of the seduction theme in *Emmeline*, the novel which brought her fame in 1788.

Emmeline is a work which demonstrates how women writers' various responses to women's situation could be interwoven in the novel. This story of the 'Orphan of the Castle', deprived of her rightful inheritance and social status, who is pursued by the hot-headed Delamere but eventually marries a worthier man, will be discussed further in Chapter 5. As far as the theme of seduction is concerned, it is not *Emmeline*'s story that is important, but the subplot concerning Lady Adelina Trelawny. The heroine and her friend Mrs Stafford meet Adelina when she is pregnant by her lover, Fitz-Edward, and in hiding from both him and her husband. Smith's treatment of Adelina is unusual, not only for the unprecedented extent of authorial sympathy with an adulteress, but for the happy ending which is allowed to follow her adultery. However, like Elizabeth Griffith before her, Charlotte Smith has a pure sentimental heroine and places the seduced woman in a marginal position in her novel.

Adelina's story contains many mitigating circumstances. She was over-persuaded into marriage when too young to judge properly for herself. 'I married him', she explains, 'and gave away my person before I knew I had an heart'.[23] Her husband turned out to be a boor and a wastrel, and it was her lover only who awakened her tender sensibilities. The husband, in fact, is practically held responsible for driving Adelina into Fitz-Edward's arms. 'In my husband', she tells Emmeline, 'I had neither a friend or a companion—I had not even a protector' (*Emmeline*, p. 216). Fitz-Edward, on the other hand, proved his love by caring for her during a stormy sea-crossing when her husband was in a drunken stupor. When her husband fled to France to avoid his creditors, Adelina found herself 'Thrown ... wholly into the power of Fitz-Edward; loving him but too well; and seeing him every hour busied in serving me ... I could not summon resolution to fly from him' (pp. 221–2). Adelina proves herself not really ruined by this one error by the extravagance of her repentance. She refuses to see Fitz-Edward or even name him once her story is finished, though she admits to Emmeline and Mrs Stafford that she still loves him. Only her love for her illegitimate baby reconciles her to life at all. The heroine gives both sympathy and practical help, not afraid of risking her own reputation in order to care for Adelina and her baby.

Adelina's chief fear is that her brother, Godolphin, will want to vindicate family honour by killing her lover. Godolphin has to learn from Emmeline that there are kinder and more useful things to do in this situation, namely to forgive and protect Adelina and adopt her child. The relationship between Godolphin and the heroine, begun through their joint care of a 'ruined' woman, eventually leads to happy union. Meanwhile Adelina's husband dies, and at the end of the novel Smith makes it clear that the adulteress is going to marry her lover and regain a place in society.

It is a mark of the general liberalism of the 1780s that this novel could be as highly praised as it was. However, Charlotte Smith did take care to make her radical treatment of adultery acceptable to her public by lavishly endowing her female characters with a feminine sensibility that blurred all their errors. One reviewer thought that Adelina, Emmeline and Mrs Stafford all had 'characters equally amiable and soft', and another called the novel 'simple, femininely beautiful and chaste'.[24] There was, however, some criticism of Smith's sentimental sympathy for a woman giving way to her passions. It came from Mary Woll-stonecraft, who, reviewing *Emmeline* in the *Analytical Review*, called Adel-ina 'a character as absurd as dangerous', whose adulterous passion, followed by extravagant despair, contrasted with the praiseworthy 'rational resignation' shown in the character of Mrs Stafford, who, 'when disappointed in her husband, turned to her children' instead of to romance.[25]

Wollstonecraft's hostility is an early indication of the feminist critique of feminine sensibility which Chapter 3 showed to be important in her *Vindication of the Rights of Woman* a few years later. By appealing to reason instead of feeling, Wollstonecraft was at one with the other leading radical thinkers of her day. Soon after *Emmeline* was written and reviewed, the French Revolution of 1789 excited widespread support among English progressives, including both Smith and Wollstonecraft. In the years immediately following, the political debate in England was sharpened as Edmund Burke attacked the French Revolution and his opponents, as well as defending it, developed far-reaching proposals for social reform at home. Thomas Paine's *Rights of Man* (1791–2) and William Godwin's *Political Justice* (1793) were the fruits of these years, as was Wollstonecraft's work on the rights of woman. These early promulgators of democratic ideas argued their case on the basis of the concept of 'right reason', rather than appealing to the radical possibilities of sentimentalism, a movement now widely distrusted. Some radical thinkers began to develop their ideas about reason and reform in the novel, already a didactic form and at this time a polemical one. Robert Bage expressed radical ideas in *Hermsprong* (1796). Thomas Holcroft, who progressed from stable-boy to shoemaker to strolling player to writer, became an important radical novelist with *Anna St. Ives* (1792) and *Hugh Trevor* (1794–7). Godwin also moved into the novel with *Caleb Williams* (1794).[26]

In the novels written in the 1790s by women sympathetic to the radical position, including Elizabeth Inchbald, Mary Hays, and Mary Wollstonecraft, revolutionary political ideas were interwoven with themes inherited from the long tradition of protest in women's novels. Because of this, the feminist analysis of seduction was enriched in their hands; and they avoided what has been seen as the radical novelists' especial shortcoming, an inadequate attention to the liberating possi-bilities of feeling. If the reasoning radicals, in Marilyn Butler's words, 'refused to exploit sexual passion as a powerful natural ally against a moribund society and its repressive conventions',[27] the criticism does not apply to Wollstonecraft's *Wrongs of Woman*; while Inchbald and Hays, if less revolutionary in their treatment of sexuality, still made advances in their revisions of the tale of seduction.

ELIZABETH INCHBALD'S *NATURE AND ART* (1796)

Elizabeth Inchbald (1753–1821), a farmer's daughter who began her career as an actress, turned to writing plays in the 1780s. Her skills are evident in her two novels, *A Simple Story* (1791), which will be discussed in Chapter 5, and *Nature and Art* (1796).

This second novel is remarkable for its dramatic rendering of the feminist point that men destroy women's chastity and then mete out punishment for its loss. William forgets his early love for Hannah Primrose, a cottager's daughter whom he left pregnant, and while he rises in the world to become a judge, she sinks into prostitution, theft, and forgery. Eventually, the man ultimately responsible for all her crimes is the one to pass sentence on them, and he does not even recognize her as he condemns her to death. The trial-scene gains power from the restrained simplicity of Inchbald's style. She reports the judge's well-meant endeavours to help the criminal: '"Recollect yourself—have you no witnesses? No proof in your behalf?" A dead silence followed these questions'.[28] Hannah's silence speaks eloquently of the innocence and the guilt which cannot be explained in court.

MARY HAYS'S *THE VICTIM OF PREJUDICE* (1799)

Mary Hays (1760–1843) went further than Inchbald in developing a feminist analysis of social institutions in her two novels, *Memoirs of Emma Courtney* (1796) and *The Victim of Prejudice* (1799). Hays, an admirer of Wollstonecraft's *Vindication of the Rights of Woman* and of Godwin's *Political Justice*, wrote her fiction to express her political ideas. She especially criticized feminine education for making women weak and too concerned with sensibility. The situation of *Emma Courtney*, in which the heroine pursues the unresponsive hero, Augustus Harley, with declarations of love, while another man, a rational radical philosopher, tries to argue her out of her enslavement to passion, illustrates women's difficulties in embracing the 'new philosophy' of reason. It was based on an episode in the author's own life, in which the part of the reasoning philosopher was played by her friend William Godwin. Emma Courtney's offer (never accepted) to live with Augustus Harley outside marriage, because, she tells him, '*the individuality of an affection constitutes its chastity*', made the novel and its author bywords for immorality, despite Hays's careful claim that her heroine's story was meant 'as a *warning*, rather than as an example'.[29]

Emma, for all her desires, remains a chaste woman, and it was in her second novel that Hays tackled the question of seduction, tracing its consequences over two generations. In the first generation, Mary is seduced, abandoned by her lover, and rejected by her parents. Soon she has no alternative but prostitution, and eventually she is condemned to death for her part in a tavern brawl that leads to murder. Her summary of her career, written just before her execution, makes it clear that Hays blames Mary's plight on the whole range of social institutions:

> The despotism of man rendered me weak, his vices betrayed me into shame, a barbarous policy stifled returning dignity, prejudice robbed me of the means of independence, gratitude ensnared me in the devices of treachery, the contagion of example corrupted my heart, despair hardened and brutality rendered it cruel. A sanguinary policy precludes reformation, defeating the dear-bought lessons of experience, and, by a legal process, assuming the arm of omnipotence, annihilates the being whom its negligence left destitute, and its institutions compelled to offend.[30]

The heroine of the story is Mary's illegitimate daughter, also called Mary. Left by her mother to be brought up by an old friend, benevolent Mr Raymond, Mary is educated to be hardy, self-reliant, and free in spirit. Not until she has fallen in love with William, one of her benefactor's pupils, does she learn that, as Mr Raymond tells her, 'In the eye of the world, the misfortunes of your birth stain your unsullied youth', and that William's father will never allow him to marry her (*The Victim of Prejudice*, I, 171).

The belief that illegitimacy is a stain is the first prejudice which causes trouble for Mary. Another is the resistance to a genteel young woman's attempts to earn her living. When she is raped by Sir Peter Osborne, yet another prejudice dooms her. She threatens legal proceedings, but he points out how difficult it is for a rape victim to get justice, in words that still have relevance now: 'Who will credit the tale you mean to tell? What testimony or witnesses can you produce that will not make against you? Where are your resources to sustain the vexations and delay of a suit of law, which you so wildly threaten? Who would support you against my wealth and influence? How would your delicacy shrink from the idea of becoming, in open court, the sport of ribaldry, the theme of obscene jesters?' (II, 85–6). When she demands to be freed, he explains to her what her 'ruin' will mean if she leaves him. 'What is called, in your sex, honour and character, can, I fear, never be restored to you; nor will any asseverations or future watchfulness (to adopt the cant of policy and superstition) obliterate the stain' (II, 85). She determines to 'seek, by honest labour, the bread of independence' (II, 87); but he warns her, 'your heroic sentiments will, I suspect, prove but a feeble support' (II, 88).

Sir Peter is right. *The Victim of Prejudice* is a study of the obstacles in the way of female independence, the ideal that animated Wollstonecraft in *The Rights of Woman*. After further troubles, including two years in debtors' prison, Mary's health is ruined and she anticipates an early death. Her last message to the reader is:

> From the fate of my wretched mother, (in which, alas! my own has been involved,) let [man] learn, that, while the slave of sensuality, inconsistent as assuming, he pours, by *his conduct*, contempt upon chastity, in vain will he impose upon *woman* barbarous penalties, or seek to multiply restrictions; his seductions and example, yet more powerful, will defeat his precepts, of which *hypocrisy*, not virtue, is the genuine fruit. (II, 231)

Mary is as thorough a victim as any Manley or Haywood heroine. The main difference between Hays's portrayal and theirs is the fruit of 1790s radicalism: Hays is explicit in tracing the heroine's wrongs to social causes, and makes an open attack on male dominance and the oppressive ideology of natural female chastity.

MARY WOLLSTONECRAFT'S *MARIA: OR THE WRONGS OF WOMAN* (1798)

The most far-reaching of the feminist renderings of the seduction tale was Mary Wollstonecraft's second novel, unfortunately left unfinished at the author's death in 1797, and published posthumously in 1798. Mary Hays attacked the 'too-great stress laid on the *reputation* for chastity in *woman*' (*The Victim of Prejudice*, Advertisement), but, forewarned by the criticisms that had been made of her after *Emma Courtney*, she was very careful not to show disrespect for chastity in itself. Mary Wollstonecraft, on the other hand, defended a heroine who acknowledged and acted upon her own sexual desires, in defiance of her marriage vows. This was far more shocking in the late eighteenth century than it would have been earlier, when Manley and Haywood were creating their heroines brought to ruin by the power of love. Wollstonecraft went much further than her contemporaries in defiance of sexual mores. In *Emmeline* Charlotte Smith had allowed her adulteress, Adelina, to be forgiven, but Wollstonecraft denied that her adulteress, Maria, had committed any crime. She also went much further than earlier novelists in the tradition of protest, by criticizing not only the seducer and the social ostracism of his victim, but the very definition of seduction.

Obviously Wollstonecraft's ideas had changed remarkably since she

had criticized Charlotte Smith for creating Adelina; yet from the beginning of her career she had felt a conflict between the radicals' faith in
reason and the women's tradition of defending their sex through praising
sensibility. Her first novel, *Mary, a Fiction*—published in the same year
as *Emmeline*—purported to describe a heroine of unusual 'thinking
powers', but she actually created the portrait of a woman more remarkable for her powers of feeling.[31] In *A Vindication of the Rights of Woman*,
she had suppressed sensibility and seen reason as the ideal, with the
result that her vision of liberation did not include any liberation of
sexuality. On the contrary, she deprecated all idea of sexual fulfilment:

> In order to fulfil the duties of life … a master and mistress of a
> family ought not to continue to love each other with passion. … I
> will go still further, and advance … that an unhappy marriage is
> often very advantageous to a family, and that the neglected wife is,
> in general, the best mother. *And this would almost always be the
> consequence if the female mind were more enlarged* … (*Rights of Woman*,
> p. 114; my italics)

A woman contemplating this projected outcome of her emancipation
might well exclaim, with Wollstonecraft's first heroine, 'have I desires
implanted in me only to make me miserable?'[32]

Between *The Rights of Woman* and *The Wrongs of Woman*, Wollstonecraft
had turned back to her earlier consideration of the importance of feeling
and sexuality. Her movement away from the position of *The Rights of
Woman* reflects the loss of revolutionary optimism in the later 1790s—
difficult years for the English radicals, when it no longer appeared that
reasoning would lead to immediate reform. However, the particular
impetus for Wollstonecraft's reassessment of her ideas came from events
in her personal life during the intervening years: her affair, in Revolutionary France, with Gilbert Imlay, who deserted her not long after
the birth of their daughter, her subsequent suicide attempts, and her
liaison with Godwin, whom she married when she became pregnant
again. These experiences, revealed by Godwin in his *Memoirs of Mary
Wollstonecraft*, written and published soon after she died from complications following her second childbirth, were long considered the
only refutation needed of her feminist arguments. Wollstonecraft had
abandoned the woman writer's respectable role with a vengeance. Today,
however, we can see that it was after losing her respectability that she
was able to explore the problems of feminine sensibility in a way that
the earlier female sentimentalists could not. Without abandoning her
feminist analysis of artificial sensibility, she developed a revolutionary
view of sexuality which she expressed in her second novel.

Maria: or, The Wrongs of Woman really has two heroines: Maria, who

has been confined in a madhouse by the husband who married her for
her money, and her wardress Jemima, who has come to her present
employment after a life of poverty, servitude and prostitution. The stories
of the two women thus show 'the wrongs of different classes of women,
equally oppressive, though, from the difference of education, necessarily
various'.[33] The friendship which grows up between Maria and Jemima
is the most positive value within the world of the novel. Instead of using
the seduced woman as a foil to an unfallen heroine, Wollstonecraft
makes a point of the connections between two women labelled by
society as irreconcilably alien to one another—one a pure woman, one
a prostitute.

Wollstonecraft goes on to attack the ideal of feminine purity itself,
and makes this novel the most radical of seduction tales by challenging
the very term 'seduction'. In the madhouse Maria falls in love with
Darnford, a young man who is also wrongly imprisoned. With Jemima's
help the lovers escape to start a new life together, but then Maria
discovers that the relationship she entered freely is construed in law as
a seduction for which her lover has to pay damages to her husband. In
a paper she writes to be read out in court, she protests against the
attempt to incriminate Darnford, pointing out that she was 26 when
she left her husband, and adding, 'if ever I am to be supposed to arrive
at an age to direct my own actions, I must by that time have arrived
at it.—I acted with deliberation' (*The Wrongs of Woman*, pp. 197–8).
Jemima's very different experience is used to make a similar point. She
was not seduced, but raped, and she remarks sardonically, 'I have since
read in novels of the blandishments of seduction, but I had not even
the pleasure of being enticed into vice' (p. 109). In each case the
woman's experience has been ignored by a society that prefers one neat
label for all illicit sexual activity.

The novel boldly vindicates its heroine's recognition of her sexuality.
Maria declares, 'When novelists or moralists praise as a virtue, a woman's coldness of constitution, and want of passion ... I am disgusted. ...
we cannot, without depraving our minds, endeavour to please a lover
or husband, but in proportion as he pleases us. Men, more effectually
to enslave us, may inculcate this partial morality ... but let us not blush
for nature without a cause!' (p. 153). Her decision to allow her feelings
to influence her life is a rebellion against all society's views of womanhood, as the judge in the adultery trial makes clear:

> The judge, in summing up the evidence, alluded to 'the fallacy of
> letting women plead their feelings, as an excuse for the violation of
> the marriage-vow. ... if women were allowed to plead their feelings,
> as an excuse or palliation of infidelity, it was opening a flood-gate

for immorality. What virtuous woman thought of her feelings? (pp. 198–9)

Wollstonecraft reveals that contradiction at the heart of the sentimental idealization of womanhood which is embodied by heroines like Brooke's Emily Montague and Harriet Lee's Sophia Vernon. 'Feeling', said to be woman's distinctive and most wonderful attribute, is only condoned when it leads to self-renunciation and a stifling of natural instinct. When feeling is in conflict with conventional morality, society's deep suspicion of women ('What virtuous woman thought of her feelings?') is revealed.

At the same time as defending her heroine's right to a sexual life, Wollstonecraft portrays Maria's love of Darnford as a romantic folly, the product of confinement and too much sentimental literature. This is not only evident from the notes the author left about the ending of the novel, which show that Darnford was to have proved unfaithful, but is implicit in the lovers' relationship from the outset. After her first glimpse of Darnford in the asylum gardens, Maria turns to Rousseau's *La Nouvelle Héloise*, and models her idea of the unknown man on the tender hero, St Preux. Even before she sees him, the marginal notes he has written in some books he sends her have made her half in love with him. She is annoyed with herself for thinking of him so much, but excuses herself by reflecting on 'the little objects which attract attention when there is nothing to divert the mind; and how difficult it was for women to avoid growing romantic, who have no active duties or pursuits' (p. 87). Here, the heroine's tendency to fall into romantic idealization is linked to women's general condition, as *The Rights of Woman* had argued. Maria's imprisonment is a metaphor for women's situation in a world that is 'a vast prison, and all women born slaves' (p. 79). The novel, then, is both a feminist analysis of the construction of an oppressive notion of 'feminine sensibility', and a defence of the heroine's right to physical love, one of the consequences of true sensibility.

Wollstonecraft defended feeling not just for the sake of her heroine's sexual life but because she saw feeling as the necessary instrument of female liberation. If feminine sensibility was an oppressive social construct, true feeling was a positive womanly quality and the hope for the future. Early in her imprisonment, Maria realizes that there are two possible reactions to her (and by implication all women's) condition: sorrow 'must blunt or sharpen the faculties to the two opposite extremes; producing stupidity, the moping melancholy of indolence; or the restless activity of a disturbed imagination' (p. 79). The second of these is the danger threatening Maria, while Jemima, her emotions stifled by her horrific experiences, suffers from the first. The nadir of her brutalization occurred when she added to the wrongs of woman by persuading her new lover to turn his pregnant mistress out of the house, thus driving the girl to suicide. But Jemima's 'humanity had rather been benumbed than killed, by the keen frost she had to brave at her entrance into life' (p. 120), and the story of Maria's sufferings 'touched her heart' (p. 79). It is when she hears that Maria's child was torn from her breast that 'the woman awoke in a bosom long estranged from feminine emotions' and she is redeemed through feeling (p. 80). *The Wrongs of Woman* turns all the assumptions of the seduction tale upside-down, and within its keen analysis of women's imprisonment within patriarchy is an optimistic vision of liberation through the feeling that in most seduction tales leads to ruin.

Wollstonecraft and Hays, with their bold revisions of the tale of seduction, opened up new possibilities for the novel, but the years that followed were not to see the realization of the new potential. In England, the conservative reaction against radicalism, a strong force since the 1793 declaration of war between England and Revolutionary France, and subsequent Government suppression of English 'Jacobins', continued into the early years of the nineteenth century.[34] After the turn of the century, radical protest practically disappeared from the novel. Attacks on Wollstonecraft and Hays, however, did not rise simply because of a change in political climate. In their treatment of sexuality they had in any case gone further than other radical thinkers, and they were attacked not just as radicals but as women. Their critics seemed to feel that the shades of Manley and Haywood were rising again. The *Critical Review* attacked Hays for arousing 'the contagious and consuming fever of perverted sensibility', and carefully distinguished, yet again, between the respectable and the unrespectable woman writer. 'The writings of a [Hannah] More, [an Anna Laetitia] Barbauld, and a [Jane] West, are monuments of well-directed genius, and will be deservedly admired when all the impassioned imitations of Rousseau and Diderot shall cease to be remembered'.[35] By the time *The Wrongs of Woman* was published, Wollstonecraft's liaison with Gilbert Imlay, and her illegitimate daughter, were public knowledge. Wollstonecraft was openly attacked for 'concubinage', and once again the connection between her life and her writing was used against a woman writer. Wollstonecraft was condemned because 'she lived and acted, as she wrote and taught'.[36] Not surprisingly, then, her novel was not well received. Her defence of Maria's adultery was 'repugnant to religion, sense, and decency',[37] and it was pronounced 'better to persuade [women] to submit to some inconveniencies, than to encourage them to break down all the barriers of social virtue'.[38]

Wollstonecraft eschewed respectability in her life and her writing, and her reputation was shadowed for over a century because of this. The position the woman writer had won by becoming a respectable spokes-woman for bourgeois morality was soon lost if she strayed from that role. *The Victim of Prejudice* and *The Wrongs of Woman* now stand out as maverick productions of a short-lived revolutionary era, and the mainstream of the English novel refused to draw such radical impli-cations from the old story of seduction and betrayal. When, over 50 years later, Elizabeth Gaskell made an unmarried mother the central figure of her novel *Ruth* (1853), she forgave rather than vindicated her heroine's lapse, and still her novel aroused strong reactions of disgust from some.

The women novelists' protest against unfair sexual conventions ran an uneven course during the century. In the early years erotic seduction-scenes caught popular taste, and were used by Manley and Haywood to criticize masculine attitudes. Later, as greater refinement in bourgeois society required greater delicacy of novelists and their heroines, erotic scenes were dropped and heroines remained unsullied. Seduction was relegated to the margins, to be re-centralized and treated more radically by the revolutionary writers at the end of the century. Women novelists shaped the development of the seduction tale through all these changes. Their feminist message was often compromised, especially in the late-century sentimental novel, by the convention of natural feminine inno-cence. Yet by criticizing mercenary marriage, parental pressure on the daughter's choice, the double standard, and the equation of a woman's virtue with her reputation, they contributed to a tradition of protest which remained alive, though subdued, after the eclipse of the more radical analyses offered by the feminists at the end of the century.

NOTES

1. *An Essay in Defence of the Female Sex* (London, 1696), p. 11; Mary Astell, *Reflections upon Marriage*, 3rd edn (London, 1706), p. 27.
2. 'Sophia', who has never been satisfactorily identified, wrote another pamphlet, *Woman's Superior Excellence over Men* (1740), a rejoinder to *Man Superior to Woman*, which appeared in response to her first essay in 1739. The three works were collected and published together as *Beauty's Triumph* (1751). It has been pointed out that 'Sophia' uses the arguments of a seventeenth-century feminist work: Poulain de la Barre's *De L'Egalité des deux Sexes* (1672) which was translated into English in 1677. See Florence M. Smith, *Mary Astell* (New York: Columbia University Press, 1916), p. 177. For the feminist ideas in Lady Mary Wortley Montagu's *The Nonsense of Common-Sense*, nos 2 and 6, see Robert Halsband, *The Life of Lady Mary Wortley Montagu* (Oxford: Clarendon Press, 1957), pp. 166–8. Lady Mary,

as Halsband points out (p. 117), was acquainted with Mary Astell, who gave her a copy of her *Serious Proposal to the Ladies*.

3. Boswell, *Life of Johnson*, ed. R. W. Chapman, corr. J. D. Fleeman (Oxford University Press paperback, 1976), p. 393.

4. John Gregory, *A Father's Legacy to his Daughters* (Dublin: Thomas Ewing and Caleb Jenkin, 1774), pp. 46–7.

5. *The Autobiography and Correspondence of Mary Granville*, Mrs. Delany, ed. Lady Llanover (London: R. Bentley, 1861), **I**, p. 24; and letter to Mrs Dewes, 16 March 1751, in *Autobiography and Correspondence*, **III**, p. 25.

6. *A Serious Proposal to the Ladies, for the Advancement of their True and Greatest Interest*. Part **I**. 3rd edn (London: R. Wilkin, 1696), pp. 99–100.

7. *Clarissa Harlowe* (London: Everyman, 1982) **I**, Letter XVII, p. 83, and Letter XVI, p. 74.

8. This point has been made by Susan Staves in her article 'British Seduced Maidens', *Eighteenth-Century Studies* **14** (1980–1), pp. 109–34: 'the pretty young girl who is seduced usually finally falls *because* she is simple, trusting, and affectionate. Although the culture laments her fall, the eighteenth century was quite certain it did not want young girls to be knowing, suspicious, or hardhearted' (p. 118).

9. Eliza Haywood, *Cleomelia: or, the Generous Mistress* (London, 1727), p. 36.

10. See John J. Richetti, *Popular Fiction Before Richardson*, p. 208.

11. It is based on the Earl of Portland's seduction of Stuarta Howard; and other seductions in *The New Atalantis* are based on well-known contemporary cases. See Köster, pp. vi–vii.

12. A Count in *The New Atalantis* says 'Courage we see in-born to many, whilst Chastity must be acquir'd, because it moves directly against the prior Law of Nature' (**I**, p. 145). Intelligence suggests that he has ulterior motives for this speech, but Astrea commends him. The claim that chastity is not numbered among the virtues is at **I**, p. 210.

13. This was a subject of interest to Manley and her contemporaries: several women in fiction are seduced or sexually assaulted by their fathers or father substitutes. Manley's story of Delia is one example, and another is found in Jane Barker's *Exilius* (2nd edn, London, 1719) where Turpius tries to rape his daughter Clarinthia (**I**, pp. 28–31).

14. Richetti, pp. 8, 162.

15. *The British Recluse: or, the Secret History of Cleomira, Suppos'd Dead*. 2nd edn (London, 1722), p. 77.

16. The hero of Frances Brooke's *Emily Montague* observes that among the Huron Indians the women choose the chief, and suggests that it would be a good idea if European women could vote for their rulers (**I**, pp. 67–9).

17. *Charlotta du Pont*, in Aubin, *Collection*, **III**, p. 17.

18. Sarah Fielding, *The History of the Countess of Dellwyn* (London: A. Millar, 1759), **I**, pp. 16–17.

19. Harriet Lee, *The Errors of Innocence* (London, 1786), **III**, p. 185.

20. *Emily Montague*, **IV**, p. 16.

21. Elizabeth Griffith, *The History of Lady Barton*, 2nd edn (London, 1773) **II**, pp. 108–09.

22. *A Series of Genuine Letters Between Henry and Frances*, 3rd edn (London, 1767), **I**, p. 44, and **I**, p. 47.

23. *Emmeline, or the Orphan of the Castle*, ed. A. H. Ehrenpreis (London: Oxford University Press, 1971), p. 213.

24. *Critical Review* **65** (1788), p. 531; *Monthly Review* **79** (1788), p. 242.

25. *Analytical Review* **I** (1788), p. 333. Wollstonecraft wrote reviews for the *Analytical* from 1788–92, and from early 1796 until her death in 1797. Her work was initialled M, W, or T: some of it was probably unsigned. See R. M. Wardle, 'Mary Wollstonecraft, *Analytical* Reviewer', *PMLA* **62** (1947), pp. 1000–9, and Derek Roper, 'Mary Wollstonecraft's Reviews', *Notes and Queries* **203**, n.s. 5 (1958), pp. 37–8.

26. Valuable discussions of these novelists are to be found in Marilyn Butler, *Jane Austen and the War of Ideas* (Oxford: Clarendon Press, 1975) and Gary Kelly, *The English Jacobin Novel* (Oxford: Clarendon Press, 1976).

27. Butler, pp. 44–5.

28. *Nature and Art* (London, 1796), **II**, p. 141.

29. *Memoirs of Emma Courtney* (London, 1796), **I**, Preface, p. 8, **II**, p. 65.

30. *The Victim of Prejudice* (London, 1799), **I**, pp. 167–8.

31. Advertisement to *Mary*; in *Mary* and *The Wrongs of Woman*, ed. Gary Kelly (Oxford University Press, 1980), n. pag.

32. *Mary*, p. 40.

33. *Maria: or, The Wrongs of Woman*, in *Mary* and *The Wrongs of Woman*, ed. Kelly, Author's Preface, p. 74.

34. For discussions of the repression of radicals see Carl B. Cone, *The English Jacobins* (New York, 1968), J. Ann Hone, *For the Cause of Truth: Radicalism in London, 1796–1821* (Oxford, 1982), and E. P. Thompson, *The Making of the English Working Class* (London, 1963).

35. *Critical Review*, 2nd ser. **26** (1799), pp. 451, 452.

36. *Anti-Jacobin Review and Magazine*, **I** (1798), pp. 97, 93.

37. *Critical Review*, 2nd ser. **22** (1798), p. 419.

38. *Monthly Review*, New Series **27** (1798), p. 326.

5
Reformed Heroines:
The Didactic Tradition

INTRODUCTION: THE CENTRAL WOMEN'S TRADITION

When Eliza Haywood's *History of Miss Betsy Thoughtless* was published in 1751, it prompted Ralph Griffith, assessing the novel in his *Monthly Review*, to ponder on the problem of feminocentric plots. The novel, he explained, was

> the history of a young inconsiderate girl, whose little foibles, without any natural vices of the mind, involve her in difficulties and distresses, which, by correcting, make her wiser, and deservedly happy in the end. A heroine like this, cannot but lay an author under much disadvantage. ... [It is a] barren foundation [for a novel].[1]

His bemusement was understandable at a time when the accepted notion of female character was static. The lustful women in bawdy stories, or the tragic women in Haywood's own seduction stories, were acceptable enough as fictional foundations. Even better was a woman like Henry Fielding's Amelia, whose story was enthusiastically reviewed in the same periodical a few months later: a 'model of female perfection, formed to give the greatest and justest idea of domestic happiness'.[2] But what sort of story could be written about Haywood's Betsy, who was neither interesting tragic victim nor model of perfection? A mixed character was all very well in a young man, and *Tom Jones* had recently brought the fallible but good-hearted hero into prominence. A female Tom Jones, however, could not be allowed his sexual adventures if she was to be the heroine of any but a totally immoral novel; and if 'vices' were avoided and only 'foibles' remained, the novel seemed to be left without a strong focus of interest, without an adequate framework.

The only explanation the baffled reviewer could give for the strengths of *Betsy Thoughtless* was that a poor subject had been enlivened by a talented writer. The novel was published anonymously but its authorship seems to have been an open secret, and having hinted at the writer's identity, Griffith suggested that 'no other hand would, probably, have more happily finish'd a work begun on such a plan' as the one described.[3] To us, with our knowledge of the novel after Haywood, this judgment is so obviously mistaken as to be comic. For the 'barren' history he outlined fits not only the plot of *Betsy Thoughtless* but the pattern of Jane Austen's *Emma*; while the feminine characterization that seemed to him so disadvantageous to the novelist produced, in Austen's Elizabeth Bennet, one of the best-loved heroines in English literature.

Betsy Thoughtless and novels like it brought about a crucial shift in the novel's presentation of women, from the stasis of perfection or villainy to the dynamics of character change. Heroines who made mistakes about the choice of friends, about reading matter, about lovers and love—in short about the young woman's place in the world—became standard in the late eighteenth century. From Charlotte Lennox's Female Quixote, deluded by romance, to Jane Austen's Catherine Morland, deluded by the gothic novel, from *Evelina* to *Camilla*, heroines amused and charmed the reader with their little foibles, involved themselves in comic and serious difficulties and distresses, were corrected, and earned their happiness. The reviewer of *Betsy Thoughtless* had unwittingly outlined the paradigm of the central female tradition in the eighteenth-century novel.

Burney and Austen are usually seen as the heirs of Richardson and Fielding, and it is true that they and other women writers used both these authors. Their pictures of the minutiae of domestic life drew on *Sir Charles Grandison*, their ironic narrative voice on Fielding's novels. However, in the development of this key character-type—the mistaken heroine who reforms—they were following a tradition begun by women and almost exclusive to them. Fielding, Smollett, and most other male novelists concentrated on the hero's education and made the heroine a static image of goodness. Richardson, who being close to the female tradition is too often taken to be its source, created mistaken but reform-worthy female characters in Anna Howe and Charlotte Grandison, but he did not make them the focus of his plots. His heroines are Pamela, the exemplar of unswerving if naive virtue, and Clarissa, the near-paragon. Harriet Byron, his third heroine, is nearest to the women novelists' type, for she has to undergo a moral and sentimental education before earning her happiness; but though she is a young lady entering the world she does not make Evelina's kind of naive mistakes, and though she needs to mature by expanding her sympathies and emulating her perfect lover, she does not need fundamentally to change her outlook as Emma does. Burney's and Austen's concern with educating and reforming the heroine has its roots elsewhere.

Those roots are in the woman novelist's accepted role and the tradition that had arisen because of it. As we have seen, it was as a teacher that the 'respectable' woman novelist found an acknowledged place in literary discourse. Ideally, from the moralist's point of view, the novel could serve as a kind of dramatized conduct book for young women. Such a novel could be written by drawing an exemplary heroine for the reader to imitate; but less flattering to the young female's proverbial vanity was the erring heroine. Her errors could not be too grave, and must not include the great error, unchastity, especially considering the perennial tendency to identify a woman writer's heroine with her creator. So women novelists developed the fallible, but unfallen heroine, who learned from her mistakes and reformed her ways.

The typical heroine in need of reform is a coquette: that is, she enjoys the courtship game and delays making her final choice of a husband, often by encouraging several suitors at the same time. It is not surprising that women novelists' interest in a mixed female character should lead them to draw the coquette, because the general view that woman's destiny was a sexual destiny and her virtue sexual virtue meant that attention was concentrated on her behaviour during the period of courtship. Vanity and unsteadiness were the coquette's distinguishing characteristics. Pope presented the portrait of such a woman in Belinda, the heroine of *The Rape of the Lock*, creating her according to the convention that woman is both irresistably charming, and faulty by nature of her sex:

> Her lively Looks a sprightly Mind disclose,
> Quick as her Eyes, and as unfix'd as those:
> ...
> If to her share some Female Errors fall,
> Look on her Face, and you'll forget 'em all.[4]

However, the behaviour of the coquette could be interpreted, not as naturally giddy femininity, but as a covert protest against female subordination. For a woman destined to be subject first to her father and then to her husband, the period of courtship, when the man was supposed to be subordinate to her, was her one experience of power; though even here, as we will see in the discussion of Burney's novels particularly, the conventions of feminine propriety eroded that power. The coquette, then, often defying propriety, tried to extend the time of her power and postpone or avoid her subjection. The heroine's attempt to make the most of her power in courtship is an important theme in most of the novels discussed in this chapter.

A novel written about the reformation of a coquette, who learns to give up her power and become a dutiful wife, has very different ideological implications from the story of the seduced and abandoned heroine, with its usual message of protest about the treatment of women. Novels with reformed heroines were about learning to repudiate faults seen as specially feminine, and accepting male authority instead of challenging it. This was a tradition of conformity and, significantly, it had a more continuous history during the eighteenth century than the tradition of protest, and led to greater achievements in the novel: Fanny Burney, Maria Edgeworth and Jane Austen all drew more or less extensively on this tradition. The question then arises: why was the central women's tradition in eighteenth-century fiction built on the character of the coquette—surely a male-created image of unstable femininity—and a narrative framework that seems to depend on anti-feminist assumptions?

There were, I think, two reasons. One was outlined in Chapter 3: women who spoke in support of masculine authority found it easier to have their work accepted than those who protested against it. This was especially so after the 1720s, when earlier and more rebellious women writers like Manley and Haywood were being discredited for their 'immorality'. The more conformist the woman writer's message, the more acceptable her novel and the more likelihood of a tradition developing from her work. The second reason had rather different implications for women's writing. However much the basic fable of the reformed heroine encouraged a message of conformity to existing patriarchal society, the working-out of her story required a concentration on female moral progress; an investigation of the woman's mind; and the conclusion that women are capable of moral growth. I suggest that women writers were drawn to the didactic tradition not because they wanted to preach female subordination, but because this tradition could be used for the development of a new and more complex treatment of female character.

It should also be noted that the tradition of conformity is hardly ever simply that: some protest about female subordination could be mingled with it, to the extent that the author sympathized with her heroine's errors. This point will emerge during the discussion, which is concerned not only with novels in which the heroine is reformed, but with several works that comment on and qualify the tradition of reform. Towards the end of the century, indeed, the reform of the heroine was so well established that the more sophisticated writers were inevitably aware that their work constituted a comment on the tradition to which they were adding.

The development of the didactic treatment of the heroine's reform can be traced from the very early days of the novel. Our discussion here includes Catharine Trotter's *Olinda's Adventures* (1693), Mary Davys's

The Reform'd Coquet (1724), and Eliza Haywood's *The History of Miss Betsy Thoughtless* (1751), after which the convention can be considered established. There were many thoughtless heroines in the second half of the century, like Arabella in Charlotte Lennox's *The Female Quixote* (1752), who has to learn to give up the illusion of life-and-death power over adoring lovers, and accept the hero's love with humility, promising to try to make herself worthy of being his wife.[5] Since Arabella's mistakes are due to the delusions of romance, her story will be considered in detail in the next chapter. Another faulty heroine, Maria in Frances Brooke's *The Excursion* (1777), whose story, though her mistakes are not those of coquetry, belongs to the didactic tradition, was discussed in Chapter 1. Our attention in this chapter will be focused rather on two of Burney's novels, *Evelina* (1778) and *Camilla* (1796), on works by Charlotte Smith, Elizabeth Inchbald and Maria Edgeworth which in various ways question the tradition of reform, and on three novels by the tradition's greatest inheritor, Jane Austen.

THE BEGINNINGS: CATHARINE TROTTER'S *OLINDA'S ADVENTURES* (1693)

Far from being a post-Richardsonian phenomenon, the fallible heroine had already begun to emerge in the era of Behn and Manley. She appeared in an attractive form in *Olinda's Adventures* (1693), which was published when its likely author, Catharine Trotter, was only 14. This short, lively epistolary novel is a work of remarkable, but certainly not impossible, precocity for a 14-year-old girl who at this time was living in much the same situation as her heroine, in genteel poverty with a widowed mother.[6] It is certainly convincing as a picture of a rebellious girl's response to parental pressure on her to marry well.

Olinda's apology for herself is one that all thoughtless young heroines could have taken as their motto. Introducing her story to her correspondent, she writes:

> tho' perhaps I have not always been so nicely cautious as a Woman in strictness ought, I have never gone beyond the bounds of solid Virtue. ... I will give you a faithful Account of all my Weaknesses.[7]

Her story of her 'weaknesses' shows her waging a covert war against the young lady's proper role and destiny. Her weapon is coquetry. She delights in admiration, plays at encouraging and then discouraging her lovers, and takes care not to be cheated into losing control of herself by falling in love or marrying. In this she is close to the abundant coquettes of Restoration and eighteenth-century comedy, apparently frivolous young women who have a good grasp of the sexual politics of coquetry, for as Congreve's Millamant points out in *The Way of the World* (1700), 'when one parts with one's cruelty, one parts with one's power'.[8] Coquettes in the novel are very like coquettes in the drama, but in the women's novels they and their education become central, and comic exposé of coquetry shades into analysis of the feminine situation that produces it.

In Olinda's case there is only the slightest hint of moral comment on her behaviour. Her ready wit and insouciance do have their dangers, as we see when Olinda falls in love with Cloridon, a married man. After avoiding the snares of unwanted matrimony she has found herself tangled in those of illicit desire, and her tone becomes more serious. The novel leaves her fate in suspense, as, after refusing to see Cloridon again, she waits hopefully for his wife to die and set him free. With its tricks and disguises, and its light attitude to the courtship game, *Olinda's Adventures* is clearly inspired by Restoration comedy; and it lets the heroine off very lightly. Olinda learns from experience, but she does not need to repent, only to acknowledge the dangers of passion. Later novels would insist on the coquette's repentance and reform.

THE LOVER–MENTOR: MARY DAVYS'S *THE REFORM'D COQUET* (1724)

We might expect that a novel tradition based on the woman writer's role as moral guide to her sex would present stories of a heroine's reform through the advice of a more experienced woman; and in fact, wise women often appear as mentors in didactic novels. Frances Sheridan's Sidney Bidulph is guided by her mother, and later guides her own daughters.[9] In Clara Reeve's *School for Widows* (1791), Mrs Strictland and Mrs Darnford exchange life-histories and promise to monitor each other's conduct; and Mrs Strictland has preserved wifely duty in a difficult marriage with the help of a motherly housekeeper's admonitions.[10] In Jane West's *The Advantages of Education* (1793) Maria Williams learns to reject an attractive rake and accept worthy Mr Herbert under her mother's wise tuition; and the importance of the female mentor is further emphasized by the fact that Mr Herbert's mother was once an equally necessary guide to Mrs Williams herself.[11] A female teacher is not always central, however. Often she plays a subordinate part while a male teacher—the heroine's lover and her mentor—takes the dominant role. The relationship between a faulty heroine and her lover–mentor conveniently combines love story and moral lesson, and reflects the sexual hierarchy established in society;

not surprisingly, then, it provides the didactic novel with its central fable.

The prototype of this relationship can be found in the century's comedies, with their coquettes and serious-minded suitors,[12] but it is only fully developed in the novel. The first novel to do this thoroughly is Mary Davys's *The Reform'd Coquet* (1724), the title of which provides an apt designation for many a heroine in the didactic tradition. Davys is at the beginning of a long line of women writers who create coquettish heroines and lover–mentors to reform them.

Davys's Amoranda, pretty and clever, spends her childhood as the centre of an admiring circle of parents and visitors, and is spoiled by indulgence. When her parents die, she is a rich, beautiful and foolish coquette, rather similar in situation and character to a later, more famous heroine, Austen's Emma Woodhouse, who begins as a spoilt young woman with 'the power of having rather too much her own way, and a disposition to think a little too well of herself'.[13]

Amoranda's dangerous independence is curbed by Alanthus, a young man who shows his love for her by disguising himself as Formator, a wise old guardian appointed by her uncle. Alanthus only reveals his true identity at the end of the story, but the reader has guessed it before. Amoranda is instructed, not wooed, by this lover–mentor, and her first sight of him as a young man is calculated to link the idea of lover and stern tutor firmly in her mind. He makes his appearance when her coquetry has placed her in the power of Berinthius, who means to rape her. Instead of rescuing her at once, Alanthus scolds her:

> I presume, Madam, you are some self-will'd, head-strong Lady,
> who, resolved to follow your own Inventions, have left the Care of a
> tender Father, to ramble with you know not who. Oh Sir! *said she*,
> some part of your guess is true; but Father I have none. Nor
> Mother? *said the Stranger*; nor Guardian? Nor Mother, *said she*, but a
> Guardian, a good one too, I have; and were I but once again in his
> possession, I wou'd never leave him while I live.
>   Well, Madam, *said the Gentleman*, I am sorry for you, but am no
> Knight-Errant, nor do I ride in quest of Adventures; I wish you a
> good Deliverance, and am your humble Servant. Saying this, he and
> his Servants rode away.[14]

He does return and rescue her from harm, but the lesson has been a severe one. Soon after this it is revealed that Alanthus and Formator are the same person, and the heroine, cured of self-will, eagerly accepts her mentor as her husband and guardian for life.

The ideological implications of this novel are clearly very different from those of the seduction tale. We only have to compare *The Reform'd*

Coquet with Manley's tale of Charlot in *The New Atalantis*. There are wicked ravishers in Davys's novel as there are in Manley's, but this does not mean, as it does in Manley's, that men are not to be trusted, but that the heroine must find an honest man, submit to his authority, and gain his protection. Whereas Manley portrays the guardian as corrupt, the abuser of his patriarchal authority, Davys makes the guardian the lover and supports his programme of courtship-by-reform. The father substitute, instead of being a quasi-incestuous ravisher, is the legitimate mate for a thoughtless young heroine. His advice is wisdom, and his lifelong control is necessary for a woman who, though basically virtuous, is inevitably subject to vanity, that 'Foible of ... [her] Sex' (II, 71). The story of Charlot is a protest against male domination: the story of Amoranda is an apology for it.

This message of conformity is found in most novels where the heroine's lover is her mentor. It is built into the very structure of the 'reformed coquette' tradition. The heroine's basic fault is usually identified as the natural concomitant of her femaleness—her vanity, her coquettishness are nearly always specifically described as female foibles. The fact that she is a virtuous and sensible woman apart from her little follies only underlines the distrust of femininity implied in her creation. Even the best of women, it would appear, cannot escape the moral weaknesses of her sex. Masculine guidance and protection are the answer to the heroine's problems, and she is given a substitute father to guard her from other men, from the evil of the world, and from her own female nature.

REFORM BY SELF-DISCOVERY: ELIZA HAYWOOD'S *THE HISTORY OF MISS BETSY THOUGHTLESS* (1751)

The change in Eliza Haywood's tone when she began writing novels again after the 1730s has already been mentioned. *Betsy Thoughtless* and *The History of Jemmy and Jenny Jessamy* (1753) differ from her earlier works not just in the greater concessions to the new feminine modesty and morality in their presentation (making the famous scenes of seduction taboo), but in their more detailed and naturalistic rendering of both outer and inner realities, the heroine's environment and her thought-processes. Haywood had evidently learned from both Fielding and Richardson, but she adapted what she learned to the development of a different tradition. In *Betsy Thoughtless*, we come to a full treatment of the theme of the reformed heroine.

Like most heroines in this tradition, Betsy is deprived of proper parental control. Early in the novel she is orphaned, and though she has two good guardians, appropriately named Sir Ralph Trusty and Mr Goodman, she comes under the influence of Mr Goodman's wife Lady Mellasin and her daughter Flora, who are far from sharing his virtue. Delighting in the admiration of the various young men who visit the house, Betsy encourages all advances equally, and becomes a coquette. The basic situation then is similar to that of *The Reform'd Coquet*, but *Betsy Thoughtless* has a more serious tone and a new, detailed, domestic realism. One example of this is found when Betsy and Flora walk in the park in Oxford, meet two students, and thoughtlessly agree to go and sit with them in a shady garden nearby. The young man who makes this request, 'on finding it so easily obtained, [begins] to form some conjectures no way to the advantage of these ladies reputation'.[15] Betsy's naive and lively responses make the situation even more dangerous:

> on entering [a dark recess in the garden] miss Betsy cried, 'Bless me! this is fit for nothing but for people to do what they are ashamed of in the light.' 'The fitter then, madam,' replied the gentleman-commoner, 'to encourage a lover ...' He accompanied these words with a seizure of both her hands, and two or three kisses on her lips. The young student was no less free with miss Flora; but neither of these ladies gave themselves the trouble to reflect what consequences might possibly attend a prelude of this nature, and repulsed the liberties they took in such a manner, as made the offenders imagine they had not sinned beyond a pardon. (*Betsy Thoughtless*, I, 83)

When Betsy and Flora go into a nearby house with the young men, Haywood's description of the ensuing display of thoughtless high spirits even has some anticipatory flavour of Jane Austen's tone:

> Persons of so gay and volatile a disposition, as these four, could not content themselves with sitting still, and barely talking,—every limb must be in motion,—every faculty employed. The gentleman-commoner took miss Betsy's hand, and led her some steps of a minuette, then fell into a rigadoon, then into the louvre, and so ran through all the school-dances, without regularly beginning or ending any one of them, or of the tunes he sung: the young student was not less alert with miss Flora; so that between singing, dancing, and laughing, they all grew extremely warm. (I, 85)

Flora, not so ignorant of the men's intentions as Betsy, soon slips away with her student, leaving Betsy alone with a young man and torn between her pleasure in his embraces and her feeling that she ought to resist them:

[He] began to kiss her with so much warmth and eagerness that surprised her; she struggled to get loose, and called miss Flora, not knowing she was gone, to come to her assistance. The efforts she made at first to oblige him to desist, were not, however, quite so strenuous as they ought to have been, on such an occasion. (I, 87)

Only her brother's sudden arrival on the scene prevents Betsy's 'ruin'; and he, enraged to find a friend of his trying to seduce his sister, challenges the gentleman-commoner to a duel. Both are wounded, and Betsy finds that the story travels all over the city. Ladies gossip about her, students write satires on her, and she hurries back to London where her reputation is still for the moment secure.

Compared to the seduction scenes in Haywood's earlier novels, this is a fresh, circumstantial account, relatively free of hackneyed situations and rhetorical clichés. Apart from the freedom of Betsy's behaviour, unthinkable in the heroines of the politer age that was soon to succeed, this incident would not be out of place in a Burney novel.

Betsy is rather like Fielding's Tom Jones. Her faults are those of carelessness, not design, and she is vulnerable to misrepresentation because of her good nature and her thoughtlessness. Whereas the jealous Blifil plots against Tom, Flora Mellasin slanders Betsy. However, while Tom has the hero's privilege of being forgiven lapses from chastity, Betsy, as a heroine, must remain chaste. Her generosity in supporting a poor washerwoman's baby leads to malicious rumours that the child is her own, but it is important that these rumours are false. Her thoughtlessness leads her into nothing worse than flirting with three admirers at once, behaviour which disgusts her one worthy lover, Trueworth. Trueworth marries another woman, but not before he has had a short-lived amour with Flora Mellasin. The narrator implies no criticism of this action, which is 'no more than any man, of his age and constitution, would have done' (III, 77).

In *Betsy Thoughtless*, Haywood accepts a double standard she had attacked in her earlier work. In *The British Recluse*, Cleomira's and Belinda's friendship was founded on their shared experience of men's treachery, and it made little difference to that friendship that Belinda had preserved her chastity while Cleomira had not. In *Betsy Thoughtless*, when the heroine's old friend, Miss Forward, turns up as a victim of seduction, Betsy is censorious, and she breaks off the friendship on learning that Miss Forward is being supported by a lover's gifts. Haywood's earlier feminist protest has been lost in her recreation of herself as a new 'moral' novelist.

The firm separation of the chaste heroine from the fallen woman is only one of many indications that in this novel Haywood is supporting her society's standards for female conduct. Like *The Reform'd Coquet*,

Betsy Thoughtless is about the dangers of too much independence for a young woman, and Trueworth, Betsy's brothers, and Lady Trusty all warn her about her behaviour. However, Betsy's mentors do not always defeat her in argument. One example of Haywood's support for her heroine's point of view is found in Betsy's exchange with her brother on the subject of virtue and reputation:

> 'What avails your being virtuous?' said mr. Francis: — 'I hope,— and I believe you are so; —but your reputation is of more consequence to your family: —the loss of the one might be concealed, but a blemish on the other brings certain infamy and disgrace on yourself, and all belonging to you.'
>
> On this, she assumed the courage to tell him, his way of reasoning was neither just nor delicate. —'Would you,' said she, 'be guilty of a base action, rather than have it suspected that you were so?' —'No,' answered he, 'but virtue is a different thing in our sex, to what it is in yours; —the forfeiture of what is called virtue in a woman is more a folly than a baseness; but the virtue of a man is his courage, his constancy, his probity, which if he loses, he becomes contemptible to himself, as well as to the world.'
>
> 'And certainly,' rejoined miss Betsy, with some warmth, 'the loss of innocence must render a woman contemptible to herself, though she should happen to hide her transgression from the world.' — 'That may be,' said mr. Francis; 'but then her kindred suffer not through her fault: — ... a woman brings less dishonour upon a family, by twenty private sins, than by one public indiscretion.'
>
> 'Well,' answered she, 'I hope I shall always take care to avoid both the one and the other, for my own sake'. (III, 108–09)

Note that Betsy does not challenge her brother's sexual division of virtue. Unlike Manley earlier, and Wollstonecraft later, Haywood here accepts the location of feminine virtue in chastity. What she does not accept is the notion that this virtue exists for its use to the woman's family and that therefore the reputation of virtue is what really counts. Her emphasis on the need for self-respect is a feature of other novels about the heroine's reform, and tends to qualify their message of conformity. The heroine who cares for the reality of virtue for her own sake finds herself in conflict with a society that cares mainly for the appearance of it.

Betsy has a longer and harder lesson than many other coquette-heroines. Where they only run the risk of choosing the wrong man, she actually marries him. Her marriage to the mean, petty and domineering Mr Munden is an ordeal during which she finally learns how to keep the self-respect she has claimed as her standard. She has to teach herself, for Haywood does not share the faith in masculine authority evident in *The Reform'd Coquet*. At Betsy's wedding Lady Trusty gives the bride advice that could have come out of any contemporary female conduct-book. Be neither too fond nor too cold, she advises, remain in your own sphere, give him his rights, and always yield to him in disputes (IV, 37). Standard advice: but Betsy's experience shows that it cannot be followed with any dignity.

The domestic scenes in which Betsy and her husband quarrel over the household accounts are among the most vivid in the novel, and Haywood's sympathies are clearly with her heroine. Munden tears up bills, refuses to pay Betsy what he agreed in the marriage contract, and kills her pet squirrel. 'How utterly impossible was it for her now to observe the rules laid down to her by lady Trusty!' comments the narrator at one point (IV, 59). Betsy eventually leaves her husband, just as her creator, 30 years earlier, had run away from Valentine Haywood.

Haywood avoids pursuing the more radical implications of this story by arranging a convenient death for Munden. Betsy's plight as runaway wife of an impossible husband reveals perhaps too much of the inadequacy of Lady Trusty's conduct-book advice. Haywood cannot applaud Betsy's conversion to prudence if this means submitting to the authority of a Munden, so she evades the issue by freeing Betsy to marry Trueworth, whose first wife died soon after their marriage. Trueworth's authority as a husband will never be improperly exercised, and Betsy, like Amoranda, ends her story reformed and under the protection of a worthy man. There is a crucial difference, though, in the process of reform. In *The Reform'd Coquet*, Formator/Alanthus reforms the woman he intends to marry. In *Betsy Thoughtless*, Trueworth's efforts as lover–mentor are singularly unsuccessful, and Lady Trusty's rules do not help much either. The heroine eventually reforms herself, when she realizes that her flirtatious conduct has gone too far—not for her 'virtue' narrowly defined or for her reputation, but too far for her own self-respect.

During her first marriage, Lord—, Munden's patron, contrives to be alone with her, and tries to seduce her. She rejects him indignantly, only to find that Munden is angry with her for offending such an important man. Betsy's chastity is not compromised, her husband does not suspect her of infidelity, and she is in no danger of losing her reputation over an incident which does not become publicly known. Yet it is now that Betsy reviews her conduct. She realizes that she has enjoyed the nobleman's admiration and might have been led into adultery. The narrative focuses on her private thoughts:

> 'The vanities of my virgin state ... might plead some excuse; —but
> nothing now can be urged in my defence for persevering in them. —
> The pride of subduing hearts is mine no more; —no man can now
> pretend to love me but with the basest and most shameful views. —

The man who dares to tell me he adores me, contradicts himself by
that very declaration, and while he would persuade me he has the
highest opinion of me, discovers he has in reality the meanest.'
    In fine, she now saw herself, and the errors of her past conduct,
in their true light. 'How strange a creature have I been!' cried she,
'how inconsistent with myself! I knew the character of a coquet
both silly and insignificant, yet did everything in my power to
acquire it: —I aimed to inspire awe and reverence in the men, yet
by my imprudence emboldened them to the most unbecoming
freedoms with me: — ... Nature has made me no fool, yet not one
action of my life has given any proof of common reason.
    'Even in ... marriage' — added she, with a deep sigh, 'have I not
been governed wholly by caprice! —I rejected mr. Trueworth, only
because I thought I did not love him enough, yet gave myself to
mr. Munden, whom at that time I did not love at all ...'
    In summing up this charge against herself, she found that all her
faults and her misfortunes had been owing either to an excess of
vanity; —a mistaken pride, —or a false delicacy. (IV, 159–61)

By using interior monologue at this point Haywood shows Betsy's reform
taking place in her mind. Here is a concern with the inner self not found
in Fielding's portrayal of Tom Jones, and an interest in the thoughtless
young girl's moment of self-knowledge not paralleled even in Richardson's work.
    Haywood's rendering of Betsy's consciousness at work foreshadows
some of the achievements of Jane Austen, whose heroines go through
comparable moments of self-knowledge. Emma reflects on her folly for
several pages when she realizes—the moment that she believes she
may lose him to Harriet—that she loves Mr Knightley. She learns to
'understand, thoroughly understand her own heart' for the first time in
the course of her reflections.[16] Elizabeth Bennet's thoughts after reading
Darcy's letter of explanation are similar to Betsy's at her moment of
truth, and are rendered in a similar manner:

She grew absolutely ashamed of herself.—Of neither Darcy nor
Wickham could she think, without feeling that she had been blind,
partial, prejudiced, absurd.
    'How despicably have I acted!' she cried.—'I, who have prided
myself on my discernment!—I, who have valued myself on my
abilities! who have often disdained the generous candour of my
sister, and gratified my vanity, in useless or blameable distrust.—
How humiliating is this discovery!—Yet, how just a humiliation!—
Had I been in love, I could not have been more wretchedly blind.
But vanity, not love, has been my folly.—Pleased with the
preference of one, and offended by the neglect of the other, on the
very beginning of our acquaintance, I have courted prepossession

and ignorance, and driven reason away, where either were
concerned. Till this moment, I never knew myself.'[17]

The moment of self-knowledge, revealed by narrative access to the
heroine's consciousness, is the turning-point of *Pride and Prejudice* as it is
of *Betsy Thoughtless*. Crude though it is in comparison to the later work,
Haywood's novel truly anticipates the moral art of Jane Austen.

THE SHY COQUETTE: FANNY BURNEY'S *EVELINA* (1778)

Fanny Burney's novels all introduce a young woman to fashionable
society, where she proves herself generally superior to the people of the
world, but often mistaken in judgment and actions. Her first and third
heroines, Evelina and Camilla, both have lover–mentors who help them
learn to perform a woman's duties properly. It has been pointed out
that *Evelina* bears close resemblances to *Betsy Thoughtless*;[18] and Evelina
could be seen as a Betsy Thoughtless with greater delicacy, living in a
more vividly rendered social world.

Though the reader sees with Evelina's eyes and is invited to share her
feelings, Burney does not show the same interest that Haywood does in
rendering the heroine's mind at the point of the self-realization that
leads to reform. In fact, it could be argued that Evelina does not really
need to reform so much as to be recognized, and at crucial moments in
the novel, attention shifts from her to people's reactions to her. Yet
although she is not typical of the coquette who needs reform, Evelina's
actions are often those of an unconscious coquette, who is in some sense
testing her power; and that a special kind of power is granted her, shows
that the conformist didactic novel has some affinities not only with the
alternative tradition of protest, but with the tradition of escape through
romance.

Evelina is so shy and retiring that it may seem wrong to place her in
the reformed coquette tradition at all. Certainly there are external
parallels between her and Betsy Thoughtless. Both are deprived of their
natural parents; both have good guardians to protect them; and both
make their entrance into the world by going to London, where they
bring embarrassments upon themselves by their unguarded behaviour.
As Betsy suffers in Trueworth's eyes after appearing in public with Miss
Forward, Evelina worries that her accidental appearance in the company
of two prostitutes will ruin her in the opinion of her lover–mentor, Lord
Orville.[19] Evelina's attitude, however, is very different from Betsy's.
Never was heroine more single-hearted in devotion to her hero. Far from
acting the coquette, she only wants to be the dutiful daughter of Sir

John Belmont, the worthy pupil of the Reverend Mr Villars, and eventually the well-directed wife of Lord Orville. Although circumstances, the faults of others, and her own ignorance continually place her in situations where the true Evelina may not be recognized, it is Lord Orville's distinction to perceive unknown Evelina Anville as a true heroine before she is revealed to the world as Evelina Belmont. At the end of her trials Evelina gains Orville as a guardian–husband, in addition to being reconciled to her father and retaining the love and care of Mr Villars, the man who has always been as a father to her.

In *The Reform'd Coquet*, the husband is established as the woman's true guide by making the old mentor and the young lover the same person. In *Evelina* the same effect is achieved more naturalistically, by means of repeated comparisons between Lord Orville and Mr Villars. Describing Orville to her guardian, Evelina writes: 'I sometimes imagine, that, when his youth is flown, his vivacity abated, and his life is devoted to retirement, he will, perhaps, resemble him whom I most love and honour [i.e., Villars himself]'.[20]

Yet, however different Evelina's desires from those of the thoughtless heroines who try to resist their guardians' control, she does make many of their mistakes. Her behaviour at the first balls and assemblies she goes to is not that of the coquette teasing her admirers, but it is nevertheless fundamentally related to the coquette's actions, because it expresses feelings of rebellion against the woman's prescribed position in courtship.

At her first ball she will not dance with Mr Lovel because he is a ridiculous fop, and accepts Lord Orville instead, thus violating the unwritten rule that a young lady cannot dance with one man after refusing another. Though Evelina claims that she was not aware of this, her mistake seems like a deliberate one. Just before Lovel approaches her, she is provoked on behalf of all the ladies, by the behaviour of the gentlemen at the ball. They 'looked as if they thought we were quite at their disposal, and only waiting for the honour of their commands'. She decides she would 'rather not dance at all, than with any one who should seem to think me ready to accept the first partner who would condescend to take me' (*Evelina*, pp. 28–9). Her phrasing suggests awareness of the price of refusal, and resentment of the rules that prescribe meekness to women; and her indecorous action expresses her desire to share the man's power of choosing a partner.

Further mistakes at her second ball make her preference for Orville even clearer, and expose her to Sir Clement Willoughby's teasing. Like the coquette, Evelina is trying to exercise some choice in the courtship ritual, and her author's sympathy with her desire is evident. In men, either negligence or insistent attention is sanctioned by the assembly rules Evelina breaks—rules that mirror those of life. It is the men's part to choose (if they wish) while women must wait to be chosen. Evelina's fears of having the wrong dancing partner thrust upon her reflect the eighteenth-century woman's fear of being made to accept an unwanted partner for life.

Burney's complaints about the woman's helpless position are made in her heroine's letters. Evelina, always bolder on paper than in action, makes sharp observations about scenes during which she was passive and frightened, so that the record of her experiences builds up into a satirical novel written by a timid heroine. There is a discrepancy, too, between the picture of men in society revealed in Evelina's satire, and the novel's didactic message. Evelina has to learn to keep the rules of assemblies and of society. The novel's conclusion denies the earlier implied criticisms of male domination by showing Evelina finding all her happiness in male protection. Burney bridges this gulf between her satire and her moral message with her creation of Lord Orville. She shows that the rules of society encourage men to treat women badly, but by introducing Orville she manages to attack only the bad behaviour, not the rules themselves. Orville is as privileged by the rules as Lovel and Sir Clement are, but he refuses to take advantage of them. Evelina's early experiences imply that there is total male control of the dance, the courtship it initiates and the marital relationship it symbolizes. This harsh idea can be evaded through the fantasy of the perfect gentleman.

In many ways, Lord Orville is reminiscent of Sir Charles Grandison, the impeccably behaved hero of Richardson's third novel, but he is much humbler in courtship. Sir Charles hesitates between two possible women, Harriet and Clementina, while Orville is devoted to Evelina alone. His love may be difficult for the reader to understand, since for much of the novel he only sees the heroine in situations that suggest she is thoughtless, flirtatious, possibly even immoral. The point is that Orville can see through false appearances, and this is crucially important to the novel. *Evelina*, like *Betsy Thoughtless*, criticizes the world's readiness to judge the heroine by appearances.

The contrast between Orville and Sir Clement Willoughby makes Burney's point. Willoughby is always ready to believe the worst of Evelina and to take advantage of it. When he finds her alone in Vauxhall gardens he assumes her to be fair game for sexual assault, and he rescues her from a group of riotous men only to make his own unwelcome advances. When he realizes she is under the care of the vulgar Branghton family, his scorn is evident. Social customs compel him to behave with restraint towards her when she is accepted among people of his own rank, but once deprived of the outward trappings of respectability, she is simply sexual prey to him. He cannot perceive that her virtue is intrinsic to her, and not dependent on circumstance. Lord Orville can. Even when he sees Evelina walking with two prostitutes he speaks politely to her, and far from doubting her virtue, he visits her later to warn her about companions whose real character he assumes she is too innocent to have realized.

Orville may be a lover–mentor like Trueworth and Formator, but in this novel the heroine is not the only one who has something to learn. From the beginning he is ready to trust to her innocence and make allowances for her inexperience, but he has to learn to trust her judgment too. When he discovers her violating the feminine proprieties by making clandestine appointments with a young stranger, Mr Macartney, he begs for an explanation, which she refuses. When she exclaims unguardedly that she would 'give the universe' for a private conversation with Mr Macartney, Orville is both anxious and jealous, but he arranges the meeting she desires, promising: 'I will ask no questions, I will rely upon [your] own purity, and uninformed, blindfold as I am, I will serve [you] with all my power!' (p. 319). The hero's concern for propriety and the heroine's fear of his disapproval may seem excessive even by late eighteenth-century standards, but the very heightened fragility of female delicacy in Burney's world makes it a striking moment when Orville decides to waive the strict rules of decorum and trust to Evelina's essential honour.

Having shown this 'blindfold' trust in Evelina, it is fitting that Orville makes her an equally blindfold offer of marriage, while ignorant of her true name, connections, rank and fortune; and during the early days of their engagement he has to contend with more mysterious behaviour. 'My beloved Miss Anville ... pardon my impatience! ... You shall tell me nothing you would wish to conceal', he responds, when his fiancée has refused to tell him her real identity (p. 354). Most critics of *Evelina* have tended to agree with Sir Clement Willoughby that Orville is 'cold, inanimate, phlegmatic' (p. 358), but his devoted trust surpasses the love of more dashing heroes.

Lord Orville is suitably rewarded for his blindfold choice when Evelina turns out to be Sir John Belmont's daughter with £30,000, but Burney has so engineered his courtship that he clearly chooses the heroine without regard to her family and fortune. Her identity, defined as society defines it by these externals, does not concern him, for he looks inward. His devotion is a triumph of faith in inner integrity over concern for outward appearance. Evidently Orville, unlike Sir Clement, believes in the reality of female virtue.

CRITICISMS OF THE LOVER–MENTOR

Sarah Fielding's and Jane Collier's The Cry *(1754)*

Evelina shows that even within the tradition of the thoughtless heroine the lover–mentor might be criticized. His role implied a suspicion not only of her conduct but of the moral capacities of women in general. For Burney, Orville was the perfect hero because at the crucial moment he abdicated his position as Evelina's moral guide. Other heroes had to learn his implicit trust. This theme gives us an indication that the women's didactic tradition was not so entirely a conformist one as at first appears. It did uphold the conventional standard of a special virtue for women, but some novels in the tradition provided a rationale for women to argue for greater freedom of action on the grounds that female virtue could be trusted. Others, less inclined to idealize natural feminine virtue, questioned whether a lover was the heroine's proper mentor. Woven into this basically conservative tradition, then, was a contrasting strand, sharply critical of masculine authority.

It was mainly towards the end of the century that protest began to surface within the women's didactic novel. An early example of it, however, was to be found in 1754 in *The Cry*, by Sarah Fielding and Jane Collier. Its hero, Ferdinand, starts off as a welcome lover–mentor to Portia, but he takes the role too far. He does not doubt the heroine's virtue or her love for him, but he wants to be sure her principles are strict enough to include a proper appreciation of *his* virtue. He devises a test for her. While he is away in Barbados, he sees that she receives false reports that he has seduced and abandoned a planter's daughter. True to her principles, Portia rejects Ferdinand when he returns to her under the assumed character of a rake.

Portia has passed the test, but in subjecting her to it Ferdinand has become unworthy of her. He is punished when Portia, on her way to France to avoid him, falls ill. By mistake Ferdinand gets a report that she is dead, and is reduced to despair. Later, he hears that she is alive after all, and he goes to confess his crimes to her and receive her reproaches. She chides him for his lack of trust: 'Was I so little known then, *Ferdinand*? or is there no force on the most innocent, as well as most ardent affection, to banish all doubt and suspicion from the mind?'[21] However, she forgives him for his 'cruel whim' (*The Cry*, III, 264), and once his 'dangerous love of refinement [is] ... rooted from his heart' the two lovers can become a 'truly happy couple', with 'nothing to conceal from each other' (III, 296–7).

Charlotte Smith's Emmeline *(1788)*

Charlotte Smith also writes of the need for masculine trust in *Emmeline*. Like Burney, she distinguishes between suitors on the basis of their faith in the heroine. Like Fielding and Collier in *The Cry*, she depicts misunderstandings between separated lovers. When Emmeline and her fiancé, Delamere, have been kept apart for some months, he hears malicious reports that she has had a baby by his friend Fitz-Edward. He claims not to believe this, but is sufficiently troubled to go secretly to the cottage where she is staying, and when he finds her with Lady Adelina's baby in her arms, he assumes the child is her own, and breaks off their engagement. Emmeline refuses to explain the situation, not only to protect Lady Adelina, but because she does not want a man who has 'so little reliance on her principles, as to be driven on a mere suspicion into rudeness and insult' (*Emmeline*, p. 296).

Emmeline's heroic silence is rather less impressive in view of her secret relief about being set free. By this time she is in love with Godolphin. Her preference is based on Godolphin's greater moral worth—which is demonstrated by the trust he, unlike Delamere, is prepared to place in her. Like Lord Orville, this hero allows the heroine to withhold vital information from him, but he does even better than Orville by showing implicit confidence in the heroine at their very first meeting. Having come to visit his sister, Lady Adelina, after a long absence abroad, he discovers that she is very ill, perhaps dying, and is being nursed by a stranger to him—Emmeline—who refuses to let him visit the patient. Not unreasonably, Godolphin asks for some explanation, but Emmeline refuses to give one. She even asks him to leave and not tell anyone where his sister is. Saying that he does not want to cause pain to Emmeline's 'generous and sensible heart', he promises her, 'Your commands shall be sufficient. I will stifle my anxiety and obey you' (pp. 267–8). When Godolphin eventually wins Emmeline, he is rewarded for the sure moral instinct that has led him to trust her on sight.

Elizabeth Inchbald's A Simple Story *(1791)*

Smith supports her heroine against masculine doubt by making her naturally good, needing no reform. Elizabeth Inchbald revises the didactic tradition differently. In *A Simple Story* (1791) the coquettish heroine needs reforming, but her lover–mentor's efforts to teach her fail. Inchbald's Protestant heroine, Miss Milner, educated at a fashionable boarding school which has taught her the usual accomplishments but left 'her mind without one ornament, except those which nature gave', is bound to clash with her guardian, Dorriforth, a Roman Catholic priest 'bred at St. Omer's in all the scholastic rigour of that college'.²² Miss Milner is 18 when her father dies, and Dorriforth is uneasy at taking on the responsibility for a 'young, idle, indiscreet, giddy girl, with half a dozen lovers in her suite' (*A Simple Story*, p. 9). However, his problems with his ward are not exactly those he anticipates. Touched by Dorriforth's earnestness and gentleness Miss Milner falls in love with him, and her coquettish behaviour towards her suitors is only adopted in order to conceal her passion for her guardian.

The barrier between Miss Milner and Dorriforth is removed on his succeeding to the title of Lord Elmwood and being released from his vows. However, their very different temperaments keep them apart for a while. Lord Elmwood now intends to marry from a sense of his duty to perpetuate his Catholic earldom, and he makes a coldly prudent decision to marry Miss Fenton, a cool and virtuous young lady. However, Miss Milner's passionate love, revealed in an outburst to her friend Miss Woodley, overcomes Miss Fenton's cold charms. Miss Woodley, telling Lord Elmwood of his ward's feelings for him, reveals to him that he loves Miss Milner.

So far this plot may seem typical of the reformed coquette novel: the guardian helps the lively heroine to learn prudence and is then metamorphosed into her lover. However, the novel casts doubt on the whole notion of reform by the lover–mentor. Miss Milner's reform, based not on reflection and self-knowledge but on passion, is incomplete, and her austere guardian, also under the influence of passion for the first time in his life, is the worst person to make allowances for her imprudences.

As her guardian, Miss Milner reveres Lord Elmwood, but once he is her lover, she expects him to revere her.

> Are not my charms [she thinks] even more invincible than I ever believed them to be? Dorriforth, the grave, the sanctified, the anchorite Dorriforth, by their force is animated to all the ardour of the most impassioned lover—while the proud priest, the austere guardian, is humbled, if I but frown, into the veriest slave of love. ... Why did I not keep him longer in suspense? ... my power over him might have been greater still. (p. 138)

Determined to prove his love stronger than his prudence, she deliberately defies his commands and goes to a masquerade, dressed as the goddess of chastity but looking like 'a female much less virtuous' (p. 155). She learns the limit of her powers when her angry fiancé breaks off their engagement.

It takes a different kind of mentor—harsher, but not blinded by passion—to bring them together again. Mr Sandford, once Dorriforth's

tutor, has continually slighted and insulted Miss Milner in the hope of
humbling and reforming her. When he sees her truly sorry for her
treatment of her fiancé he tells Lord Elmwood, 'take this woman's
marriage vows; you can ask no fairer promises of her reform' (p. 191).
Instead of going abroad to avoid Miss Milner, Lord Elmwood marries
her.

Lord Elmwood's inability to be both lover and mentor is symptomatic
of *A Simple Story*'s challenge to the fundamental assumptions behind the
didactic tradition. A novel like *Evelina* suggested that the tutor and lover
could properly be found in the same person, and that the right husband
was one who would take over the functions of father and guardian. Only
by giving her heroine such an excess of delicacy that she seems quite
impervious to sexual desire did Burney avoid the incestuous implications
of this relationship, which had been so clear to earlier women writers
like Delariviere Manley. Inchbald challenges the narrowing definition
of female delicacy in the late eighteenth century by suffusing her story
of a guardian and his ward with convincing passion. Miss Milner feels
love for Dorriforth when it is doubly forbidden, by the code of feminine
delicacy and by his priesthood, and her frank declaration, 'I love him
with all the passion of a mistress, and with all the tenderness of a wife'
(p. 72), heralds the return of women's sexuality to the women's novel.
By sexualizing a de-sexualized novel convention, Inchbald undermines
that respect, preached in the more conservative didactic novels, for the
purely virtuous influence of the authoritative male.

Having brought sex back into the relationship between hero and
heroine, Inchbald cannot bring her story to a happy resolution. The
convention that virtue implies sexlessness is too strong for her, and the
second half of *A Simple Story* is an attempt to cancel out the boldness of
the first. Set 17 years later, the second part takes a retrospective view
of Lord and Lady Elmwood's marriage, which has not been a success.
During Lord Elmwood's absence abroad, Lady Elmwood had an affair
with her old suitor Lord Frederick Lawnly, and her husband has never
forgiven her. The narrative traces the process of reconciliation in the
second generation. Lady Elmwood dies, and her daughter, Matilda, is
left to the care of the father who has refused to see her since her mother's
adultery. Eventually, father and daughter are reunited, and Matilda
marries Harry Rushworth, Elmwood's nephew.

Characterization is simplified to the point of crudity in this second
part of the novel. Impulsive Miss Milner, a fine and subtly drawn
example of the thoughtless heroine, is replaced by her dutiful and
colourless daughter. The sensitive Lord Elmwood of the first two
volumes, struggling between rigid notions of virtue and sudden passionate love, is transformed into the monstrous tyrant of volumes three
and four, who evicts a whole family of poor dependants because one

member of it inadvertently mentions his disgraced wife to him. The novel does not offer any definite criticism of this hyperbolic excess of patriarchal authority: Inchbald presents the final reconciliation as a proper recompense for any undue harshness. Lord Elmwood's love for his daughter is awakened only in defence of the virginity that now constitutes his definition of female virtue. He rescues her from a kidnapper, and there is no authorial suggestion that the reconciliation between father and daughter, when she 'falling on her knees [clings] round his legs, and [bathes] his feet with her tears' (p. 328–9), leaves anything to be desired. The second half of *A Simple Story* bears witness to the difficulties of questioning masculine authority and acknowledging feminine desire in the late eighteenth-century novel.

Maria Edgeworth's Belinda *(1801)*

Maria Edgeworth (1768–1849), an Anglo-Irish novelist and educational writer, is now most often remembered as an early regionalist, whose Irish stories—the most famous of them *Castle Rackrent* (1800)—influenced Walter Scott. She is also important, however, for carrying the women's didactic tradition into the nineteenth century, especially in novels like *Belinda* (1801) and, much later, *Helen* (1834). *Belinda*, a work which Jane Austen included with *Cecilia* and *Camilla* as evidence in the novel's favour when giving fiction its famous defence in *Northanger Abbey*,[23] is, like Burney's novels, about a young woman's entrance into the world. Belinda, however, is wittier and more independent-minded than any of Burney's heroines. A full discussion of this work would include the ways Belinda develops through her experiences, and her relationship with her friend and hostess Lady Delacour, whose sparkling conversation is one of the book's strongest points.[24] Here we are only concerned with one strand of the plot, the hero's involvement with a young girl he names Virginia, who serves as a foil to the heroine. In this episode, Edgeworth attacks the lover–mentor convention more consistently and more effectively than Inchbald in *A Simple Story*.

Edgeworth mocks the male fantasy of a woman educated entirely for her future husband's benefit, found in Rousseau's *Émile* and in the real-life experiment of her father's friend, Thomas Day, who planned to have a young girl, Sabrina Sidney, brought up in seclusion as a preparation for being his wife, but quarrelled with her (she later married a friend of his).[25] Edgeworth's hero, Clarence Hervey, adopts an orphaned cottage girl and keeps her in seclusion, meaning to preserve her innocence, superintend her education, and make her into a suitable wife for himself. His benevolence masks a will to dominate and control, shown first in his insistence on renaming his protegée according to his own romantic ideas: 'the name of Rachel he could not endure ... he thought it so unsuited to her ... he was struck with the idea that she resembled the description of Virginia in M. de St. Pierre's celebrated Romance; and by this name he always called her'.[26] The name he chooses indicates that virginal innocence is the girl's attraction; and his literary model for the perfect woman, the heroine of St Pierre's _Paul et Virginie_ (1788), is so obsessed with maiden modesty that she drowns rather than take off her clothes and swim to safety.

Clarence is attracted by female purity because it offers him the dream of total possession. 'All that was amiable or estimable in Virginia had a double charm, from the secret sense of his penetration, in having discovered and appreciated the treasure' (_Belinda_, III, p. 111). Having done his best to erase Virginia's past life and identity, he thinks of her as a blank sheet on which he can write his own romance; but Virginia's true romance, her love for a man she saw before she met Clarence, has already begun, and she does not fall in love with her lover–mentor. Her virginal innocence is real enough but it does not mean the infinite pliability he expects. Moreover, Clarence discovers for himself that the Rousseauistic ideals of female blankness and malleability will not bring him happiness. He discovers his mistake when he falls in love with Belinda, who, unlike Virginia, is his equal in intelligence and sophistication. Finding Virginia insipid compared to the heroine, Clarence is nevertheless bound in honour to offer marriage to the woman he believes he has taught to love him. Not until Virginia's true feelings are revealed towards the end of the novel can the hero be released to marry Belinda. Before this happens he has been suitably punished for his attempt at courtship by total male domination, by being placed in the position of helplessness usually reserved for heroines. Like many a thoughtless heroine, he is wrongly suspected of dishonour, and unable, from motives of delicacy, to clear himself. Belinda believes him to be keeping Virginia as his mistress, and on this supposition decides to forget him. Clarence has to endure this passively. Instead of planning and conducting his own courtship, he has to wait until other people's actions clear up the mystery and prove his innocence. Instead of claiming Virginia's love as his reward, according to his original idea, Clarence has Belinda bestowed upon him. Edgeworth, with gentle mockery, reforms her hero by taking away his masculine prerogatives, and rewards him for reforming by giving him Belinda, whose virtue does not imply blankness, and whose love will not mean submission.

THE SMOTHERED HEROINE: FANNY BURNEY'S
CAMILLA (1796)

The element of protest in the didactic tradition surfaces most strongly in writers like Smith, Inchbald and Edgeworth, who were to a greater or lesser extent in sympathy with the progressive political movements of the late eighteenth century. For Fanny Burney, firmly conservative in her views, the radical ideas of the 1790s posed a difficult problem. Like other women novelists she wanted to criticize masculine mistrust of women, but she also wanted to defend the established authorities of her society from attack. The result of her dilemma can be seen in her third novel, *Camilla* (1796).

Camilla is another story of a young heroine who errs from ignorance and inadvertence. Edgar Mandlebert, her exacting lover–mentor, is her father's ward and has known her since childhood. Though he is not much older than her, he seems, like other lover–mentors, to combine the wise old man with the young lover: 'can you condescend', he asks Camilla, 'to suffer an old friend, though in the person of but a young man, to offer you, from time to time, a hint, a little counsel, a few brief words of occasional advice?'[27] Camilla, like Evelina, is only too ready to be advised, but various obstacles lie in the lovers' way. Edgar does not, like Lord Orville, trust implicitly in his heroine's virtue. His tutor, Dr Marchmont, teaches him to doubt Camilla. She, for her part, fuels his doubts by the heedless behaviour which leads her to appear in a number of compromising situations. Her friendship with Mrs Arlbery, a witty, worldly and capricious lady who fascinates her, makes matters worse. Though Mrs Arlbery is in fact a perfectly chaste woman, her 'wilful strangeness of behaviour' is enough, under the severe moral code that operates in this novel, to make association with her a kind of threat to the heroine's sexual innocence (*Camilla*, p. 194).

Edgar and Camilla's story follows a pattern of repeated misunderstandings and reconciliations. Each breach, always more serious than the last one, marks a worsening of the heroine's situation. Before their final reconciliation she has been reduced to debt, estrangement from her parents, and near-fatal illness. The tone throughout the novel is much darker than in *Evelina* or indeed any other reformed coquette novel. The message is that the slightest mistake can have disastrous consequences.

Whereas Evelina's timidity is offset by the satirical perception her letters reveal, Camilla, surrounded by sombre-toned and moralizing narrative, rarely shows the vivacity that is supposed to be her charm and her danger. She is more often seen in distress than in thoughtless gaiety. Fanny Burney, it would seem, had grown much less indulgent to youthful errors: this was certainly the judgment implied by the contemporary reviewer who protested that 'The errors of Camilla are not errors in one who is almost a child'.[28] The change between *Evelina* and *Camilla* can be seen as the triumph of didacticism over entertainment, of the conservative conduct-book over the novel.[29]

Yet it has also been claimed that there is a 'growth of feminism' in Burney's later novels. Though her heroines cause many of their own problems they always suffer more than they deserve, and their vulnerability can be seen as a metaphor for women's plight. This is clearest in the last novel, *The Wanderer* (1814), with its revealing subtitle, *Female Difficulties*; but submerged feminist protest can be found in *Camilla* with its rather appealing 'rebel', Mrs Arlbery, and its victimized heroine.[30] There is much to be said for this view. Certainly Edgar is shown to be too mistrustful of Camilla, and the novel ends with a warning about the dangers of making harsh judgments. Dr Marchmont has to acknowledge the 'injustice ... narrowness ... [and] arrogance' of his prejudices against women in general and Camilla in particular (p. 913). However, the standards these men have applied to the heroine—female propriety and delicacy—do not themselves come under attack. *Camilla* is not feminist in the sense that *The Wrongs of Woman* or *The Victim of Prejudice* are feminist. Its attitude to woman's position is more resigned gloom than protest.

We can detect this in Mr Tyrold's letter of advice to his daughter— a letter so famed in its day for good morality that it was separately bound, along with Gregory's *Father's Legacy*, to make up a double conduct-book of real and fictional paternal care. Mr Tyrold does not actually protest against woman's condition, but he certainly laments it. 'The temporal destiny of woman is enrapt in still more impenetrable obscurity than that of man. She begins her career by being involved in all the worldly accidents of a parent; she continues it by being associated in all that may environ a husband', he writes (p. 356). Since a girl's career cannot be planned, because it depends on the will and 'humour' of that unknown male, her future husband, 'the proper education of a female, either for use or for happiness, is still to seek' (p. 357). Mr and Mrs Tyrold, parents of three daughters, have therefore been faced with an insurmountable problem, and 'mutually deliberating upon the uncertainty of the female fate, [they] determined to educate [their] girls with as much simplicity as is compatible with instruction, as much docility for various life as may accord with invariable principles, and as much accommodation with the world at large, as may combine with a just distinction of selected society' (p. 357). In other words, they have tried to reconcile opposites: to create women of judgment, with their personalities left blank for their unknown husbands to fill in later. This is only one of

many places in *Camilla* where Burney reveals that the various virtues
society requires of women are mutually contradictory.

We see the heroine placed in an impossible position when Edgar,
taking Marchmont's advice, decides not to ask her to marry him till he
is sure of her love. Marchmont, embittered by his own marriage, believes
women to be heartless creatures who marry only to gain financial
support. He implies that only by clearly proving that she loves Edgar
for himself, not his money, can Camilla free herself from the suspicion
of sharing the deceitful nature of all womankind. Every instance of
apparent caprice or coquetry—neglect of Edgar's advice or a smile for
another man—appears not merely as youthful error, but the sign of a
universal female frailty. Edgar, then, waits to be allowed 'the independent, unsolicited, involuntary possession' of Camilla's heart, as the
proof of her *virtue* as well as her love (p. 160); but as her father's advice
makes clear, for Camilla to reveal her love unasked would be a violation
of the female delicacy that is the essential sign of that virtue.

Mr Tyrold exhorts Camilla to keep her love a secret. His explanation
of the reason reveals his, and his author's, uneasiness about this advice.
Although he admits that 'nature', 'theory', and even 'common sense'
allow women, like men, to fall in love without being asked, more
important than all these are the 'feelings of delicacy', the 'notions of
propriety', which dictate that a woman cannot choose, but must wait to
be chosen (p. 358). He advises Camilla both to 'shut up every avenue
by which a secret which should die untold can further escape', and to
behave towards Edgar 'with the same open esteem as in [her] days of
unconsciousness' (p. 360). This is admitting defeat from the start.
Camilla can hardly prove to Edgar that she is free from woman's wiles,
when she is forced to simulate an ideal virginal 'unconsciousness' which
falling in love has destroyed.

Mrs Arlbery's advice to Camilla, that she should play the coquette
so as to make Edgar doubt his hold over her, only makes matters worse.
Like Marchmont, she treats courtship as a war between the sexes, and
advises calculation rather than trust. The mistaken advice of both these
faulty mentors is intended to contrast with the truly virtuous counsel
offered by Mr Tyrold. Yet if we compare Mrs Arlbery's ideas with Mr
Tyrold's, we can make a connection Burney may not have intended. His
motives and methods may be more virtuous than hers, but he tacitly
admits what she says openly, that a woman has to practise deceit.

Camilla, pushed into coquetry by the feelings of delicacy, often appears
to Edgar to be turning lightly from one man to another. Even when they
become engaged, further misunderstandings arise and compel Camilla to
break off the engagement. Misfortune strikes again when her father is

arrested for debt, partly on account of her own unconfessed extrava-
gances. Her failure to confide properly in either her lover or her parents
thus receives a heavy punishment, and at the crisis of the story, Camilla
is isolated from all her family and friends, mad with remorse and self-
hatred, and to all appearances dying. Only in this last extremity can
she tell her estranged fiancé of her love:

> She ... had only written 'O Edgar! in this last farewell be all
> displeasure forgotten! — from the first to the final moment of my
> short life, dear and sole possessor of my heart!' — when the
> shooting anguish of her head stopt her hand ... she, with difficulty
> added, '*Not to be delivered till I am dead;*' and was forced to lie down.
> (p. 870)

When Camilla recovers and is reconciled to her family she finds that
Edgar has seen this note, and 'every doubt [is] wholly, and even mir-
aculously removed' by this revelation of 'the true feelings of her heart'
(p. 898). They marry.

Only an unambiguous declaration of love can win Edgar's trust: only
imminent death can excuse (or validate) such a declaration. The
demands made of the heroine in *Camilla* push the novel to the brink of
tragedy. Through her picture of Camilla's dilemma and its drastic
results, Burney reveals the unbearable position of a woman who possesses
the female delicacy her society requires. She does not share Wollstonecraft's feminist ideas, and cannot therefore condemn the female delicacy
that she has shown to be the cause of Camilla's problems. Her conscious
intent is that of the conservative conduct-book writer, sharing Mr Tyrold's dilemma and offering his uneasy solution. The uneasiness pervades
the novel. Burney avoids tragedy, brings the lovers together, and reconciles her heroine to the world: but at a very high price.

Before she can be reconciled to Edgar and fulfil her destiny as loving
wife, Camilla has to be reduced to total helplessness. When she finds
herself accepting the ministrations of her estranged lover, in the guise
of a clergyman charitably visiting her to read prayers for the dying over
her sick-bed (pp. 874–8), she has lost all a heroine's dignity. Equally
important is her unbounded humiliation in front of her mother. While
she lies conscience-stricken and (she believes) dying, her mother visits
her. Camilla leaps out of bed onto the floor, and stays there: 'Camilla
would not be aided; she would not lift up her eyes; her face sought the
ground, where leaning it upon her hands, without desiring to speak,
without wishing to stir, torn by self-reproaches that made her deem
herself unworthy to live, she remained speechless, immoveable' (p. 881).
After this Camilla never really stops prostrating herself. She is forgiven,

she is reconciled to Edgar, she is happy—but only at the cost of making her whole life a reflection of this scene of self-abnegation.

Evelina marries a man who will take over her guardian's role, but at least her entrance into the world demands that she learn to act for herself. Camilla's requires just the opposite. Once reconciled to Edgar she gives him, as the final proof of her trust, 'the fullest, most candid, and unsparing account of every transaction of her short life, from the still shorter period of its being put into voluntary motion'. The effect is to cancel out that 'voluntary' past life, especially as Edgar, listening to her, finds 'himself the constant object of every view, the ultimate motive to every action' (pp. 902–3). Camilla has never really been free at all and she certainly will not be in the future. Her only voluntary acts now are abdications of will: she 'voluntarily' promises, for example, to let Edgar choose her acquaintances from now on (p. 903). Our last glimpse of her shows her smothered in the care of parents and husband together: Edgar, now 'the repository of her every thought ... rarely part[s] her from her fond Parents and enraptured Uncle' (p. 913). Burney has shown, with great perception, the difficulties of growing up as a woman in eighteenth-century society; but the solution she offers is a perpetual childhood.

JANE AUSTEN AND THE TRADITION OF THE REFORMED HEROINE

The work of Jane Austen (1775–1817) comes after over a century in which women novelists played an important part in forming the novel's conventions, and her achievement, so much greater than the achievements of her precursors, arises out of the tradition they established. In *The Rise of the Novel*, Ian Watt describes her strength as the ability to unite Fielding's external and Richardson's internal techniques for rendering character,[31] and the skill with which she does so entitles her to the praise Barbara Hardy gives her as a great, if quiet, innovator in fiction, the creator of the modern novel.[32] Several studies have pointed out Austen's indebtedness to earlier novelists, particularly the Richardson of *Sir Charles Grandison*, and Fanny Burney, and also to the work of those sentimentalists and Gothic novelists whom she mocked in her juvenilia and the early novels.[33]

The women's didactic tradition had a particularly strong influence on Austen. She read and admired not only Burney and Edgeworth, but lesser-known writers like Charlotte Lennox and Jane West, and she also read Charlotte Smith with much attention, though she enjoyed mocking her for sentimental excess.[34] More important, though, than possible

direct influences, or even particular points of resemblance between
earlier women novelists and Austen, is the fact that these precursors
had established the woman novelist's didactic role, and built up a
tradition of the thoughtless heroine who needs an education in discretion
and moral awareness. Austen's work is part of this tradition, though her
attitude to it is complex, and her adaptations of it subtle and far-
reaching. We can get some idea of Austen's place within the women's
didactic tradition by examining the way she treats the convention of the
lover–mentor in three of her novels: *Pride and Prejudice* (1813), *Mansfield
Park* (1814) and *Emma* (1815).

To place Austen within a tradition characterized by its message of
conformity is to oppose the view, offered by several recent critics, that
she is a feminist novelist deeply critical of her society.[35] Certainly, like
Wollstonecraft in *The Rights of Woman*, she criticizes the reduction of
female education to the pursuit of trivial accomplishments. On the other
hand, so does the conservative writer, Hannah More, in *Strictures on the
Modern System of Female Education* (1799), a work conceived of as a
refutation of Wollstonecraft. More, who considered that 'the imposing
term of *rights* has been produced to sanctify the claims of our female
pretenders ... with a view to excite in [women's] hearts an impious
discontent with the post which God has assigned them', actually sounded
like Wollstonecraft at certain points. When she recommended serious
study to women because 'it corrects that spirit of trifling which [a woman]
naturally contracts from the frivolous turn of female conversation and
the petty nature of female employments',[36] she echoed the complaint
made in *The Rights of Woman* that the 'love of pleasure, fostered by the
whole tendency of their education, gives a trifling turn to the conduct of
women in most circumstances; ... they are ever anxious about secondary
things; and on the watch for adventures instead of being occupied by
duties' (*The Rights of Woman*, p. 151). That More and Wollstonecraft
shared a belief in taking women seriously is not so much a tribute to
the success of Wollstonecraftian feminism as an indication that the
revolutionary feminist writer and the reactionary were both heirs to a
long tradition of women's didactic writing—as Jane Austen was, too.
An exposure of the shortcomings of the usual female education is central
to her work, and the Austen heroine is a woman who can rise above
trifling and frivolity and deserves to be treated as a rational creature,
as Elizabeth Bennet asks Mr Collins to treat her. Yet, unlike Wollstonecraft in her novels, Austen integrates her thinking heroines into
society as it is. Didacticism is not, for her, a method to be transformed
into an attack on male authority and prerogative. Unlike Wollstonecraft
she upholds the status quo, and has her heroines marry landowners or
other leaders of the community, thus underlining her approval of the

established hierarchy when those at the top fulfil their moral responsibilities.

Yet Austen does want a better status for women within that hierarchy. When we look at her as part of the long tradition of heroine-centred moral writing, we can see that she shares some of Edgeworth's and Inchbald's reservations about didactic men. In contrast to the excessive faith placed in the hero's guidance in some novels—notably Richardson's lover–mentor novel, *Sir Charles Grandison*, and Burney's *Camilla*—she brings her lovers to positions of moral equality. Unlike Burney, Austen never offers retreat into childhood as a solution to the heroine's problems. Central to her work is the belief in women's capacity for intellectual and moral growth that underlies most novels of the reformed coquette tradition, and makes for the progressive element within the tradition of conformity. Feminist argument had gone much further than this in the years before Austen's work, but her novels, nevertheless, give a new view of women, because within them, the picture of the learning heroine, sketched in earlier reformed coquette novels, is most fully and convincingly developed.

Pride and Prejudice

Begun in the later 1790s but not published until 1813, *Pride and Prejudice* contains the liveliest of heroines to be reformed, Elizabeth Bennet. The hero, Darcy, corresponds to the lover–mentor of other novels. Unlike most of them, he is no morally superior guardian; rather he is a truth-teller, who dispels the heroine's illusions. Darcy's letter revealing the truth about George Wickham is the turning-point of the novel because it initiates the self-examination which leads to Elizabeth's reform. She is made to reassess her unreasonable prejudices in favour of Wickham and against Darcy; and the turn inward to self-analysis marks the beginning of her moral progress. The change in the heroine is reflected in a change of emphasis in the novel's narrative method.

The 'light, and bright, and sparkling' qualities Austen pretended to sigh over are especially in evidence in the first half of the book, where the emphasis is on dialogue and on Elizabeth's witty and dominating part in it.[37] Adept at the surfaces of social life and convinced that this makes her a 'studier of character', Elizabeth actually misinterprets many key conversations and builds up a false picture of the people and events around her.[38] She announces to Mr Bingley that she understands him perfectly, and believes that she understands Mr Darcy equally well; but her dislike of him, founded on his slighting remarks about her overheard at their first meeting, and fuelled by the enjoyment she gets out of being witty at his expense, blinds her to his good qualities.

When Elizabeth makes the crucial mistake of believing Wickham's story about Darcy's treatment of him, we see how she is tricked by her delight in his indiscreet words into being indiscreet, and undiscriminating, herself. Having witnessed the two men's cold meeting she longs to hear what 'she could not hope to be told, the history of his acquaintance with Mr. Darcy. ... Her curiosity however was unexpectedly relieved. Mr. Wickham began the subject himself' (*Pride and Prejudice*, p. 77). It is Elizabeth, however, who is 'unwilling to let the subject drop' (p. 77), and she encourages him to continue by revealing her own low opinion of Darcy.

Jane Austen is always interested in what is passing in her heroine's mind, but in this scene her investigation is limited to a few references to Elizabeth's 'thought' and 'reflection'. The brief glimpses we get of Elizabeth's mind show her deceiving herself with surface impressions of Wickham. Hearing Wickham announce that he will never publicly disgrace Darcy out of respect for his father's memory, 'Elizabeth honoured him for such feelings, and thought him handsomer than ever as he expressed them' (p. 80). She does not reflect that he is at this moment doing his best to publicize his view of Darcy by giving it to a stranger. Throughout this dialogue, whenever Elizabeth is said to be thinking, the thoughts themselves do not appear but the rash speeches that result from them do:

> 'I ... did not suspect [Darcy] of descending to such malicious revenge, such injustice, such inhumanity as this!'
> After a few minutes reflection, however, she continued, 'I *do* remember his boasting one day ... of the implacability of his resentments ... His disposition must be dreadful.' ...
> Elizabeth was again deep in thought, and after a time exclaimed, 'To treat in such a manner, the godson, the friend, the favourite of his father!' (p. 80)

Elizabeth is *said* to be deep in thought, but what the narrative conveys is her lack of true reflection.

In the later scene, when she receives Darcy's letter explaining his connection with Wickham, her behaviour is very different. She is not impervious to truth clearly stated and backed up with evidence. Her mind begins to work properly, and she reads closely, 'command[ing] herself so far as to examine the meaning of every sentence' (p. 205). She 'read[s], and re-read[s] with the closest attention' (p. 205), all Darcy's details. She begins to think back on her blind approval of Wickham, and this time her thoughts lead her not to hasty words, but to fresh attention to the evidence: 'She could see him instantly before her, in every charm of air and address; but she could remember no more substantial good than the general approbation of the neighbourhood ... After pausing on this point a considerable while, she once more continued to read' (p. 206). Eventually she looks back to the conversation with Wickham, and gives it the reflection she has never allowed it before:

> She perfectly remembered every thing that had passed in
> conversation between Wickham and herself ... Many of his
> expressions were still fresh in her memory. She was *now* struck with
> the impropriety of such communications to a stranger, and
> wondered it had escaped her before. She saw the indelicacy of
> putting himself forward as he had done, and the inconsistency of his
> professions with his conduct. (pp. 206–7)

These reflections lead to the conclusion, dramatically presented in interior monologue: 'Till this moment, I never knew myself' (p. 208).

From now on Elizabeth reflects more often, and we are more often inside her mind as it goes through its prolonged task of reassessment. Her family's behaviour, her father's attitude to her mother, her visit to Pemberley and the changing feelings about Darcy that it encourages, are all subjects of reflection. Witty Elizabeth, deceived by appearances and unwary in conversation, has learned to weigh things in her mind, and as a result she improves not only in judgment but in feeling, learning not only to be fair to Darcy but to love him.

Though Elizabeth has to move from witty speech to serious thought, Austen does not finally attack the liveliness of a heroine she thought 'as delightful a creature as ever appeared in print'.[39] Her lively spirits are important moral agents for Darcy. As she herself informs him later, he is first attracted to her by her impudence, so unlike the flattery he is used to as a rich and powerful man. Her scornful rejection of his first proposal is the trigger for his reformation. He learns from her that his pride threatens to ruin his virtues; whereas he thinks his rank above hers, she tells him that his haughty manners debase him. Her assurance that she would not have accepted him, but might have felt some sympathy for him, if he had proposed 'in a more gentleman-like manner' (p. 192), reminds him that being a gentleman is a matter of behaviour, not merely of social standing; and her refusal rebukes him for pride of sex as well as pride of rank. His evident expectation that she will accept his first proposal links him to Mr Collins, whose earlier proposal to Elizabeth showed his belief that a woman must be eager to grasp any eligible offer of marriage. Darcy, though never so scornful of women as to believe, with Mr Collins, that a woman's no is a coy yes, is equally convinced of his own irresistibility. His arrogant assumption of the man's privilege of choice is shown in his first remarks about Elizabeth: 'not handsome enough to tempt *me* ... I am in no humour ... to give consequence to young ladies who are slighted by other men' (p. 12). It has to be replaced by respect for the woman's privilege of refusal, evinced when he proposes for a second time and tells her 'one word from you will silence me on this subject for ever' (p. 366). As he confesses later, Elizabeth herself has brought about the change: 'By you, I was properly humbled. I came to you without a doubt of my reception. You shewed me how insufficient were all my pretensions to please a woman worthy of being pleased' (p. 369).

Pride and Prejudice is very different from the reformed coquette novels in which the hero is right and the heroine wrong, but neither does it present the opposite extreme, the ideal heroine who guides a man to morality. Darcy and Elizabeth are equals, and each has something to teach the other. Romantic comedy becomes Austen's means of reforming her heroine without elevating her hero's authority. Elizabeth is reformed without being subdued, and her spirits are understandably 'soon rising to playfulness again' (p. 380).

Mansfield Park

In *Mansfield Park*, a work of much darker tone, it is not so easy for erring lovers to reform each other. In fact, it is here that the lover–mentor convention is given its most thorough dissection. The relationship between hero and heroine begins in the tradition of mentor and pupil: like Burney's Edgar and Camilla, Austen's Edmund Bertram and Fanny Price grow up together. He begins to take the part played by lover–mentors in other novels: 'he recommended the books which charmed her leisure hours, he encouraged her taste, and corrected her judgment'.[40] As she grows into a shy and awkward girl in her teens he offers her good advice and gently checks her excessive sensitivity.

The stage seems set for a love growing out of the tutor–pupil relationship; but Edmund falls in love with Mary Crawford instead. Mary has all the vitality and wit Fanny lacks, but none of her steady principles, and Austen's irony is directed against this mentor who so little understands the value of the mind he has helped to form that he falls for its opposite. With amusement we see the tables turned on the mentor. Fanny, more clear-sighted than he, sees all the faults of Mary and her brother, Henry, and maintains her objections to the thoughtless conduct that both Crawfords and Bertrams indulge in. Edmund, initially sharing Fanny's assessment of the Crawfords, is led by his admiration for Mary to join in the activity that expresses the young peoples' irresponsibility and potential immorality—the performance of *Lovers' Vows*.[41]

Edmund now needs Fanny's advice instead of the other way round, and with a fine irony Austen makes him both recognize the fact and refuse to follow it to its logical conclusion. Wondering if he should retract his objections to private theatricals in order to act with Mary as her lover, he comes to the schoolroom to ask Fanny for her advice. It soon appears, however, that he actually thinks there is 'but *one* thing to be done' (*Mansfield Park*, p. 154). He wants to act. Fanny hesitates to offer an opinion, and his apparent deference to her judgment masks determination to have his own way. 'I see your judgement is not with me. Think it a little over' he begins, and is soon urging her, 'Give me your approbation ... I am not comfortable without it' (pp. 154–5). She does not, but he pretends to himself that she has done, and decides to join the acting, leaving Fanny to the bitter knowledge that he is inconsistent and self-deluded, and that it is 'all Miss Crawford's doing' (p. 156).

Worse is to come from Edmund. When Henry Crawford proposes marriage, Fanny expects that Edmund, if not his father, will agree that it is right to refuse a man she cannot love. Yet though he agrees that her initial refusal was right, he confounds her immediately afterwards with the plea, 'let him succeed at last ... prove yourself grateful and tender-hearted' (p. 347). He expects her to alter her feelings to suit his, and provide in her love for Henry a neat parallel to his love for Henry's sister.

Fanny's distrust of the Crawfords is borne out by events; and when Henry Crawford by adultery, and Mary by frivolity, have put themselves out of Fanny and Edmund's sphere, Edmund is ready to acknowledge himself mistaken. 'How have I been deceived! Equally in brother and sister deceived! I thank you for your patience, Fanny' (p. 459). He means her patience in listening to the story of his final disillusionment; but in fact Fanny has been waiting patiently throughout the novel, for this admission and the love which soon follows it. 'Even in the midst of his late infatuation, he had acknowledged Fanny's mental superiority [over Mary]. What must be his sense of it now, therefore? She was of course only too good for him; but ... nobody minds having what is too good for them' (p. 471). Austen's irony undermines the conventional transformation of mentor into lover. What could be more natural than Edmund's changing from Mary to Fanny, she asks, 'Loving, guiding, protecting her, as he had been doing ever since her being ten years old, her mind in so great a degree formed by his care[?]' (p. 470). Most of the love, guidance and protection, in fact, has come from Fanny.

Austen, however, does not simply reverse the usual tradition, substituting a female lover–mentor for the male. In *Mansfield Park* she attacks the whole idea of either good man or good woman reforming the opposite sex through love and guidance. Edmund's attempt to reform

Mary Crawford provides plenty of evidence against the practice. He sees her faults but spends his time making excuses for them; and instead of influencing her he merely deceives himself about the amount of goodness behind her coquetry. Fanny does better not because she makes a better lover–mentor, but because she refuses to be one.

Henry Crawford's courtship gives Fanny every chance of playing this role. He resolves to marry her because he has 'too much sense not to feel the worth of good principles in a wife, though he [is] too little accustomed to serious reflection to know them by their proper name' (p. 294). He believes Fanny will be a wife in whom he can 'wholly and absolutely confide' (p. 294); and that, without taking the trouble to be virtuous himself, he will have all the credit for recognizing virtue and raising it from its lowly estate. Edmund's arguments in favour of their marriage place Fanny as Crawford's mentor:

> 'a most fortunate man [Henry Crawford] is to attach himself to such a creature—to a woman, who firm as a rock in her own principles, has a gentleness of character so well adapted to recommend them. He has chosen his partner, indeed, with rare felicity. He will make you happy, Fanny, I know he will make you happy; but you will make him every thing.'
>
> 'I would not engage in such a charge,' cried Fanny in a shrinking accent—'in such an office of high responsibility!'
>
> 'As usual, believing yourself unequal to anything!' (p. 351)

Edmund's retort here is unfair: Fanny's shrinking is evidence of a humility he needs himself. To try to 'make' another person is certainly too high a responsibility for a fallible human being to undertake in Jane Austen's world. Edmund, in his pride of virtue, is trying to 'make' Mary Crawford 'everything' that she is not; but Fanny, with greater moral sensibility, refuses to 'make' Henry. When he tries to win her by asking her advice, telling her 'Your judgment is my rule of right', she refuses the flattering role he offers: 'Oh, no!—do not say so. We have all a better guide in ourselves, if we would attend to it, than any other person can be' (p. 412). Edmund later learns what Fanny already knows—that only conscience can effect true reform. Any attempt at influence which goes beyond awakening the other's own conscience is doomed to failure. Fanny can offer a kind of moral guidance to Edmund but it is by example, not advice, and it only works once he has become aware of his own errors. Fanny's marriage to Edmund has disturbed many readers, who prefer the idea of marriage to a reformed Henry Crawford, showing that balancing of opposites that Elizabeth favours in *Pride and Prejudice*. But Jane Austen is deliberately undercutting the complacent belief in the power of love to reform. Elizabeth and Darcy influence each other for good, but the change comes from within. Without that inner moral life, which neither Mary nor Henry possesses, no-one can be reformed by a lover–mentor.

Emma

In *Emma*, on the other hand, the hero is able to influence the heroine for good. He is like Grandison or Orville humanized, his occasional irascibility and his jealousy of Frank Churchill stopping him from being one of the blank 'pictures of perfection' Austen disliked.[42] The transformation of mentor into lover is made more acceptable to her by Mr Knightley's awareness of incongruity between the two roles: 'I have blamed you, and lectured you, and you have borne it as no other woman in England would have borne it ... God knows, I have been a very indifferent lover', he tells her.[43] The good of his advice is increased by his humility about its effect: 'My interference was quite as likely to do harm as good. ... The good was all to myself, by making you an object of the tenderest affection to me' (p. 462). If he underestimates his influence here, his diffidence as lover–mentor saves him from doing harm in the role. Reform has come from Emma herself, and through Austen's portrayal of her interior monologue we have witnessed the inner change.

The tradition in the feminine didactic novel for rendering the heroine's thought-process in narrative reaches its highest degree of refinement here. We are inside Emma's consciousness for much of the narrative, yet we are continually invited to take a critical attitude to the workings of her mind. One of the pleasures of reading the novel is registering the irony against the heroine when she wilfully suppresses her own honest and intelligent reactions—for example, in favour of Robert Martin's letter against Mr Elton's pretentious charade—so as to persuade herself into the opinion that best suits her favourite schemes. Emma is descended from the eighteenth-century coquette, but she differs radically in one important respect: she does not have the conventionally 'feminine' vanity about her own powers of attraction. She does plan some flirtation with Frank Churchill, but she does most of her scheming on behalf of other people: believing herself to have smoothed the way for Mrs Weston's marriage, making up a guilty passion for Jane Fairfax, trying to marry Harriet to Mr Elton and then to Frank Churchill. Her faults could be seen as much more serious than the coquette's because she interferes with other people's lives; but the effect of her lack of coquettish vanity is to make her likeable in the midst of her self-delusion.

Austen advocates self-knowledge and shows her heroines reaching it through introspection, but she also sees moral dangers in too much thought about the self. It is because Emma is not self-centred that Austen finds her errors easy to forgive. As we follow Emma's thoughts we are invited to register her mistakes but also to recognize that they are not the mistakes of solipsism. One example of the complex mixture of faultiness and saving grace in Emma's unselfconsciousness is her misinterpretation of Frank Churchill at the famous Box Hill party. When Frank asks her to choose a wife for him, Emma, wilfully stupid, manages to hear this as encouragement for her secret scheme of marrying him to Harriet: 'Would not Harriet be the very creature described?—Hazle eyes excepted' (p. 373). Self-blinded like this, she carries on flirting with Frank, unwittingly hurting Jane Fairfax and hardly acting well towards the woman she intends to make Frank's wife. Yet if Emma's love of manipulating others leads her to deceive herself, a better side of her aids the deception—her habitual unconsciousness of her own beauty. This scene calls to mind the earlier one in which, Emma being absent, Mrs Weston admires her hazel eyes and Mr Knightley adds in her favour that she is not 'personally vain' (p. 39). Obviously this amiable trait is far from keeping Emma from doing wrong: her intellectual vanity has worse consequences than conventional 'feminine' vanity. Yet it does indicate that her thoughts are not fixed on herself, and that therefore she has the potential for moral growth.

Emma's love for Mr Knightley, the one person who does not flatter her, is to her credit. She puts her power of quick thinking to good use for the first time when, realizing she loves him, she comes to know herself: 'It darted through her, with the speed of an arrow, that Mr. Knightley must marry no one but herself' (p. 408). Long, painful and accurate self-assessment follows. In learning to use her thinking powers correctly, Emma has to learn to think both more, and less, about herself. More in the sense that she realizes she too is involved in the world of love and marriage, less in that she learns the folly of trying to mould other people to fit her ideas. When she thinks Mr Knightley wants to tell her about his love for Harriet, she forgets self in her endeavour to help him: 'cost her what it would, she would listen' (p. 429). She is immediately, and comically, rewarded. Mr Knightley wants to talk about his love for her, not her friend. In fact Emma has never been more mistaken in her judgment than when she believes that Mr Knightley may marry Harriet. Her reform is not complete without the realization that her self-abasement can go too far, and 'that Harriet was nothing; that she was everything herself' to Mr Knightley (p. 430). Emma learns the self's claims as well as its limits, and her self-denying intention of remaining single for her father's sake is soon overcome by Mr Knightley's practical suggestion of moving into Hartfield, which combines unselfish consideration of Mr Woodhouse with a sense of what is due to himself and Emma.

Mary Wollstonecraft's feminist endeavour in *Mary* was to create a heroine with 'thinking powers',[44] but the novel's first really full presentation of such a heroine is Jane Austen's. Misused, Emma's intelligence almost brings about catastrophe, but it is not only, as she wryly reflects in one of her penitent phases, 'too late in the day to set about being simple-minded and ignorant' (p. 142), it is undesirable. Emma's silliest mistake is the idea that silly Harriet will be a better wife to Mr Knightley than her intelligent self. Once she has learned to know herself, Emma's thinking powers will make her the equal of her lover–mentor as the conventionally 'feminine' woman she praises, 'such a girl as Harriet ... exactly what every man delights in ... what ... bewitches his senses' (p. 64), could never be.

Austen's critical attitude to the workings of her heroine's mind leads her to new depths in the portrayal of women in fiction. The rational heroine, whose good sense may be used in support of her author's feminism, tends to be a static figure. This is true of Charlotte Smith's heroines, who though they are said to learn their unusual powers of mind from experience, are rarely shown in the process of learning. It is true to some extent of Edgeworth's Belinda, for though we often see her mind at work, she tends to become a model of good sense against whom coquettish Lady Delacour and simple Virginia are measured. Paradoxically, Emma, the heroine who learns to distrust her own mind, gives greater evidence of the heroine's 'thinking powers', and does more to establish complexity of female character in fiction.

The tradition of the reformed heroine, however much its basic fable worked in the opposite direction to feminist protest, did contain the implicit assumption that women's moral growth was both more important and more interesting than had usually been thought. The novelists discussed here challenged the fictional convention Wollstonecraft complained of, whereby 'the hero is allowed to be mortal, and to become wise and virtuous as well as happy, by a train of events and circumstances. The heroines, on the contrary, are to be born immaculate'.[45] Austen took this development further. It is not just that, as one critic pointed out, Emma 'has a moral life as a man has a moral life',[46] but that she is the first character in English fiction, male or female, to have a moral life so richly created and yet ironically analysed. Characterization of men in the novel only reached a comparable level after Austen's example had shown the way. The tradition of the lover–mentor and the reformed coquette grew out of a narrow didactic role prescribed for the woman writer; but in using it, women novelists expanded and deepened the fictional presentation of human character.

NOTES

1. *Monthly Review* **5** (1751), p. 394.
2. *Monthly Review* **5** (1751), p. 515.
3. *Monthly Review* **5** (1751), p. 394.
4. *The Rape of the Lock*, Canto II, in *The Poems of Alexander Pope*, ed. Butt (1-volume Twickenham edn), p. 223.
5. See *The Female Quixote*, ed. M. Dalziel (London: Oxford University Press, 1970), p. 383.
6. See R. A. Day, introduction to *Olinda's Adventures: Or the Amours of a Young Lady* (Augustan Reprint Society Publication No. 138. University of California, Los Angeles: Williams Andrews Clark Memorial Library, 1969), pp. ii–v.
7. *Olinda's Adventures*, p. 134.
8. *The Way of the World*, Act II, in *The Works of Congreve*, ed. F. W. Bateson (London, 1930), p. 326.
9. See *Memoirs of Miss Sidney Bidulph, Extracted from Her Own Journal, And now First Published* (Dublin, 1761). Sidney's daughters appear in the sequel, *Conclusion of the Memoirs of Miss Sidney Bidulph* (1767).
10. See *The School For Widows* (Dublin, 1791).
11. See *The Advantages of Education*, by 'Prudentia Homespun' (London: Minerva Press, 1793).
12. The comedy of the coquette finally cured of frivolity and won by a serious-minded man has been dated from Crowne's *The English Friar* (1690): see John Harrington Smith, *The Gay Couple in Restoration Comedy* (Harvard University Press, 1948) pp. 142–3. A similar pattern is found in the sub-plot of Cibber's *The Careless Husband* (1715) which Betsy Thoughtless goes to see in Haywood's novel.
13. Jane Austen, *Emma, The Novels of Jane Austen*, ed. R. W. Chapman, **IV** 3rd edn (London: Oxford University Press, 1966), p. 5.
14. *The Reform'd Coquet*, in *The Works of Mrs. Davys* (London, 1725), **II**, pp. 83–4.
15. *The History of Miss Betsy Thoughtless* (London: T. Gardner, 1751), **I**, p. 82.
16. *Emma*, p. 412.
17. *Pride and Prejudice, The Novels of Jane Austen*, ed. R. W. Chapman, **II**, 3rd edn (London: Oxford University Press, 1967), p. 208.
18. See J. P. Erickson, *Evelina and Betsy Thoughtless, Texas Studies in Literature and Language* **6** (1964), pp. 96–103.
19. See Erickson, p. 97.
20. *Evelina*, p. 72.
21. *The Cry: A new dramatic fable* (London: R. and J. Dodsley, 1754), **III**, p. 258.
22. *A Simple Story*, ed. J. M. S. Tompkins (Oxford University Press, 1977), pp. 3 and 5.
23. "'It is only Cecilia, or Camilla, or Belinda;" or, in short, only some work in which the greatest powers of the mind are displayed, in which the

most thorough knowledge of human nature, the happiest delineation of its varieties, the liveliest effusions of wit and humour are conveyed to the world in the best chosen language.' *Northanger Abbey* in *The Novels of Jane Austen*, ed. R. W. Chapman, **V**, 3rd edn (London: Oxford University Press, 1969), p. 38.

24. Marilyn Butler discusses *Belinda* in her *Maria Edgeworth: A Biography* (Oxford: Clarendon Press, 1972); see esp. pp. 307–15.

25. See Butler, *Maria Edgeworth*, p. 39n.

26. *Belinda*, 3rd edn, (London: J. Johnson and Co., 1811), **III**, pp. 104–5.

27. *Camilla*, ed. Edward A. Bloom and Lillian D. Bloom (London: Oxford University Press, 1972), p. 267.

28. *Critical Review*, 2nd ser. **18**, (1796), p. 40.

29. This view is argued by Joyce Hemlow in *The History of Fanny Burney*: see Chapter X, '*Camilla: or, A Picture of Youth*'.

30. See Rose Marie Cutting, 'Defiant Women: The Growth of Feminism in Fanny Burney's Novels', *Studies in English Literature 1500–1900* **17** (1977), pp. 519–30. Cutting's claim for Burney's 'growing rebellion against the restrictions imposed upon women' (pp. 519–20) is not in my view entirely convincing. I agree rather with Patricia Spacks that Burney's later work 'acknowledges more openly the high psychic cost of female compliance' with social restrictions, but does not challenge the view that this compliance is necessary. See *Imagining A Self*, p. 181.

31. 'Jane Austen's novels ... must be seen as the most successful solutions of the two general narrative problems for which Richardson and Fielding had provided only partial answers. She was able to combine into a harmonious unity the advantages both of realism of presentation and realism of assessment, of the internal and of the external approaches to character.' *The Rise of the Novel* (Harmondsworth: Penguin, 1977), p. 338.

32. Barbara Hardy, *A Reading of Jane Austen* (London: Peter Owen, 1975), p. 11.

33. See especially Kenneth Moler, *Jane Austen's Art of Allusion* (Nebraska, 1968). Moler argues that Austen revises the relationship between heroine and 'patrician hero' found in Richardson and Burney, making the heroine challenge the hero's authority: I have drawn on his work in the discussion of *Pride and Prejudice*. Marilyn Butler, in *Jane Austen and the War of Ideas*, presents Austen as a conservative writer reacting against the radicalism of the popular novel in the 1790s. Both these writers stress Austen's disagreements with the traditions she inherits: for a different view, placing Austen in relation to the Gothic and characterizing her as 'almost an imitator ... an heiress of Radcliffe', see Judith Wilt, *Ghosts of the Gothic* (Princeton: Princeton University Press, 1980), pp. 130–1.

34. For Austen's remarks on Lennox and West see *Jane Austen's Letters*, ed. R. W. Chapman (Oxford University Press, 1979), pp. 173 and 466. Mary Lascelles points out Austen's possible parody of Smith's heroine Emmeline in Catherine Morland of *Northanger Abbey*. See *Jane Austen and her Art* (Oxford University Press paperback, 1983), p. 60.

35. This view is most extensively argued by Margaret Kirkham in *Jane Austen, Feminism and Fiction* (Sussex: Harvester Press, 1983), where she links Austen

and Wollstonecraft together as 'feminist moralists' (p. 48). While agreeing
with Kirkham that both writers inherit the eighteenth-century tradition of
women's writing which insists that women are rational moral beings, I find
this insufficient to place Austen in the forefront of feminism, in an age
when feminist argument had gone far beyond this contention to include a
radical critique of the social institution of male dominance in the marriage
laws and women's forced economic dependence. What Austen's cham-
pionship of women's rationality shows is rather the successful integration
of an earlier phase of feminist argument into the women's didactic novel,
without disturbing its basic message of conformity.

36. *The Works of Hannah More*, **V** (London: T. Cadell, 1830), pp. 136 and 230.
37. Letter to Cassandra Austen, 4 February 1813; in *Jane Austen's Letters*, p. 299.
38. *Pride and Prejudice*, p. 42.
39. Letter to Cassandra Austen, 29 January 1813; in *Jane Austen's Letters*, p. 297.
40. *Mansfield Park, The Novels of Jane Austen*, ed. R. W. Chapman, **III**, 3rd edn (London: Oxford University Press, 1966), p. 22.
41. The German playwright Kotzebue's *Lovers' Vows*, translated by Elizabeth Inchbald, was popular in England between 1798 and 1802. It concerns a Baron who is persuaded to marry the peasant woman he once seduced, and the Baron's daughter, who persuades a clergyman to overlook their differences of rank and marry her. The play thus subverts social and sexual conventions: see Butler, p. 234. For a different view of the play's significance within *Mansfield Park*, suggesting that what Austen opposes in Kotzebue is his sentimentalization of women, see Kirkham, pp. 110–16.
42. Letter to Fanny Knight, 23 March 1817; in *Jane Austen's Letters*, p. 486.
43. *Emma*, p. 430.
44. Advertisement to *Mary*, in *Mary* and *The Wrongs of Woman*, n. pag.
45. Preface to *The Wrongs of Woman*, in *Mary* and *The Wrongs of Woman*, p. 73.
46. Lionel Trilling, '*Emma* and the Legend of Jane Austen' (1957); rpt. in David Lodge, ed., *Emma: A Casebook* (London: Macmillan, 1968), p. 154.

6

Romance Heroines:
The Tradition of Escape

Romances oppose reality. That is the substance of the realist's attack on them, and early novelists never tired of assuring their readers that their works, unlike romances, were real and true. *The Fair Jilt*, said Behn, was not 'a feign'd Story, or any Thing piec'd together with romantick Accidents; but every Circumstance, to a Tittle, is Truth.' Defoe shielded his *Farther Adventures of Robinson Crusoe* (1719) from charges of unreality: 'All the Endeavours of envious People to reproach it with being a Romance, to search it for Errors in Geography, Inconsistency in the Relation, and Contradictions in the Fact, have proved abortive', he claimed.[1] Characterized by feigning, improbable coincidence, errors, inconsistency and contradictions, clearly romance was being rejected as inferior to reality. The realistic novel is in part an expression of reaction against romance, and its beginnings have been traced in Cervantes' *Don Quixote*, which takes as its subject the confrontation between reality and the illusions of romance.[2] The quixote who is deluded by romantic expectation is a favourite butt for satire from Cervantes onwards.

Yet the novel depends heavily on those romantic elements at which novelists like to laugh. Novels use structures derived from romance such as the quest, the rise and progress of a low-born or apparently low-born hero, the unknown protagonist's discovery of his or her real identity and parentage. Northrop Frye has called the novel 'a realistic displacement of romance', which uses 'the same general structure' as romance but adapts it to 'a demand for greater conformity to ordinary experience'.[3] The difference between the two genres would seem from this point of view to be one of degree rather than kind.

Certainly 'romance' and 'novel' were not always distinguished from each other in the eighteenth century. Critics mentioning 'romances' sometimes referred to fiction in general—often signalled by their putting 'novels and romances' together as sharing the same faults—and sometimes to an older form of writing like the medieval romance or the seventeenth-century French romance, which they distinguished from the novel (or, confusingly, 'modern romance'). Later in the century the distinction between romance and novel became better established, and Clara Reeve gave it clear expression in her history of fiction: 'The Romance is an heroic fable, which treats of fabulous persons and things.—The Novel is a picture of real life and manners, and of the times in which it is written'.[4] Novelists had good reason to insist on this difference, because while the novel was associated with romance it had the same reputation for unreality. Hume criticized novels and romances for their 'false Representations of Mankind', and Fielding censured improbability equally in the works of 'the Authors of immense Romances, or the modern Novel and *Atalantis* Writers'.[5] On the other hand, Reeve, writing after the realistic novel—not least by Fielding's own efforts— had made its mark, reserved her charges of improbability for the French romances, which, she wrote, falsified history.[6]

Yet no sooner had the anti-romantic standard of 'a picture of real life and manners' been raised than the impulse to deal with 'fabulous persons and things' cropped up again in a new guise. Novelists moved the settings of their work away from 'the time in which it was written' to explore medieval (Gothic) times, and use them as a pretext for fantasy. What are now called Gothic novels were often called romances when they first appeared. Horace Walpole, complaining that in the modern novel 'the great resources of fancy have been dammed up, by a strict adherence to common life', produced what he claimed was 'a new species of romance' in *The Castle of Otranto* (1765).[7] Ann Radcliffe's *Mysteries of Udolpho* and *The Italian* were both described on their title pages as 'A Romance'.[8]

Romance obviously held a continuing appeal for the novelist and the novel-reader; and it held an especially strong appeal for women. We have already seen that the romance was one source of a role-model for the woman writer. It is also noticeable that all the most 'romantic' kinds of fiction were strongly associated with female authorship or audience, from the French romances, through the amatory fictions of Manley and Haywood, to the Gothic novel, whose greatest practitioners included Ann Radcliffe and Mary Shelley. Even in the more realistic women's novels of the eighteenth century the influence of the French romance can be found.[9] A similar phenomenon has been noted in earlier times. In his study of Elizabethan culture, Louis Wright claims that John Lyly and Robert Greene catered to a courtly feminine audience in their romances, and to explain this he universalizes the connection between romance and women: 'Since women in general have never subscribed to realism, romance in strange opera lands and love stories with happy endings found favor with the Elizabethans even as with feminine readers today'.[10]

Without resorting to the eternal feminine for explanation, we need to examine this connection, which has meant that much of women's fiction has been devalued as unrealistic. Why should women in general, and hence women writers, not subscribe to realism? It depends who decides what reality is. As Chapter 3 showed, eighteenth-century upholders of the realistic as opposed to the exemplary treatment of character considered it their task to show 'the world as it is' with all its unpleasant aspects. Early realistic novelists, as Ronald Paulson points out, see the real in whatever is opposed to the illusions of idealists: to them 'the ugly and the gross, the sensual and fecal, are real in contrast to the beautiful and harmonious; the middling and commonplace, the urban and local, are real in contrast to the heroic and extraordinary', and the picaro, antithesis of the romantic hero, is the proper realistic protagonist.[11] These realities were precisely what respectable women writers were not supposed to deal with. So far as the ordinary experience the novel depicted was the picaro's experience, it was outside women's range.

Yet women novelists writing about the lives of young ladies in their own society were, of course, dealing with reality and ordinary experience. The reason their work was not interpreted as realistic has to do with society's attitude to the young lady's life. It was a life cut off, to a large extent, from what is too often termed 'the real world'—that is, the world outside the home. The young lady's concern with dress, amusements, accomplishments and attracting a husband was seen as frivolous and somehow not truly real. The ordinary experience of the proper woman was supposed to be mainly emotional experience: romantic love was considered to be at the centre of her life. Yet the very term *romantic* love shows that this experience is thought of as in some sense unreal, opposed, for example, to the economic reality of property-based marriage contracts. The feminocentric novel of the century was thus inescapably bound to the 'unreality' as well as the love-theme of romance.

What was 'unreal' about romance was precisely women's importance in it. In the seventeenth-century French romances the lover's humility and his lady's despotic power were legendary. Here is a typical romance hero addressing the beloved in Madeleine de Scudéry's once-famous work, *Clelia*: 'the boldnesse which I assume in loving you, has no ingredient in it which can displease you: ... I do not desire any thing from you in my advantage, but onely [sic] that you will give me leave to adore you'.[12] Of course, this kind of thing was not new: it had long been an accepted poetic convention that in the love relationship (when idealistically viewed) the normal hierarchy of the sexes was reversed, and the woman reigned; but the romance writers of seventeenth-century France pretended that this convention had a decisive power in real life. They related historical events with the stress on romantic love as the cause of actions that changed the world. These romances, much read in England in the seventeenth century, were soon overtaken in popularity by the novel in the eighteenth; but when the novel centred on a heroine, it usually reproduced the romance's emphasis on the power of love. Even when concerned with everyday life in a contemporary setting, novelists could still retain that vital feature of the French romance, the importance of women and their power in love. This, surely, was the main appeal of romance for the female reader: it offered escape from male-dominated reality through a fantasy of female power.

Over the whole of our period, women's novels of very diverse kinds contain elements of romance used for the purpose of creating this fantasy. This is especially noticeable in the sentimental novel. The world it portrays, more circumscribed than the world of romance, does not allow the heroine's charms to decide the outcome of war and the downfall of kingdoms. The ideals for hero and heroine are rather different from the ideals of romance: soft feeling and delicate sentiment are more prominent than formality and reserve in the lady, and the hero proves his worth not by military prowess but by sharing the feminine virtues. The relationship between hero and heroine, though, is reminiscent of romance. Despite their frequent mockery of romantic devotion, sentimental writers copy the romance's submissive lover in their own pictures of love relationships.

One early example of the sentimental reworking of romantic devotion is found in the work of Mary Collyer, a writer whose first publication was a translation of French sentimental writing: Marivaux's *La Vie de Marianne*, which appeared in Collyer's English version as *The Virtuous Orphan* in 1742. Soon afterwards Mary Collyer's own novel, *Felicia to Charlot* (1744), appeared. It has a typical sentimental theme: the war between love and duty, finally resolved so as to satisfy both. The story is told in the heroine's letters, which she writes as a parody of romance. She mocks her friend's supposedly romantic expectations: 'You are now ready to imagine I shall describe him throwing himself at my feet, while with a flow of rapture, he admires my superlative goodness, ... if these were your thoughts, you were extremely mistaken'.[13] The hero, Lucius, 'too good a christian to deify his mistress', wins the heroine with his conversation about the beauties of nature and the delights of virtue, not by paying her silly compliments. Yet the descriptions ostensibly contrasting Lucius with romance heroes only underline his resemblance to them. He does not flatter Felicia because, when he sees her alone, he is tongue-tied with diffidence. When he eventually confesses his love, he is as humble as any hero in romance: 'He opened his lips several times, but, quivering with fear, they instantly closed, without uttering a syllable; but at last, seeming to collect all his fortitude, Forgive me, Miss, said he, giving me a look inexpressibly tender; ... I saw his face covered with a deep blush' (*Felicia to Charlot*, I, 40). Felicia laughs at romances, but in the end she admits, 'I seem to be writing one myself' (I, 68).

Elements derived from romance were also exploited in the sentimental novels written in the 1760s and 1770s by Frances Brooke and Elizabeth Griffith. Both these writers stress the feminization of the hero. In Brooke's *Emily Montague*, Edward Rivers, who claims that his 'heart has all the sensibility of woman', is terrified of confessing his love: 'the timidity inseparable from love', he explains, 'makes me dread a full explanation of my sentiments' (II, 39 and II, 123). Henry Mandeville, hero of Brooke's *Lady Julia Mandeville*, has similar fears, and his devotion to Julia would not disgrace a romance hero: 'every action of my life', he reports, 'is directed to the sole purpose of pleasing her; my noblest ambition is to be worthy her esteem'.[14] In Elizabeth Griffith's *Lady Juliana Harley*, Charles Evelyn leaves the country rather than offend the heroine with his presence, and he even calls her, in the romance-fashion so favoured by Lennox's Arabella 'arbitress of my fate!'[15]

These writers, like Mary Collyer, include some mockery of romantic sentiment. It is usually provided by the heroine's livelier and wittier female friend. In *Lady Julia Mandeville* Anne Wilmot sprinkles her letters with sardonic comments on the lovers' extravagant feelings, and in *Emily Montague* Arabella Fermor mocks Emily's romantic attitudes. In *Lady Juliana Harley* Lucy Evelyn compares the hero and heroine to those of French romances. After a tearful parting scene between the lovers she writes to the heroine, 'Why surely since the days of Cassandra and Orondates [sic], and such other silly gentlemen and ladies of absurd memory, there never was, and I hope never will be, such a pair of ridiculous noodles as Lady Juliana Harley and Charles Evelyn' (*Lady Juliana Harley*, I, 149). She warns Charles Evelyn that his attitude will 'reinstate our mortal sex in their former rank of deities', exclaims against the boredom of a 'Platonic courtship', and laughs at his 'romantic strains' (II, 1–2). Yet the novels only incorporate these anti-romantic jibes in order to refute them. In the midst of her liveliness, Arabella Fermor acknowledges that Emily Montague's romantic attitudes place her love for Edward Rivers on a higher plane than her own for Fitzgerald: if both women marry their lovers, she reflects, Emily 'will certainly be more exquisitely happy than I shall' (*Emily Montague*, II, 180). The sad endings of Lady Julia's and Lady Juliana's love stories (Lady Juliana flees from the world to become a nun, while Julia Mandeville dies of grief after her lover has been killed in a duel) teach their mocking friends greater sensibility, and help them understand the romantic attitude.

The pervasiveness and persistence of romance elements affected the morality of women's fiction. We saw in Chapter 5 that women's central tradition in the novel was a didactic one, with a basically conformist message for the young female reader. Novels could even become fictional illustrations of the female conduct-book precepts, recommending modesty, gentleness, obedience to parents and guardians, and so on. Yet they were rarely just that. Didactic novels and nonfictional conduct books tended to agree on every point but one: romantic love, disparaged by moralists, was essential to most novels. This softened the didactic message. For instance, in Orville's trusting devotion to Evelina, the heroine regained the female power apparently lost through her intense desire to conform to feminine propriety. Other heroines, dutifully putting obedience to a father's authority before their own inclination for marriage, were often rewarded with love and happiness anyway, the novel's romantic theme thus subverting its moral point. In many cases, then, the appeal of romance within a novel worked against its conduct-book precepts, bringing internal contradiction to romantic fiction.

For this reason, many eighteenth-century writers saw in the novel the same dangers to female chastity and subordination that had formerly been attributed to the romance. Seventeenth-century moralists had predicted that reading romances would make young girls deceive their parents, run away with their lovers, and so be 'ruined', all in imitation of what they had read. Romances, it was argued, encouraged those who ought to be subordinate—men of the lower orders, and women of all ranks—to indulge in dangerous dreams of pre-eminence, imagining themselves kings and queens.[16] These fears were echoed in eighteenth-century comments on the novel. Novels, it was claimed, threatened chastity. The writer Hester Chapone (formerly Hester Mulso, and one of Richardson's correspondents) contended that novels were likely 'to inflame the passions of youth, whilst the chief purpose of education should be to moderate and restrain them'.[17] In 1790, one writer even attributed the recent 'alarming increase of prostitutes' to depravity caused by reading novels.[18] Other commentators feared not so much for the readers' chastity as their sense of reality. The novel, like the romance, was thought to encourage allegiance to the unreal. It was attacked for arousing 'extravagant desires, and notions of happiness alike fantastic and false', and for having such an influence on 'unguarded readers' that 'the whole system of life seems converted into romance'.[19] It was thought to destroy women's contentment with the realities of their lives. A woman entranced by the novel's version of love might refuse real offers of marriage. One writer claimed to know 'several unmarried ladies, who in all probability had been long ago good wives and good mothers, if their imaginations had not been early perverted with the chimerical ideas of romantic love' found in novels.[20] In her essay 'On the Origin and Progress of Novel-Writing' (1820), Anna Laetitia Barbauld wrote that novels 'paint too high' the passion of love, and credit it with a power in the world that it does not possess. They do not prepare the young girl for 'the neglect and tedium of life which she is perhaps doomed to encounter'.[21] Behind these criticisms lies an admission that explains the novel's appeal: an admission that the young lady's life was tedious, that she experienced regret, that marriage (if she was offered it) was not likely to satisfy all her desires. The continuing appeal of romance within the women's novel can be seen as a covert protest against the neglect and tedium of women's lives.

The 'romance' element in women's novels, then, is important as a fantasy of female power, through which women could escape in imagination from the reality of their oppression. This chapter will examine three novels where this fantasy can be clearly seen: Charlotte Lennox's anti-romantic novel *The Female Quixote* (1752) which clarifies fantasy by subjecting it to satire; and two Gothic novels, Sophia Lee's *The Recess* (1785) and Ann Radcliffe's *The Romance of the Forest* (1791) in which, freed from some of the realistic conventions, the writers push the implications of the fantasy of power much further than they are taken in the domestic sentimental novel.

A SATIRE ON FANTASY: CHARLOTTE LENNOX'S *THE FEMALE QUIXOTE* (1752)

No-one understood the appeal of romance better than Charlotte Lennox, whose novel *The Female Quixote: or, the Adventures of Arabella* is an analysis of romance as a fantasy of female power. Like its model, *Don Quixote*, it has a protagonist captivated by the visions of romance and comically blind to the real world. The difference is that the romances which have deluded Arabella are the seventeenth-century French romances with their pictures of the romantic heroine's absolute power over her lovers. Arabella's story is thus closely related to the reformed coquette tradition. Like the coquette, she is reluctant to give up the woman's power in the courtship game; and also like the coquette, she has a lover—mentor who tries to guide her into a more realistic frame of mind. Realism for Arabella, as for Amoranda or Betsy Thoughtless, means giving up the illusion of power and accepting the proper, subordinate role of the young woman in society. In the didactic tradition to which all these novels belong, there is a connection between the anti-romantic and the anti-feminist elements.

Arabella, brought up in the country by her widowed father, has seen nothing of the world, and she believes that the romances she reads are reflections of life. Her entry into wider society, in Bath and later in

London, provides opportunities for satirical contrast between her ideals and reality, in which fashionable society is Lennox's target as much as romantic illusion. Eventually Arabella, cured of her delusions, marries her cousin Glanville, who has been patiently waiting for her to come to terms with the real world.

Comedy in *The Female Quixote* is generated by Arabella's application of the expectations, moral standards and elevated diction of the French romances to the incidents of everyday life. When one of her father's gardeners is caught trying to steal fish from the pond, Arabella insists on believing him to be a young nobleman in disguise, trying to drown himself out of hopeless love for her. When a young gentleman rides towards her with perfectly innocent intentions, she accuses him of trying to abduct her. The comedy has its serious side, as Lennox indicates the moral dangers in Arabella's attitude. Quixotism leads the heroine not to the sexual 'ruin' that anti-romantic moralists predicted for female readers, but to a perversion of her naturally likeable personality. Centring all her thoughts on her imaginary vision of herself, she loses all touch with the real feelings of the people around her. Believing it to be a fatal necessity that heroines' beauty must kill, she contemplates with serenity the supposed deaths of rejected lovers, or Glanville's risking his life in a duel, and when Glanville is dangerously ill of a fever she imperiously commands him to live. To her, his illness 'is no more than what all do suffer, who are possessed of a violent Passion; and few Lovers ever arrive to the Possession of their Mistresses, without being several times brought almost to their Graves'.[22]

Arabella's romantic delusions cause so many complications that eventually Glanville attacks his rival, Sir George Bellmour, in a moment of jealous rage, while she herself becomes ill after attempting to swim heroically across the Thames to escape supposed ravishers. When she recovers, a good clergyman argues her out of her obsession. Once she is convinced that her romances are not true, her sympathies are reawakened. She feels remorse, not because she has made a fool of herself but because she has come close to harming other people. 'I tremble ... to think how nearly I have approached the Brink of Murder, when I thought myself only consulting my own Glory; but whatever I suffer, I will never more demand or instigate Vengeance, nor consider my Punctilios as important enough to be ballanced against Life', she concedes (*The Female Quixote*, p. 381).

Lennox handles Arabella throughout with a sympathy the self-centred heroine may seem at first not to deserve. We can understand and share this sympathy if we examine how Lennox portrays Arabella's preposterous imaginary world as her refuge from a reality that deprives women of power. Arabella's belief in the despotic power of her charms makes up to her for her lack of power in real life. In fact, she is the obedient daughter of a man who keeps her in isolation. Going to church is a privilege that the Marquis 'sometimes allow[s] her' (p. 8), and an occasional ride in the countryside attended by servants is described as 'the only Diversion she was allowed, or ever experienced' (p. 19). Her notion of her power over her lovers comes up against her father's mundane plans for her marriage. He recommends her as a suitable wife to her cousin Glanville, and expects the courtship to take 'a few Weeks' (p. 31). Arabella is attracted towards her cousin, but she expects years of silent devotion before a proposal. While she is still unsure whether she ought to grant him the favour of walking alone with her, he, to her horror, declares his love. Her ideas about a heroine's prerogative and a lover's duties are challenged at every turn. When she is offended with Glanville, she orders him out of the house, but her father makes her write and ask him back again. Her claim that Glanville has performed none of the services required of a hero in romances meets her father's insistence on reality. 'What Stuff is this you talk of? ... I perceive you have no real Objection to make to him', he tells her (p. 42).

Male-centred reality keeps on imposing itself on Arabella's feminocentric fictions. When Glanville learns that Arabella's notions are taken from romances about the distant past, he dismisses them, assuring her that 'The World is quite different to what it was in those Days' (p. 45). As he courts Arabella, he posits unheroic, male-dominated modernity against 'the illustrious Heroines of Antiquity' (p. 44). Romances, in his view, 'contradicted the known Facts in History, and assign'd the most ridiculous Causes for Things of the greatest Importance' (p. 273). He asserts the primacy of the masculine realm of politics and war, 'Things of the greatest Importance', and derides the notion that they are governed by the feminine influence of love. He tries to lead Arabella from feminine 'error' to masculine 'truth'.

When Arabella does give up her illusions, she gives up her power. There is nothing left for her to do but accept Glanville and submit to real life. Lennox makes it clear that this will be far less exciting than the fictions she has used to challenge it. The reality she is going to have to come to terms with is described by the benevolent Countess, who, trying to argue Arabella out of her romantic obsession, presents her own calm, uneventful life as a model of female experience:

> when I tell you ... that I was born and christen'd, had a useful and
> proper Education, receiv'd the Addresses of my Lord— through the
> Recommendation of my Parents, and marry'd him with their
> Consents and my own Inclination, and that since we have liv'd in
> great Harmony together, I have told you all the material Passages
> of my Life, which upon Enquiry you will find differ very little from

those of other Women of the same Rank, who have a moderate
Share of Sense, Prudence and Virtue. (p. 327)

In effect, the Countess is telling Arabella (and by implication every
woman) not to be a heroine. This smooth ideal of a woman's life is
disrupted not only in Arabella's romances but in every eighteenth-
century novel which centres on the heroine. Whether deprived of parents
and guardians or persecuted by them, whether she defies authority to
marry the man of her choice or becomes a martyr to duty, the young
woman in the novel becomes a heroine only by departing from this
uneventful norm: otherwise there would be nothing to say about her.

Of course the ideal woman in eighteenth-century society is the woman
about whom there is nothing to say. Deluded Arabella thinks that a
heroine's good reputation depends on the 'Noise and Bustle she makes
in the World' (p. 128), but she has to learn a woman's best fame is to
be unknown. In eighteenth-century parlance the very word *adventures* in
connection with a woman implies a loss of virtue. In Arabella's romance-
world, a heroine's adventures mean abductions, disguises, and escapes,
none of which derogate at all from her honour; but in reality, the
Countess tells her, a woman's adventures can only be illicit sexual
relations: 'The Word Adventures carries in it so free and licentious a
Sound in the Apprehensions of People at this Period of Time, that it
can hardly with Propriety be apply'd to those few and natural Incidents
which compose the History of a Woman of Honour' (p. 327). To retain
her virtue, Arabella must relinquish her adventures: but as we can see
from the subtitle of the novel, *The Adventures of Arabella*, this means giving
up the story of her life and her identity as heroine. The Countess's
advice to Arabella implies the most extreme anti-feminist attitude to
women's fictions: any woman whose life is eventful enough to be the
subject of romance has compromised feminine virtue. The ideals offered
to Arabella are silence, anonymity, and the end of the story—or rather,
no story at all.

But that ideal cannot possibly be attained in a novel. Arabella *is* a
heroine and she does have a story. Like Don Quixote, she has heroic as
well as ridiculous qualities: in contrast to the vanity and spite of the
fashionable young lady Miss Glanville, Arabella's idealism appears in a
positive light.

Like Don Quixote, too, she has some power to impose her romantic
visions on the real world. She turns Glanville's courtship into something
closer to the long-term devotion required in romance than to the busi-
ness-like few weeks projected by her father. When Glanville realizes that
Arabella is modelling herself on the romance heroine, he knows that
'the Oddity of her Humour would throw innumerable Difficulties in his
Way, before he should be able to obtain her' (p. 45), and being really

in love with her, he rises to the challenge. For all his intention of weaning her from her romantic follies he finds himself acting the part of a romantic hero, and though at first this is an assumed role, it tends to come closer and closer to the reality of his feelings, and we soon learn that 'he stood in such Awe of her, and dreaded so much another Banishment, that he did not dare, otherwise than by distant Hints, to mention his Passion' (p. 81). Here, Lennox parodies the terms of romance, but her hero is beginning to take them seriously.

Glanville's endeavours to guide Arabella towards truth lead him deeper into romantic fiction. When they are out riding together, Arabella sees a former admirer, who, she believes, is trying to kidnap her. She wants to know if Glanville is brave enough to defend her. He almost loses his temper as he tells her that no-one is trying to harm her, but when Arabella rides away, and the supposed kidnapper jokes that she is 'fit for a Mad-house' (p. 157), Glanville fights with the man for insulting her. Arabella has the gratification of seeing her lover literally (though luckily not fatally) shed blood in her defence. On another occasion Glanville rescues Arabella from a real ravisher—though she comically fails to recognize the fact—and towards the end of the novel he fights and wounds his rival. When she accuses him of perfidy, he is frightened that she is losing her wits rather than stricken with remorse, but his reaction is that of a lover in romance:

> [He] threw himself on his Knees before her, and taking her Hand, which he tenderly prest to his Lips,
> Good God! my dearest Cousin, said he, How you distract me by this Behaviour! ... Can I have offended you so much?—Speak, dear Madam—Let me know my Crime. Yet may I perish if I am conscious of any towards you—(p. 352)

Arabella relinquishes her role as heroine, but not until she is sure of love from a man who offers all the devotion of a hero.

The Female Quixote is not only a satire on Arabella's adventures, it is the story of her actual courtship and marriage, and she is necessarily at the centre of it. The novel has some of the same kind of appeal as the romance it mocks. At one point, Arabella promises Miss Glanville her story:

> another time, you shall know my History; which will explain many things you seem to be surprised at, at present.
> Your History, said Miss *Glanville*! Why, will you write your own History then?
> I shall not write it, said *Arabella*; tho', questionless, it will be written after my Death.
> And must I wait till then for it, resumed Miss *Glanville*, gaily?

No, no, interrupted *Arabella*: I mean to gratify your Curiosity
sooner; but it will not be yet a good time; and, haply, not till you
have acquainted me with yours.

Mine! said Miss *Glanville*: It would not be worth your hearing;
for really I have nothing to tell, that would make an History.
(p. 110)

Miss Glanville, like the Countess's sensible young woman, has no history;
but as readers we can see that this is because she is insipid and unheroic.
Arabella, on the other hand, is a heroine and her history, of course, *has*
been written as she anticipates. Therefore she is an example that a
woman can be essentially virtuous and yet escape the anonymity the
Countess advocates. Despite Lennox's conservative moral view, *The
Female Quixote* with its romance appeal gives its virtuous woman power,
importance and a history.

THE GOTHIC NOVEL

Charlotte Lennox's female quixote had to learn that history and romance
were distinct; but later in the century, the Gothic revival mixed them
up again. The popularity of 'Ossian's' poems, of stories of the Middle
Ages, of ancient history, all showed people's delight in the past for the
charm of its remoteness. Novels with a historical theme became popular,
and gave women writers new opportunities to rewrite history with the
focus on love and female influence.

The heroine of Austen's *Northanger Abbey* evidently reads Gothic novels
because they reinterpret women's historical position. When asked why
she does not read history, Catherine Morland replies, 'history, real
solemn history, I never could be interested in ... the men all so good
for nothing, and hardly any women at all'.[23] Her reason for preferring
Gothic fiction is the same as Arabella's for preferring the versions of
history that she gets in the French romances: women are acknowledged
there as they are not in history books. Women's fiction has always been
concerned with redressing the balance and restoring women to the
record: whereas the domestic novel does this implicitly, Gothic fiction
can make the claim explicit.

The Gothic reinterpretation of history was no more historically accurate than that of the French romances. The Gothic novelists used a
historical setting in order to create a fantasy world. They took the
heroine out of the constricting world of the realistic novel into an
imaginary world of adventure, and widened the fantasy of female power
offered by romance by exploring other kinds of power than that of

heroine over adoring lover. They also combined fantasies of power with expressions of fear about women's vulnerability in the real world.

The focus in the Gothic novel is on the heroine's mind: it is not only what happens to her that concerns us, but how she reacts to it. Her travels and her adventures can be seen as journeys into the self, or investigations of possible selves. The mysterious castles that imprison her and the sublime landscapes on which she gazes can be interpreted as projections of herself. Ann Radcliffe's heroines can always be soothed, even at times of the most complicated distress, by contemplating the beauties of nature. Emily St Aubert, heroine of Radcliffe's most famous novel, *The Mysteries of Udolpho* (1794), spends much of her time in the power of the villainous Montoni. When he has imprisoned her in the gloomy castle of Udolpho, she relieves her mind by looking out of the window onto 'the wild grandeur of the scene', with its 'delightful' woods. She watches while the morning mists clear:

> as the veil drew up, it was delightful to watch the gleaming objects, that progressively disclosed themselves in the valley—the green turf—dark woods—little rocky recesses—a few peasants' huts—the foaming stream—a herd of cattle, and various images of pastoral beauty. Then, the pine-forests brightened, and then the broad breast of the mountains, till, at length, the mist settled round their summit, touching them with a ruddy glow. The features of the vista now appeared distinctly, and the broad deep shadows, that fell from the lower cliffs, gave strong effect to the streaming splendour above; while the mountains, gradually sinking in the perspective, appeared to shelve into the Adriatic sea, for such Emily imagined to be the gleam of blueish light, that terminated the view.
>
> Thus she endeavoured to amuse her fancy, and was not unsuccessful. The breezy freshness of the morning, too, revived her. She raised her thoughts in prayer, which she felt always most disposed to do, when viewing the sublimity of nature, and her mind recovered its strength.[24]

Radcliffe's description belongs to the late eighteenth-century picturesque tradition, and also to a wider tradition of women's special use of land-scape.[25] In passages like this the natural world functions in the way Simone de Beauvoir describes it working for women generally, as an emblem of the young girl's free self which is threatened by her entry into the male-dominated social world. De Beauvoir describes the 'refuge' which the young girl finds in nature:

> among plants and animals she is a human being; she is freed at once from her family and from the males—a subject, a free being. She finds in the secret places of the forest a reflection of the

solitude of her soul and in the wide horizons of the plains a tangible
image of her transcendence; she is herself this limitless territory, this
summit flung up towards heaven; she can follow these roads that
lead towards the unknown future, she will follow them; seated on
the hilltop, she is mistress of all the world's riches, spread out at
her feet, offered for the taking.[26]

Radcliffe's Emily finds just this refuge in natural beauty. In this scene
she is not alone on a hilltop (though she and other Gothic heroines do
wander alone in the hills and woods when they get the chance) but
confined in a castle, so this image of her 'transcendence' is doubly
important. She may be subject to Montoni's tyranny but nature is not,
and so because of her affinity with the natural world, neither, ultimately,
is she. Significantly, Emily's aunt, who has married Montoni and will
never escape his power alive, is unable to respond to the beauties of
nature.

If the natural world represents female freedom, the castle can often
be seen as a symbol of the trap of womanhood. Sometimes heroines are
transported into castles by evil men, as Emily is brought to Udolpho
by Montoni. At other times the castle is where the heroine is brought
up. This is the case in Charlotte Smith's *Emmeline*, a novel which includes
elements of the Gothic fantasy as well as sentiment and Burneyan social
comedy. Emmeline grows up secluded from society in a Pembrokeshire
castle belonging to her uncle, who keeps her out of the way because he
does not want to acknowledge that she is the rightful heiress of his
estate. The castle therefore represents Emmeline's unfair exclusion from
the male-dominated world of power: but it also becomes a refuge from
that power. In her lonely retreat she grows up perfect in feminine
virtue, and when her retirement is broken by her cousin Delamere's
inconsiderate courtship, the castle keeps her safe. She escapes from him
by running through the dark passages which she knows well and in
which he is soon totally lost. At this point in the novel, the impenetrable
castle is being used as a symbol of the unviolated heroine.

The women's Gothic expresses an ambivalent attitude to womanhood:
it is both confinement and refuge. Women are always represented as
persecuted, deprived of power, and imprisoned, yet the places which
confine them often protect them too. The heroine escapes from imprisonment into a natural world that symbolizes her own free nature, the
spiritual freedom which she always maintains under physical oppression.
The adventures that break into the Gothic heroine's life as a proper
young lady serve to express women's fears and simultaneously offer a
fantasy of escape from them.

REWRITING HISTORY: SOPHIA LEE'S *THE RECESS* (1785)

Sophia Lee (1750–1824) ran a school in Bath with her younger sister Harriet Lee, author of *The Errors of Innocence*. She also wrote drama, translations and fiction. *The Recess*, her first work of prose fiction, is one of the earliest historical novels, combining an escape from the contemporary world with the psychological interest typical of the Gothic writers. The novel purports to restore lost records of women's lives to history. The heroines, Ellinor and Matilda, are twin daughters of Mary Queen of Scots by her secret marriage to the Duke of Norfolk. They spend some time at the Elizabethan court, at one point appearing incognito as waiting maids to the Queen. They are involved with some of the most powerful men of their time, Matilda marrying Lord Leicester and her sister being in love with Lord Essex. Yet their names have never reached the history books.

The story is supposed to be derived from an 'obsolete manuscript'— claiming, like many novels of the century, to be truth, not fiction. The difficulty of distinguishing the two is one of Lee's main themes. Her 'Advertisement' states that it is difficult to ascertain the truths of history because unremembered emotional events are often of more significance than recorded facts: 'the best and worst actions of princes often proceed from partialities and prejudices, which live in their hearts, and are buried with them'. Lee promises to disinter some of these buried truths through the story of these two sisters, revealed in their own writings, which were preserved for posterity by being entrusted to a female friend. Thus women's autobiography, women's friendship, and the 'historical' research of the woman writer, Lee herself, combine to reinstate women in a properly prominent place in history. This is done by turning history into romance.

Significantly, Lee chooses a woman's reign for the setting of her history–romance, and uses Elizabeth's name to authenticate her improbable story. The sisters' narratives, she acknowledges, might seem farfetched to modern readers, but they must remember that 'the reign of Elizabeth was that of romance', and what seems incredible to the eighteenth century would have been possible then.[27] The fantasy of female power, central to women's romance, is thus set in a historical period when one woman did wield great power. In *The Recess* Elizabeth's power dominates the story, and she causes the deaths of Essex and Leicester. The struggle, so fatal to the men in the novel, originates in female rivalry: Elizabeth's hatred of Mary Queen of Scots is her prime motive. This is history, not as the actions of great men but as the jealousies of great women.

Elizabeth, who dominates the masculine world of politics and war, is the villain of the story, a woman who has turned away from womanly values, and is therefore doomed to long in vain for the romantic devotion that an unwomanly woman cannot inspire. Good women—real women— are the victims not the rulers of history, as the heroines of Lee's story demonstrate by their virtue and unhappy fate. They are brought up in isolation, hidden in the recess that gives the novel its title, for fear of what Elizabeth—who has beheaded their father and imprisoned their mother—would do if she found out about them.

Romantic love rules their lives. When they meet Lord Leicester and shelter him in the recess from assassins, Matilda falls in love with him on sight, marries him secretly, and enters on a life of romance and persecution. The loss of her husband, shipwreck and four years spent as a captive in a Spanish colony with her young daughter are among her sufferings. Meanwhile Ellinor, imprisoned by Elizabeth, is tricked into believing she can save both Lord Essex and her mother from the Queen's anger by repudiating her own claim to be Mary's daughter and marrying Lord Arlington. Later she learns that her mother has been executed. This experience, and her later suffering when Essex is executed, combine to drive her mad.

The Recess interprets history as a series of love entanglements, distorting historical personages like Essex and Leicester by presenting all their actions as the result of love for two unhistorical romantic heroines. From the point of view taken by Lennox's Glanville, this is certainly a romance assigning 'the most ridiculous Causes for Things of the greatest Importance' (*The Female Quixote*, p. 273). However, *The Recess* does not simply offer the attractions Arabella found in romance. Its emphasis is on suffering and the absence of reconciliation, and its narrative is structured so as to call into question the whole idea of romance and its attendant fantasy of female power.

Matilda narrates the first and final sections of the story, while Ellinor's narrative appears in the middle. The same events are presented from two different viewpoints, and the reader is left wondering which is the truer interpretation. From Matilda we get a picture of Leicester as devoted lover. When we get to Ellinor's narrative we learn that she interpreted his behaviour very differently. 'His heart', she writes, 'not warm by nature, has been rendered in a great degree callous, from having always passed his life in the chilling atmosphere of a Court' (II, 160). She claims that Leicester could safely have acknowledged his marriage to Matilda, and chose not to for political reasons. Romantic love, it seems, does not rule history after all. Ellinor is not without romantic illusions of her own, though. She is full of praise for the 'passionate ingenuousness' of that 'romantic spirit', her lover Essex (II,

173 and 274). He, she believes, acts only out of love, but her friend, Lady Pembroke, makes additions to her narrative, offering a different view. 'When this heartbreaking narrative came into my hands,' she comments, 'I could not but observe that the sweet mistress of Essex had a very partial knowledge of his character ... the early habits of power and distinction had seized on his affections' (III, 153). At another point, Lady Pembroke has added her remarks on Ellinor's plan to join Essex's fight for power in Ireland: 'I cannot agree with this fair visionary, who so easily adopts the romance of her lover' (III, 47). The heroines, indulging in romance, forget that masculine ambition determines history. Each accuses the other of being romantic and claims to have a better grip on reality, but neither will admit to any faults in her own lover.

The sisters not only suffer from romantic illusions: they feel that they themselves are unreal. Ellinor writes of their lives at court, 'Ah, how visionary seems on recollection our new situation! seen without being known; adored, without being esteemed; punished, without being guilty; applauded, without being meritorious, we were all an illusion' (II, 165). For Matilda and Ellinor womanhood means being—from the point of view of the powers that be—illusory. As romantic figures governed by romantic love, they are subject to the ambitions and violence (both witness wars and are captured on battlefields) of the real world in which they can never take their place. The heroines' defeat is the defeat of female power. They do not succeed to the throne after Elizabeth's death: their half-brother, James, does. With his accession masculine domination returns to history after the 'romance' of Elizabeth's reign, and the new king spurns any connection with feminine power. He refuses to acknowledge any relationship to his sisters, though he has seen proofs of their birth; and in denying his sisters he rejects his mother and repudiates (even while benefiting from) the female line of inheritance. 'Anxious without doubt to center in himself every right of his mother, he voluntarily renounced all regard for either her ashes or her offspring ...—What after this is to be hoped from the King of Scots?' (III, 31). What indeed. Denying the truth, he shuts his sisters out of history and confines them to romance.

In *The Recess*, romantic love does not give women power but takes it away, dividing women from each other and blinding them to reality. There is another kind of romance in the novel, though, which has more positive connotations. This is the 'romantic secret' hidden in the recess— the secret of the heroines' birth. Once they reach womanhood their foster-mother, Mrs Marlow, tells them of their origin, and they cherish hopes of being reunited with their mother. Matilda vainly imagines that by marrying Leicester she might achieve this:

[I believed] I gained to that dear mother ... a powerful friend in the
favourite of her unjust rival. I hoped he might yet be prevailed on
to attempt her freedom; and I already placed myself at her feet,
overcome with the dear idea of having been the instrument of her
deliverance. Alas, Madam, were it not for such vague imaginary
joys, how could we exist? All our real pleasures fall infinitely short
of these. (I, 164)

The tragedy of *The Recess* is that this romance of reconciliation can never
become reality.

Images of mystery, madness and confinement surround the heroines:
the Gothic machinery is used as a means of covertly exploring the female
condition. The romance tells of women's exclusion from the 'real world'
of power and recorded history. The central image for Sophia Lee is that
of the recess itself: an enclosed space, secluded from the world, it
represents woman's destiny of confinement, and hidden female powers.
It is part of a ruined abbey that was once the home of nuns, and so is
a reminder of lost female communities and lost female power. Matilda
tells of first coming to consciousness in an entirely female environment.
'As soon as capable of reflection, I found myself and a sister of my own
age, in an apartment with a lady, and a maid' (I, 2–3). Soon after, we
become aware of Father Anthony, the priest who is their link with an
outside world he teaches them to fear and despise. 'From him we learnt
there was a terrible large place called the world, where a few haughty
individuals commanded miserable millions, whom a few artful ones
made so; that Providence had graciously rescued us from both, nor
could we ever be sufficiently grateful' (I, 4). The girls' different reactions
to their seclusion give an early indication of the ambiguous status of the
recess:

Ellinor, whose lively imagination readily imbibed the romantic and
extravagant, conjectured we were in the power of some giant; nay,
such was her disgust to Father Anthony, that she sometimes
apprehended he was a magician, and would one day or other
devour us. I had a very different idea; and fancied our retreat a
hallowed circle to seclude us from the wicked, while Father Anthony
was our guardian genius. (I, 6–7)

Matilda calls her sister's idea romantic and extravagant, but her own,
as she says, is fancy, and her ensuing narrative makes us wonder which
of these conceptions of their hiding place is closer to reality. If at
first the recess favours female safety and independence, having 'all the
advantages of a nunnery, without the tie to continue in it' (I, 48–9),
later it becomes a 'horrible den' in which both sisters are imprisoned
separately. Throughout the novel the recess, and other places secluding

the heroines from the world, appear alternately as refuge and prison, and in this way Lee expresses ambivalent feelings towards the restriction and the shelter of virtuous womanhood.

The most explicit identification of the recess with the female self comes when Ellinor is living near it with the man she has been forced to marry. In her relations with Arlington she has maintained a spiritual independence despite sexual submission, and she describes herself as 'a wild wretch, whose weary spirit threatened every moment to escape, and leave in his arms the vile dross he thus purchased' (II, 276). Full escape, this implies, would mean death; but Ellinor still has some refuge in life, for she can revisit the scenes of her girlhood. She writes:

> Often did my feet wander towards the cell and the Recess. Often, in
> the well-known windings of that wood, where once we carolled
> together notes as careless and pleasant as those of the birds around
> us, have I paused, my sister, and watered with embittered tears the
> precious memorials of days that never could return. (II, 280)

Here, the recess and its surroundings together represent the independent self of Ellinor's childhood, now under threat. Lord Arlington, she reports, jealous of her spending her time in this manner, 'resolved to exterminate those ruins where I had owned I passed my childhood, and which, he thought, still kept alive embittered remembrances' (II, 283). These remembrances are now Ellinor's only source for a sense of her identity: 'it was dreadful', she writes, 'to think of annihilating every trace of my youth; every object which could remind me I had ever been beloved' (II, 283-4). When Arlington dies he leaves a will stipulating that Ellinor is to be kept as a lunatic, confined in the abbey. The familiar movement from refuge to prison thus occurs again, with the added twist that Ellinor is now imprisoned in her own mind, too: 'deliberately to condemn me to an imprisonment so shocking, and render it perpetual!—human nature could not resist so pungent a pang—it *made* the misery it punished; and I sunk into the dreary gulph once more from which I was lately emerging—my brain still fires but to remember it' (III, 21). Ellinor later escapes from bodily confinement, but never from her madness.

Ellinor's madness is also a kind of protection for her, sheltering her even from the agony romantic love brings, for when she is taken to say goodbye to Essex before his execution, she does not recognize him. She lives on for many years without 'those intellects which might only have proved an additional misfortune' (III, 179); and when, at last, another sight of Essex's portrait triggers her mind to recollection, she dies in the same moment. Ellinor's madness, like the recess where it begins, is an expression of women's exclusion from the 'real world'. In creating her, Lee anticipates a modern feminist analysis of women's madness as a reaction to oppression. Her heroine is one of the women who, in Phyllis Chesler's words, 'denied the experience of cultural supremacy, humanity and renewal based on their sexual identity ... are driven mad by this fact. Such madness is essentially an intense experience of female biological, sexual and cultural castration, and a doomed search for potency'.[28]

It is significant that the sister who goes mad is also the one who first chafed at the confinement of the recess and called Father Anthony a tyrant. Ellinor speaks out directly and bitterly about women's fate. When she meets Essex after a long absence, she notes the different effects their troubles have had on them:

> While he ... surveyed in tender sorrow, the ravages grief and
> disappointment had thus early made in my wan countenance ... I
> beheld with surprise the advantages he had acquired ... his graceful
> flower of youth was settled into firmer manhood ... Ah man, happy
> man! how superior are you in the indulgence of nature! blest with
> scientific resources, with boldness, and an activity unknown to more
> persecuted woman; from your various disappointments in life ever
> spring forth some vigorous and blooming hope, insensibly
> staunching those wounds in the heart through which the vital
> powers of the feebler sex bleed helplessly away. (III, 27–8)

Ellinor ascribes man's advantages to 'nature', though she also says that woman is 'more persecuted'. *The Recess* gives a catalogue of those persecutions, and it is Ellinor's madness that licenses her to complain about them. In the Gothic imagery of historical romance, Sophia Lee expresses an anger about women's condition that respectability forbade the woman writer to display openly.

The Recess is romance's revenge on recorded history. It asserts that the 'truth' of history is a lie, based on denying women their rightful place. The real truth, it suggests, is to be found in romance and in madness. Therefore Ellinor, the mad sister, is made more clear-sighted than Matilda, as we recognize when she tells her sister, 'as the apparent passion of Lord Leicester had to you the charms of reality, I am to blame perhaps thus to represent it: but the season of dissimulation is past, and my tortured heart will utter nothing but truth' (II, 161). In fact this truth, that can only be conveyed in romance, is the revelation that the form of romance allowed to women—that is, romantic love— is an illusion standing in the way of women's access to the romance of mother–daughter reconciliation and female power. Ellinor even understands, in her 'cruel wanderings', that she has had illusions about her own lover: 'I dreamt of Essex—Ah, what did I say? I dreamt of Essex?— Alas, I have dreamt of him my whole life long' (II, 243). When she relates how she heard of Essex's marriage to Lady Sydney, her memory of the shock unhinges her reason and disrupts her narrative. Soon after, she resumes, 'I perceive I have in the wild colourings of a disordered imagination, unfolded a truth my heart almost burst with' (II, 245). Her comment is not only relevant to the style of her own narrative but to the novel's whole method. The novel reveals the 'femininity' it praises as a prison, yet a necessary refuge from oppression; and shows women's ultimate refuges as madness and death. Without the vision of possible liberation the feminist writers of her time added to this analysis, Sophia Lee's truth is certainly one the heart can burst with. No wonder it is revealed obliquely, in the wild colourings of the romance writer's imagination.

ROMANCE AND ESCAPE: ANN RADCLIFFE'S *THE ROMANCE OF THE FOREST* (1791)

Ann Radcliffe is connected with Sophia Lee in more ways than one. She grew up in Bath, and probably attended the Lee sisters' school; and when she began to write she turned, like Sophia Lee, to the Gothic novel. Her work, though far more polished than Lee's, echoes some of the themes of *The Recess*, for it too rewrites history to include woman. Though Radcliffe, famous for developing the 'tale of terror', induces more fear and suspense in the reader than Lee does, she actually makes a much more optimistic equation of womanhood with romance. In her work, especially in the comparatively neglected *The Romance of the Forest* (1791), we can see how the Gothic novel presented a fantasy of female power. Set in seventeenth-century France, this novel concerns the adventures of Adeline, who both encounters and embodies mystery. The puzzles which confront her lead to the discovery of her own identity, which includes the discovery that the powers of mystery and romance are ultimately benign, and work in her favour.

Significantly, Adeline is first presented to us through the consciousness of another character, to whom she appears as a figure of mystery and romance. Pierre de la Motte, a gentleman morally and financially ruined by the 'gaieties of Paris', seems on the evidence of the opening pages to be the protagonist.[29] Losing his way as he flees from Paris and his creditors, La Motte asks for help at a lonely house on a wild heath: he is admitted only to be immediately imprisoned. Alone and helpless, he is overcome by fear: 'he endeavoured to await the event with fortitude; but La Motte could boast of no such virtue' (I, 10). By presenting us with a *man* who almost loses his mind through terror, Radcliffe contributes to a widening of the fictional portrayal of masculinity that has been described as a particular achievement of women Gothic novelists.[30]

However, if La Motte feels the fears once reserved for heroines, he lacks the heroinely virtue of courage under oppression. As we shall see, passive suffering and passive fortitude are necessary for the ideal, feminized male who is the hero of Radcliffe's romance.

La Motte's captors free him once he agrees to take with him another person who has been imprisoned in the house—a beautiful girl called Adeline, who arouses his pity as a powerless victim and his wonder as a mystery. Once he and Adeline are riding away in the La Motte coach, we are told of his reflections on the incident: 'he ruminated on the late scene, and it appeared like a vision, or one of those improbable fictions that sometimes are exhibited in a romance: he could reduce it to no principles of probability, or render it comprehensible by any endeavour to analize [sic] it' (I, 19). By looking after Adeline as if she were his daughter, this corrupted man of the world begins to redeem himself.

However, we learn at the outset that La Motte's 'virtue, such as it was, could not stand the pressure of occasion' (I, 5). At the Abbey of St Clair he attacks and robs a man who turns out to be its owner, the Marquis de Montalt. The Marquis exploits the hold he has over his attacker, threatening to turn him over to justice unless he helps him to gain possession of Adeline. From fatherly protector La Motte becomes fatherly tyrant, urging Adeline to accept a man abhorrent to her. This metamorphosis is associated with a wilful rejection of the romance which surrounds Adeline and represents feminine power. La Motte scoffs at reports that someone has been imprisoned and murdered in the abbey as 'a romantic tale to excite wonder' (I, 246), though he knows himself— from having discovered the skeleton—that in this case romance and reality are one; and this romantic tale turns out to contain the key to the mystery of Adeline's identity. When trying to persuade Adeline to accept the Marquis he appeals to 'prudence', and cannot believe her repeated refusal: 'is it possible that you can persist in this heroism of romance[?]' he asks her (II, 36 and 66).

Of course it is, and La Motte should be glad of it. It is the heroism of romance which ultimately is to save him, but not before he has given it a chance to act. Unwilling to carry out the Marquis's final command to murder Adeline, he lets her escape. The Marquis carries out his threat and La Motte is prosecuted, but Adeline pleads his pardon with the king, and his death-sentence is reduced to banishment. At the end of the novel we learn that her 'kindness operated so powerfully upon his heart ... that his former habits became odious to him, and his character gradually recovered the hue which it would probably always have worn had he never been exposed to the tempting dissipations of Paris' (III, 324).

This is not, however, primarily the story of Pierre de la Motte, but of Adeline herself. She has been persecuted all her life by the man she

believes to be her father. At the opening of the story he has sent her
away in the custody of strange men because she has refused to take the
veil. Once handed over to La Motte, she finds refuge in the abbey in
the forest of Fontainville, which eventually yields the secret of her true
parentage.

A motto from *As You Like It* ('Are not these woods / More free from
peril than the envious court?') adorns the third chapter, in which Adeline
and the La Mottes settle down in the abbey. The forest of Fontainville
is therefore compared to the forest of Arden, as a refuge from the corrupt
world and the tyranny of powerful men. Adeline, like Rosalind, gains a
new freedom in the forest. Its 'sweetly romantic' and 'luxuriant woods'
make a fitting setting for a heroine of romance (I, 57), and we learn
that Adeline 'forgot for a while the desolation of the abbey in the beauty
of the adjacent scenery. The pleasantness of the shades soothed her
heart, and the varied features of the landscape amused her fancy; she
almost thought she could be contented to live here' (I, 62). She often
wanders alone into the forest, where the beauties of nature give her
visions of 'ideal happiness' and inspire her to write poetry.

Adeline finds her hero in the forest. One day she has walked further
than usual into the forest, entranced by its signs of awakening life. She
sings one of her songs, a 'sonnet' to the lily, and suddenly realizes she
is being observed:

> repeating the last stanza of the Sonnet, she was answered by a voice
> almost as tender [as her own echo] ... She looked round in surprise,
> and saw a young man in a hunter's dress, leaning against a tree,
> and gazing on her with that deep attention, which marks an
> enraptured mind.
> A thousand apprehensions shot athwart her busy thought; and
> she now first remembered her distance from the abbey. (I, 190)

At first it seems that the man is a hunter and Adeline will be his prey,
but the stranger does not give chase: seeing her 'timid looks and retiring
steps' he pauses and Adeline goes on her way (I, 190). He later reappears
in the abbey as Theodore Peyrou, accompanying the Marquis de
Montalt. Adeline gets to know him, and begins to fall in love with him,
in a properly chaperoned setting. Yet he remains associated with the
forest. On a later occasion he appears while she is indulging her melancholy thoughts in 'a little lonely recess, formed by high trees'. She is
'interrupted by a rustling among the fallen leaves' as the hero arrives,
begging her to 'Pardon this intrusion' (I, 250–1).

Theodore's combination of wild natural setting and impeccable draw-
ing-room manners establishes him as a hero created to allay sexual fears.
He belongs to the natural world which we have seen as an emblem of

the heroine's independent self, and therefore his gentle intrusion will not threaten her independence. Significantly, this young hunter is never seen to hunt, any more than Valancourt, the hero of *The Mysteries of Udolpho*, who uses hunter's garb to mask his real identity of nature-lover, explaining 'I am pleased with the country, and mean to saunter away a few weeks among its scenes. My dogs I take with me more for companionship than for game. This [hunter's] dress, too, gives me an ostensible business, and procures me that respect from the people, which would, perhaps, be refused to a lonely stranger'.[31] The Radcliffe hero is truly a sheep in wolf's clothing.

While the forest frees Adeline's creative powers and fulfils her desires, the abbey in the middle of the forest contains the secret of her identity. It is said to be haunted, and the La Motte family hear reports that someone was imprisoned in it some years ago. It is La Motte who first investigates the abbey's hidden passages, and finds the victim's prison and skeleton, but it is Adeline who is haunted. She has a night full of strange dreams in which she repeatedly sees the same man, sometimes healthy, sometimes dying, finally dead. He is trying to contact her:

> he suddenly stretched forth his hand, and seizing her's, grasped it with violence: she struggled in terror to disengage herself, and again looking on his face, saw a man, who appeared to be about thirty, with the same features, but in full health, and of a most benign countenance. He smiled tenderly upon her and moved his lips, as if to speak, when the floor of the chamber suddenly opened and he sunk from her view. (I, 270)

The next evening she discovers a secret passage from her room, which leads her to chambers like those of her dreams. She finds a manuscript written by the victim of the abbey during his imprisonment, describing his sufferings and begging, 'O! ye, who may hereafter read what I now write, give a tear for my sufferings: I have wept often for the distresses of my fellow-creatures!' (II, 55). Compassionate Adeline grants the writer's wish, and by her tears she establishes the contact desired by the man in her dreams, who is evidently to be identified with the long-dead murder victim.

Reading the entire manuscript takes Adeline several evenings, and meanwhile life in the abbey is becoming more oppressive. Theodore has left to join his regiment, having failed in his promise to tell her about the dangers he says threaten her. The Marquis de Montalt is making dishonourable proposals to her and La Motte is not providing the protection she asks for. She overhears a conversation between these two men which leads her to believe that her father is pursuing her, and though this is inconsistent with his former haste to get rid of her, the idea fills her with fear. Trapped between cruel father and wicked Marquis, Adeline begins to revise her former trust in humanity. 'Is this human nature?' she wonders (II, 19). The dreams and the manuscript put her in touch with another kind of man, gentle and benign. Perhaps human nature is not so bad after all. La Motte, posing as the advocate of reason, dismisses the manuscript as a 'strange romantic story' (II, 86), but in Radcliffe's work as in Lee's, romance contains the truth. La Motte is hiding his knowledge of the skeleton and lying to Adeline about her supposed father, while the manuscript turns out not only to be true, but to have been written by the heroine's real father.

This is the common romance theme of true birth discovery. Whereas for the heroines of *The Recess*, search for the mother was all-important, for Adeline (as for Burney's Evelina), finding her father is most significant. She does meet a maternal relation who gives her a portrait of her 'mild and beautiful' mother, long dead (III, 315), but this is something of an afterthought. The concentration on the father is fitting in a narrative that, unlike the covertly rebellious and overtly pessimistic *The Recess*, accommodates its heroine happily within the established patriarchal order. There is however a fundamental revision made to that order in the switch from Adeline's tyrannical false fathers to her true father, who shared her feminine virtues and the usually feminine position of passive victim.

In this novel the 'romantic story' mocked by La Motte is powerful and true; and, despite its horror, it contributes to the eventual revelation that the world is a better place than it first appears to be. While the Marquis and La Motte try desperately to conceal their guilty pasts, the tales told by superstitious villagers and the mysterious manuscript help bring the truth to light. The Marquis's crimes are revealed, and Adeline, even across the barriers of death, communicates in some sense with a father worthy of her love. No wonder that at the end past events seem to her 'no longer ... to be a work of chance, but of a Power whose designs are great and just' (III, 304).

In keeping with this ultimate faith in the divine order *The Romance of the Forest* presents the female condition much more optimistically than *The Recess* does. Imprisonment is used to symbolize the trap of womanhood as it is in Lee's novel, but in *The Romance* the contrast between prison and external nature represents the contrast between natural and artificial womanhood, and the heroine easily escapes the trap. The Marquis, intending to seduce Adeline, has her carried by force to a house on the borders of the forest. Here she finds herself in a 'magnificent saloon', where silks, silver, Ovidian scenes in fresco, busts of Horace and Anacreon, and a table covered with fruit and drink make a display of wealth, classical culture and sensuality. In contrast to Theodore, who is associated with the forest and virtue, the Marquis offers Adeline an artificial life of luxurious interiors and illicit sexuality. He uses all the refinements of civilization to trap her in the false role of a kept mistress. In Adeline's instinctive reaction, natural virtue triumphs over artifice and vice. Barely glancing at the temptations she is offered, she takes the first opportunity of jumping out of the window.

Once Adeline is outside among the trees again, it is no surprise to the reader that Theodore appears. Having helped her into a waiting carriage, he shows himself once more to be a model of propriety and respect, and as timid as one of the female quixote's favourite heroes. 'I am sensible of the impropriety of pleading my love at present ... If I could, however, now be certain that I possess your esteem, it would relieve me from much anxiety', he tells her (II, 153). Such concern for decorum is necessary to veil the way Radcliffe's plot works to satisfy Adeline's sexual desires, unacknowledged though these are by heroine or author. Adeline has after all run away from the undesired, older, rich and powerful man, whose addresses are supported by her present guardians, straight into the arms of the young lover she wants: exactly what opponents of fiction thought novels encouraged young women to do. By making the Marquis's love and La Motte's support of him criminal, and Theodore's love so utterly correct, Radcliffe transforms social realities in a romance wherein duty coincides with desire.

It is not only his propriety that makes Theodore a hero, though. He proves his worth still further by becoming, along with the heroine, a victim of powerful men. The tyrannical Marquis is Theodore's commanding officer. Having deserted his regiment in time of war, resisted arrest, and wounded the Marquis, all in order to save Adeline, Theodore faces the death-sentence on a number of counts. While he suffers long imprisonment, and is deprived of the hero's usual prerogative of rescuing the heroine, Adeline herself escapes from the Marquis a second time. This time she flees to Leloncourt at the foot of the Savoy Alps, where she is adopted by the benevolent clergyman La Luc, his sister, and his daughter, Clara, and spends her time sharing their virtuous country life. Eventually La Luc turns out to be Theodore's father, and what at first seemed an untimely pastoral digression in the midst of crisis is shown as the ultimate end of Adeline's quest. She has found a haven for female virtue. In the end Adeline and Theodore will settle in Leloncourt with his family, leaving the gaities of Paris, the seclusion of convents, the disturbing memories associated with the abbey—and the freedom of the forest—firmly behind. Leloncourt is the home of nature socialized and domesticated, under the control of La Luc, the benevolent minister who is revered by all the villagers as a father. Having resisted illegitimate masculine authority, Adeline will be protected by benevolent paternal care. However, before this reunion of feminine virtue and patriarchal control can take place, Theodore, the eventual inheritor of the father's authority, has to show that he shares womanly virtues. His long imprisonment and the threat of execution allow this. He has no resource but passive fortitude—that heroinely virtue that Adeline's father had and that La Motte so conspicuously lacks. In Radcliffe's next novel, *The Mysteries of Udolpho*, Montoni taunts Emily when she is his prisoner: 'You speak like a heroine ... we shall see whether you can suffer like one' (p. 381). In *The Romance of the Forest* it is Theodore who proves his worth by suffering like a heroine.

Evil male authority figures and persecuted heroines recur in *The Mysteries of Udolpho* and *The Italian*. Both novels end with defeat for the authoritarian male and the heroine's marriage to a feminized hero. In *Udolpho* Valancourt plays a singularly passive role in the narrative, even leaving the hero's traditional job of rescuing the heroine to another man, and it is his chastity rather than his valour that Emily is interested in. Vivaldi, the hero of *The Italian*, is more memorable for suffering than for acting, and his passive fortitude in the face of the Inquisition is worthy of a Gothic heroine. Emily's and Ellena's happy endings with these heroes are escapes, like the conclusion of *The Romance of the Forest*, and as the villains and the Gothic terrors are more prominent in these later novels, the idyllic conclusions appear more and more as retreats from the world. Radcliffe actually calls La Vallée, the childhood home where Emily settles with Valancourt, 'the *retreat* of goodness, wisdom and domestic blessedness' (*The Mysteries of Udolpho*, p. 672; my italics), and writes of Ellena and Vivaldi's eventual home, 'It was, in truth, a scene of fairy-land'.[32] Radcliffe's themes are similar to Sophia Lee's, but her conclusions are happier because she allows the power of romance to prevail. Hers are novels of escape, criticizing the status quo of male authority but not ultimately challenging it. Her solution is retreat into an idealized pastoral world, where womanly virtue and patriarchal authority are no longer in conflict.

THE CONTINUING APPEAL OF ROMANCE

I have said that conventional moralists felt threatened by romance's fantasy of female power; but, from a feminist point of view, the danger was that this power would remain a fantasy. In a work like *The Romance of the Forest*, it could be accommodated in a romance-world of idealized paternal authority, and the issue of women's powerlessness in the real world be raised only to be dropped. During the eighteenth century feminist writers attacked romance. Seduction novels often claimed that romances offered the young woman an illusory power over men only to deliver her into the real power of the seducer. It was also observed that

the obsequious lover could turn into a tyrant after marriage. A sharp
feminist analysis of the shortcomings of romance is found in *The Cry*.
The heroine ridicules the female education that makes women 'lead their
whole lives in expectation', waiting passively for romantic love to appear
and be the fulfilment of their lives. 'Little miss is taught by her mamma,
that she must never speak before she is spoken to. On this she sits
bridling up her head, looking from one to the other, in hopes of being
call'd to and addressed by the name of pretty miss' (*The Cry*, I, 62).
Later on, the young girl will think only of trying to please lovers,
hoping to get the humble adoration ascribed to heroes in romance. The
fashionable women of Portia's audience are obviously romance-readers,
and the authors of *The Cry* understand romance's attraction: 'From the
time that Portia began to describe the goddess on her throne, with her
adoring lover at her feet,' they tell us, 'a sympathizing pleasure over-
spread the countenances of the female part of the Cry' (I, 69). Portia
soon jolts her audience back to reality with a devastating exposé of the
lover's romantic adoration:

> An adulation, which, translated into p!ain *English*, means no more
> than an address of the following kind. 'Madam, I like you (no
> matter whether from fortune, person, or any other motive) and it
> will conduce much to my pleasure and convenience, if you will
> become my wife: that is, if you will bind yourself before God and
> man to obey my commands as long as I shall live. And should you
> after marriage be forgetful of your duty, you will then have given
> me a legal power of exacting as rigid a performance of it as I
> please. (I, 70)

The harsh reality of the marriage law destroys the dream of romantic
power. Yet Fielding and Collier stop short of attacking the reality of
male domination. They criticize the romantic illusion that obscures
masculine power, not the power itself. Portia's substitute for romantic
adoration is marriage as sentimental friendship, based upon the young
woman's sensible choice of 'the man she can obey with pleasure' (II,
244)—a solution just as romantic as the one she exposes.

Mary Wollstonecraft also attacked romantic fiction. Her early work
for the *Analytical Review* makes the conventional complaints about its
dangers. Reviewing *Emmeline*, she wrote, 'the false expectations which
these wild scenes excite, tend to debauch the mind, and throw an insipid
kind of uniformity over the moderate and rational prospects of life,
consequently *adventures* are sought for and created, when duties are
neglected, and content despised'.[33] In *The Wrongs of Woman*, as we
saw in Chapter 4, Wollstonecraft analysed the problem of romantic
expectation from a feminist point of view. Yet while attacking romance

in one form—as the ideology of romantic love—she embraces it in another more radical form, as a device for enlarging the possibilities of the novel of purpose. She deliberately creates the wild scenes and adventures she had once despised, decrying moderate and rational prospects as illusory for women in a world of male tyranny. In Lee's and Radcliffe's fiction, Gothic horrors act implicitly as imaginative parallels for women's condition. In Wollstonecraft's novel the connection is made explicit. For her, the wild scenes of the Gothic imagination differ from reality only in being too pale a reflection of women's oppression, and her allusions to Gothic romance give imaginative force to her feminist analysis of the realities of women's condition.

Wollstonecraft and Hays were only taking the women novelists' use of romance a step further when they openly proclaimed that the horrors they described were a reflection of reality. The *Analytical Review* supported Wollstonecraft in this, describing *The Wrongs of Woman* as 'a very simple and very probable story, founded upon daily occurrences and existing laws', but her opponents attacked her for being unrealistic. The *Critical Review* disputed the claim that the institutions of society would support a husband like Venables, and, missing the point of Wollstonecraft's attack on the ideology of romantic love, insisted that it was Maria's own fault if she was oppressed since 'She married Mr. Venables, because she was in love with him'. The same review described *The Victim of Prejudice* as 'a gross outrage on probability'.[34] The charge of being unrealistic and 'romantic' was easily made against women who wanted to change the realities of their society, and 'romantic' was an adjective frequently used of feminist characters in novels. In *The Young Philosopher* (1798), Charlotte Smith makes the heroine's mother defend her daughter's adherence to the romantic ideas that violate prescribed feminine behaviour:

> if it be romantic to dare to have an opinion of one's own, and not
> to follow one formal tract ... because our grandmothers and aunts
> have followed it before; if not to be romantic one must go through
> the world with prudery, carefully settling our blinkers at every
> step ... oh! let my Medora ... still venture to express all she feels,
> even at the risk of being called a strange romantic girl.[35]

Here Smith, like Wollstonecraft, uses 'romantic' ideas as a deliberate criticism of the reality of women's oppression.

The appeal of romance, then, was—and is—complex and contradictory. Romantic love provides a false panacea for women, and the idyllic world where romantic couples in novels find their happiness is a retreat from the real world, where changes need to be made. Yet romance in the widest sense has its feminist uses. Through the heroine's romantic adventures the eighteenth-century woman novelist could express the fears and anger that could not openly be acknowledged; and equally, romance allowed for the expression of women's hopes and desires. The novelist creating an ideal romantic world might run the risk of escapism but also had the chance to create visions of a better future, and these are an essential part of feminist thought. The new feminized heroes of Ann Radcliffe's and Charlotte Smith's novels, and Mary Wollstonecraft's glimpses, in *The Wrongs of Woman*, of women's condition transformed by sisterhood, are romantic visions of possibility.

Elements of romance have always persisted in women's fiction, and have much the same functions now as they had in the eighteenth century. We can buy escape in any number of novels written to the hugely successful Mills and Boon formula, sure of being offered a haven from the struggles of twentieth-century life in the arms of a rugged heroic male. Or we can find romance used in a different way, in the novels of feminist-inspired utopia produced by such diverse writers as Doris Lessing, Ursula K. LeGuin or Marge Piercy. Visionary blueprints for social change, and cosy retreats into an idealized version of old values, have a common ancestor in the women's novel of the eighteenth century. Both fictional traditions demonstrate the continuing—and continually double-edged—appeal of romance for women.

NOTES

1. Aphra Behn, *The Fair Jilt*, in *Works*, ed. Summers, **V**, p. 74; Daniel Defoe, Preface to *Farther Adventures of Robinson Crusoe*, rpt in *Novel and Romance 1700–1800: A Documentary Record*, ed. Ioan Williams (London: Routledge and Kegan Paul, 1970), p. 64.
2. See Ronald Paulson, *Satire and the Novel in Eighteenth-Century England* (New Haven: Yale University Press, 1967), for a discussion of sixteenth- and seventeenth-century anti-romance as developing 'various conventions of realism that played an important part in the eighteenth-century English novel'. (p. 13)
3. Northrop Frye, *The Secular Scripture: A Study of the Structure of Romance* (Cambridge: Harvard University Press, 1976), pp. 38–9.
4. Clara Reeve, *The Progress of Romance*, **I**, p. 111.
5. David Hume, *Essays Moral and Political* (Edinburgh, 1741); p. 70; Henry Fielding, *Joseph Andrews*, **III**, ch. 1, p. 167.
6. *The Progress of Romance*, **I**, pp. 65–6.
7. *Three Gothic Novels*, ed. Mario Praz (Harmondsworth: Penguin Books Ltd, 1968) pp. 43 and 48.
8. Their full titles are *The Mysteries of Udolpho: A Romance, interspersed with some Pieces of Poetry*, and *The Italian: or, the Confessional of the Black Penitents, a Romance*.

9. See Philippe Séjourné, *Aspects généraux du roman féminin en Angleterre de 1740 à 1800* (Aix-en-Provence: Publications des Annales de la Faculté des Lettres, 1966) for a discussion of romance elements in eighteenth-century women's novels.

10. Louis B. Wright, *Middle-Class Culture in Elizabethan England* (Chapel Hill: University of North Carolina Press, 1935), p. 110.

11. Ronald Paulson, *Satire and the Novel in Eighteenth-Century England*, p. 24.

12. *Clelia An Excellent New Romance, dedicated to Mademoiselle de Longeville. The Third Volume. Written in French by the Exquisite Pen of Monsieur de Scudéry* [really by Madeleine de Scudéry]. Trans. J. Davies (London, 1656), I, p. 37.

13. *Felicia to Charlotte: being Letters from a Young Lady in the Country, to her Friend in Town* (Dublin, 1765), I, p. 41.

14. Frances Brooke, *The History of Lady Julia Mandeville*, ed. E. Phillips Poole (London: Scholartis Press, 1930), p. 116.

15. Elizabeth Griffith, *The Story of Lady Juliana Harley* (London: T. Cadell, 1776), I, p. 140.

16. One moralist, Richard Allestrye, wrote that 'When a poor young creature shall read [in romances] of some triumphant Beauty, that has I know not how many captive Knights prostrate at her Feet ... her business will be to spread her nets; lay her toils to catch somebody, who will more fatally ensnare her ... those Authors ... will instruct her in the necessary Artifices of deluding Parents and Friends, and put her ruine perfectly in her own power'. *The Ladies Calling* (Oxford, 1673), p. 121. In 1692 a correspondent in the early periodical *The Athenian Mercury* was assured that it was 'lawful' to read romances if the readers were 'Persons of Quality', but romances were 'not at all convenient for the Vulgar, because they give 'em extravagant Idea's ... make 'em think themselves some King or Queen, or other ... and so for the Women, no less than Queens or Empresses will serve 'em'. Quoted in *Novel and Romance*, p. 29.

17. *Letters on the improvement of mind, addressed to a young lady* (Dublin, 1773) II, p. 204.

18. *General Magazine and Impartial Review* 4 (1790), p. 158.

19. James Fordyce, *The Character and Conduct of the Female Sex*, p. 48.

20. Richard Berenger, *The World*, 4 July 1754; rpt in *Novel and Romance*, p. 214.

21. *The British Novelists; with an Essay, and Prefaces Biographical and Critical*. New edn, I (London: F. C. and J. Rivington, 1820), p. 51.

22. *The Female Quixote*, ed. Margaret Dalziel (London: Oxford University Press, 1970), p. 132.

23. *Northanger Abbey*, p. 108.

24. *The Mysteries of Udolpho*, ed. Bonamy Dobrée (London: Oxford University Press, 1980), p. 242.

25. See the discussion of 'female landscape' in Ellen Moers, *Literary Women* (London: Women's Press, 1980), pp. 252–64.

26. Simone de Beauvoir, *The Second Sex*, tr. H. M. Parshley (Harmondsworth: Penguin Books Ltd, 1976), p. 386.

27. 'Advertisement' to *The Recess* (London, 1785), I, n. pag.

28. Phyllis Chesler, *Women and Madness* (New York: Doubleday, 1972), pp. 30–1.

29. *The Romance of the Forest* (London, 1791), **I**, p. 5.
30. See Margaret Anne Doody, 'Deserts, Ruins and Troubled Waters: Female Dreams in Fiction and the Development of the Gothic Novel', *Genre* **10** (1977), pp. 529–72.
31. *The Mysteries of Udolpho*, p. 32. Radcliffe's heroes fit the description of the 'green-world lover', non-threatening and associated with nature, identified as a type of woman writer's hero in Annis Pratt, *Archetypal Patterns in Women's Fiction* (Bloomington: Indiana University Press, 1981).
32. *The Italian*, ed. Frederick Garber (London: Oxford University Press, 1968), p. 412.
33. *Analytical Review* **I** (1788), p. 333.
34. *Critical Review*, 2nd ser. **22** (1798), p. 418; and 2nd ser. **26** (1799), p. 452.
35. *The Young Philosopher: A Novel* (London, 1798), **II**, pp. 14–15.

Index